BUDDHIST WOMEN AND SOCIAL JUSTICE

SUNY series, Feminist Philosophy

Jeffner Allen, editor

BUDDHIST WOMEN AND SOCIAL JUSTICE

Ideals, Challenges, and Achievements

EDITED BY
Karma Lekshe Tsomo

STATE UNIVERSITY OF NEW YORK PRESS

Cover art: Courtesy of Daphne Chu.

Published by
State University of New York Press, Albany

Printed in the United States of America

For information, address State University of New York Press,
90 State Street, Suite 700, Albany, NY 12207

Production by Marilyn P. Semerad
Marketing by Susan M. Petrie

Library of Congress Cataloging in Publication Data

Buddhist women and social justice : ideals, challenges, and achievements /
edited by Karma Lekshe Tsomo.
p. cm. — (SUNY series, feminist philosophy)
Includes bibliographical references and index.
ISBN 0-7914-6253-6 (alk. paper) — ISBN 0-7914-6254-4
(pbk. : alk. paper)
1. Buddhist women—Social conditions. 2. Monasticism and religious orders for women, Buddhist. 3. Feminism—Religious aspects—Buddhism. 4. Social justice. I. Karma Lekshe Tsomo, Bhiksuni, 1944–
II. Series.

BQ4570.W6B82 2004
294.3′082—dc22

2003070446

10 9 8 7 6 5 4 3 2 1

Contents

INTRODUCTION

Family, Monastery, and Gender Justice: Reenvisioning Buddhist Institutions

KARMA LEKSHE TSOMO

Buddhist women have actively worked for more than two millennia to implement Buddhist social ideals, yet rarely have their stories been told. Through the tarnished lens of history, men's achievements have dominated the narrative of Buddhist scholarship and practice. Now, at long last, a new generation of scholars is turning its attention to the recovery of the neglected contributions made by Buddhist women.

During the past fifteen years, feminist ideas have been the source of some major shifts within Buddhism, and the dialogue between feminists and Buddhists is all the richer for the multiplicity of these feminist perspectives and the Buddhist traditions that have informed them. As Buddhist thought and practice continue to enter the mainstream, international attention is focused on a range of social issues that includes both a critical appraisal of Buddhist women's historical and contemporary experiences, as well as a feminist analysis of Buddhist texts. International conferences and symposia are frequently held to evaluate the extent to which Buddhist thought is liberating or limiting for women. Eminent Buddhist scholars, including His Holiness the Dalai Lama, have publicly expressed their support for the full ordination of women, yet there remains an enormous inertia and opposition from within traditional Buddhist societies, particularly those that lack lineages of full ordination for women. The increased awareness that has resulted from global networking has inspired an international Buddhist women's movement that is dedicated to bringing Buddhist social realities more closely in tune with Buddhist ideology.

The various Buddhist traditions present the goal of spiritual awakening (*nirvāṇa*) not simply as an abstraction, but as a concrete eventuality for all human beings. Buddha Śākyamuni is recorded as having explicitly affirmed the potential for women to achieve the highest spiritual goal, yet despite the rhetoric of spiritual equality in the Buddhist texts, women, in actual practice, continue to face many obstacles in their efforts to gain access to Buddhist education and full ordination. Women today have little, if any, voice in Buddhist institutions. The de facto exclusion of women from Buddhist institutions, whether conscious or unconscious, is surprising in view of Buddhist egalitarian theory. Women's theoretical equality can even be used to mask social inequities. For example, the oft-repeated claim that women are totally equal in Buddhism diverts attention from some very blatant inequalities that exist within the Buddhist community, such as the superior status, support, and opportunities that monks enjoy. The exclusion of women from positions of power within Buddhism is currently being challenged by a growing number of women and men from a wide range of Buddhist cultures and philosophical perspectives. Efforts are being directed toward research on Buddhist women's history, the creation of more opportunities for education, the acceptance of full ordination for women, and the full participation of women in both the practice and interpretation of the tradition.

BUDDHISM AND GENDER JUSTICE

Some people look upon gender discrimination as a problem that has already been solved. There are even some young Western women who declare that they have never experienced gender bias in their lives. This is doubtful, however, since sexism is prevalent in the media as well as in many other aspects of daily life. Gender-biased images stream from magazines, films, and the music and television industries. It is nearly impossible to avoid gender-biased images in the Western world, and these images have a powerful effect on the way women and men view themselves and each other.

In other parts of the world, some women are acutely aware of gender inequalities, some sense a problem they are unable to articulate, while others may be completely oblivious to the problem. In Asian societies, many women simply accept gender bias because they feel helpless to change the situation. Not only is gender discrimination pervasive, but many women also feel they lack a support system or the skills necessary to effectively confront it.

This book examines gender attitudes in Buddhist societies and how these attitudes affect the lives of women, both lay and ordained. The chapters examine how gendered attitudes are learned and how they can be unlearned through the use of philosophical, historical, and biographical approaches, as well as hands-on practical applications. The goal of all these approaches is to examine issues of gender in Buddhist societies, to raise awareness of the gender bias that exists in Buddhist institutions, and to explore the implications of gender bias in society. The authors' conclusions suggest that, despite the gender bias in Buddhist texts and societies, the Buddha's teachings present a viable theoretical framework for spiritual and social transformation that not only empowers women, but also provides a useful perspective for addressing gender discrimination.

No matter what potential a person is born with, many human behaviors, both beneficial and harmful, are learned. Buddhism posits that if behavioral patterns are learned, they can be unlearned. Because consciousness by its very nature is impermanent, the mind is mutable and flexible, therefore unskillful behavior patterns such as aggression, attachment, and jealousy can be unlearned, and positive behavior patterns such as kindness, compassion, and wisdom can be learned. Until now, many societies have been operating on what Riane Eisler, in *The Chalice and the Blade*, calls the dominator/dominated model of human interaction.[1] The result is a world of conflict, exploitation, and injustice. By recognizing the problems inherent in this model of human interaction, human beings can create a new, more viable model based on shared responsibility and decision making. Emerging global programs for gender justice, human rights, and economic justice are evidence that this shift has already begun to occur, and it is important that a multiplicity of voices inform these initiatives.

Early Buddhist monastic communities were based on the ideals of shared responsibility and decision making. Women in Buddhist societies have generally had more freedom and independence than women in neighboring societies, but the structures of most families and institutions, especially—and ironically—Buddhist religious institutions, are distinctly patriarchal. These social and institutional realities contrast starkly with Buddhism's cherished ideals of equal access to spiritual awakening for all sentient beings. This clash between ideals and actualities has become more obvious to both practitioners and observers as Buddhism continues to move westward. A new awareness of gender inequalities in Buddhism has occasioned a reexamination of old and valued traditions, and stimulated a reenvisioning of the tradition that is predicated on equal access.

GENDER RELATIONS IN BUDDHIST FAMILIES

In Buddhist societies, as in many Asian societies, expressing respect to parents, elders, teachers, and especially religious practitioners, is an integral and valued cultural norm. Specific patterns of expressing respect and deference to elders are taught to children starting at a young age. These patterns are reinforced in Buddhist societies by praise and admiration for people who are humble and polite. The high value placed on humility and polite conduct has given women a legitimate means of achieving social esteem, but it may also have conditioned them to be docile and subservient. Typically, the ideal woman is a loyal, chaste wife and mother rather than an active participant in the public sphere.

Learning and expressing respect in culturally appropriate ways to people in positions of authority and seniority is an integral aspect of life in Buddhist societies. It is difficult to determine how children in Asian societies learn gendered patterns of expressing respect from early childhood, but it has been my experience that Asian Buddhists express greater respect to men than to women. Although mothers, sisters, and daughters may be deeply loved and honored, a greater respect toward males is evident in families and in monasteries, where traditional values are most carefully maintained.

People's dissimilar behavior and attitudes toward women and men are often largely unconscious. My observation is that gendered patterns of behavior stem from early childhood acculturation in the family, where girls and boys are socialized differently in both subtle and overt ways. Although parents usually declare that they love their daughters and sons equally, girls are expected to shoulder a larger share of work responsibilities and receive fewer advantages than boys. Because daughters are seen as vulnerable to pregnancy and marriage outside the family, girls in many Buddhist cultures receive less encouragement to pursue higher studies and are unlikely to receive the same educational opportunities as their brothers. These gendered attitudes, learned in the family, are internalized and carried over into adulthood and into the monasteries.

Generally speaking, Buddhists do not intentionally behave differently or disrespectfully toward women, much less to nuns. Instead, different behavior toward female and male monastics appears to be largely unconscious and the result of gendered patterns of childhood socialization. People are often completely unaware that they behave differently toward nuns than they do toward monks, and would probably be surprised, even incredulous, if this was pointed out. When Buddhist nuns notice these inequalities, they generally ignore them, since it may be awkward or appear self-serving to point them out. Gendered behaviors are so common that many people fail to recognize them at all. Culturally appropriate training in gender awareness is therefore essential in Buddhist cultures, for both men and women. Women can take the lead by developing an awareness of their own gendered attitudes and behaviors and by devising ways to correct inequalities in Buddhist society.

To understand the underpinnings of gender inequality in Buddhism, it is necessary to examine not only the texts and structures of Buddhist institutions, but also the attitudes and patterns of socialization that have evolved within these institutions. I use the terms "gender imbalance" and "gender inequality" instead of "gender injustice" and "gender oppression" because, although gender injustice and oppression certainly occur in Buddhist societies, these terms imply conscious, intentional behavior, unlike gender imbalances and inequality, factors that unconsciously influence behavior, but are remediable through consciousness raising. Equally as important, gender imbalances and inequalities are often the basis for gender injustice and oppression, and therefore raising awareness of gender imbalances and inequalities may go a long way toward correcting injustice and oppression. For example, to my knowledge, most Buddhist associations in traditionally Buddhist societies are entirely male, yet few people have even noticed this fact, and many would even contest the assertion that gender discrimination exists within Buddhism. With the exception of a few Buddhist women's organizations, most national or international Buddhist institutions have less than a fair representation of women members, or no women members at all, not to mention women in positions of authority. Women are underrepresented at national and international Buddhist conferences, and even in countries where women are gaining admission to institutions of higher learning, they continue to be poorly represented in Buddhist institutions.

Buddhist women frequently express a lack of interest in power or status, and many women in developing countries are understandably more concerned about obtaining their basic requirements, such as adequate food, shelter, health care, and education, than about attending conferences. When women are not provided with their basic needs, their potential is squelched and they find themselves perpetually disempowered and subordinated. Some even argue that it is futile to struggle for equal representation in Buddhist institutions at all, since most are hierarchically organized and emblematic of male authority. Meeting the basic needs of women is obviously a priority, yet at the same time, I feel that women must begin to take positions of leadership and responsibility in Buddhist institutions soon, or else remain indefinitely on the margins of social transformation. Women must gain their voice and begin to help transform Buddhist institutions from within, lest gender inequalities become even more firmly inscribed. Gradually, as international awareness of women's issues heightens, a few nuns and laywomen are being included in some national and international Buddhist conferences. Although this token inclusion does not fairly represent women's voices, it is a step in the right direction since it does give women a voice for expressing concerns and pressing for changes within Buddhism.

BUDDHIST WOMEN IN MONASTIC LIFE

For over 2500 years, monasticism has been fundamental to Buddhist societies and religious institutions. Although women have not always had equal access to the benefits of monastic life, and nuns living a monastic life do not always have the same opportunities as monks, monastic life has been meaningful and beneficial for countless women. Monastic life offers women an alternative to marriage and procreation. It provides knowledge, independence, a sense of community, and the spiritual benefits of Buddhist practice—mental clarity, balance, inner peace, wisdom, and loving-kindness.

The role of monastic practitioners is a greatly valued one in Buddhist societies, and the highest expressions of respect are generally reserved for monastics, especially male monastics. My experience of living in Buddhist cultures over a period of twenty years has taught me that, overall, there is a marked difference between the way people regard monks and nuns. Even among monastics themselves, the exemplars of cherished Buddhist values, disparities exist in attitudes toward nuns and monks. Many times I have observed that, when a visiting monk appears, Buddhists rise, hasten to receive him, arrange a comfortable seat, and offer tea, hospitality, and other services, yet when the visitor is a nun, these same behaviors are not generally applied. Instead, people, including women, generally do not rise, offer her a place to sit, serve her before themselves, or offer her the same courtesies that are commonly extended to monks. When people do show respect toward nuns, it is generally less deferential than the respect expressed to monks. In my opinion, these gendered patterns of behavior toward nuns both reflect and perpetuate the lower status of nuns—and, by extension, all women—in Buddhist societies.

Nuns receive material support at a subsistence level from the laity and enjoy the protection of the monastic precepts, which, according to Buddhist tradition, benefit them in both tangible and intangible ways. Tangibly, the precepts protect women against exploitation by providing both a strong foundation for ethical decision making as well as membership in a safe community of spiritual practitioners. Less tangibly, the precepts are thought to enhance concentration and discipline, and the mental stability developed during meditation increases alertness and sensitivity to the nuances of situations. The wisdom and loving-kindness developed through meditation practice help the practitioner to deal more skillfully with difficult life situations, and dealing with difficult situations skillfully is thought to engender greater wisdom and compassion. On a totally intangible level, the monastic precepts are believed to be meritorious and the source of protective power. When I survived a near-fatal viper bite in India some years ago, several Tibetan lamas said it was due to the power of the precepts.

This is not to say that Buddhist monastic life is always without problems. Just like people everywhere, monastics have different personalities, backgrounds, and expectations. Just like people in ordinary society, monastics can be temperamental, sluggish in their practice, or careless in their behavior. Monastic practice is designed to nurture enlightened character, but beginners (and we are all beginners) may exhibit jealousy, anger, attachment, greed, and all the usual imperfections. Monastic life is a crucible for character development, not a panacea.

My experience of visiting and living in Asian Buddhist monasteries has given me some experience with monastic protocol. After receiving novice ordination in 1977, I studied for fifteen years in a Tibetan settlement in Dharamsala, India. In 1982, I received full ordination in Korea and then went to Taiwan for further monastic training. These experiences of monastic life in different countries have given me some insight into the lifestyle of Buddhist monastics in various traditions.

The tradition of showing respect to elders in the family is replicated in the monastery. Bowing to senior practitioners not only helps monastics express respect for one another, it also sets an example for the laity. The tradition of bowing establishes clear lines of seniority within the monastery and within the monastic order as a whole, whereas in the West structures of authority are often confused with authoritarianism and therefore rejected. Having clear lines of authority in a monastic setting can be extremely useful, not only for the functioning of the monastery, but also for maintaining discipline, harmony, and an environment that is favorable for Dharma practice.

My experiences in Asian monasteries over the years have been instrumental in shaping my understanding of gender in Buddhism. For example, in the Tibetan tradition it is rare to see anyone bow to a nun, perhaps because there are no fully ordained nuns. In the Korean tradition, by contrast, all junior nuns pay respect by bowing to senior nuns. There is a precise protocol for showing respect for those who are senior in ordination status. When a fully ordained nun (*bhikṣuṇī*) visits a monastery in Korea, junior nuns immediately gather and express their respect to her by bowing in the traditional way. In Taiwan, junior nuns express respect by bowing to senior nuns as soon as they enter a monastery, immediately after paying respect to the Buddha.

In the Buddhist traditions that offer full ordination for women, nuns are generally ordained by senior, fully ordained nuns. In traditions that lack full ordination for women, nuns are ordained by monks. This custom has been standard practice for centuries in Cambodia, Laos, Myanmar, Thailand, Tibet, and Sri Lanka. Many women also prefer to take ordination with respected monks, even when fully ordained nuns are available to ordain them. To receive ordination from a highly respected monk is regarded as a blessing.

In countries where there are no *bhikṣuṇī*s to perform the ordination of nuns, monks often take the responsibility. The monks are acting compassionately when they ordain nuns, since nuns in countries without *bhikṣuṇī*s could not become ordained without the monks' help. At the same time, if the monks ordain women without careful selection criteria, or without the provision of adequate training and education, the procedure can cause many problems in the nuns' communities—problems that are beyond their control. When monks ordain nuns, they effectively decide who will join the nuns' community, but they do not always know the applicants well and do not have a stake in the admission process since they live elsewhere. Because the monastic ideal is so highly valued, new candidates may be encouraged to join, but may not be temperamentally suited to monastic life. This openhearted attitude toward admissions becomes a problem for women's communities if sufficient care is not taken in the selection process. Nuns therefore need to think carefully about investing monks with the power to ordain nuns. Although their options are limited by the absence of *bhikṣuṇī*s, nuns literally become disempowered by relinquishing their monastic authority.

BUDDHIST RESPONSES TO GENDER IMBALANCE

Over the years, I have encountered a variety of different attitudes toward the gender imbalance in Buddhism. The most common attitude is to ignore the problem altogether, dismiss it, deny it, and trivialize it. On the other hand, there are people who have recognized the gender imbalance in Buddhism and have set about to redress it, often in very creative ways, and the result has been a resurgence of interest in Buddhist women's issues. However, there are still many challenges that lie ahead on the journey toward realizing true gender equality.

First, most people are blind to gender inequalities, just as I was when I began practicing Buddhism thirty-five years ago, even though such inequalities were strikingly evident. When I became an ordained Buddhist nun in 1977, I continued to be unaware of these inequalities, or even that I was entering a tradition in which women lacked the same opportunities for education and full ordination as men.

Second, people often dismiss the gender imbalance and say that gender equality is not necessary for Dharma practice. They may recognize that there is a gender imbalance in Buddhism and acknowledge that monks have more opportunities than nuns, but believe that gender differences are irrelevant to achieving enlightenment. Even if there is gender discrimination in Buddhism, many claim it cannot prevent women from achieving *nirvāṇa*. Teachers in all the Buddhist traditions support this view by saying that women have the same spiritual potential as men. It is very easy to dismiss the problem by saying, "In Buddhism everyone can achieve enlightenment," and go on to the next question.

Third, people may deny that there is a problem by asserting that no gender imbalance or discrimination exists in Buddhism, because women can do anything that men can do and women are able to achieve whatever goal they strive for. If women want enlightenment, they can get it, if they are determined and work hard. Nothing is preventing women from achieving enlightenment. Using this reasoning and substantiating it with actual examples of women who have achieved realization in the tradition, many people deny that there is a gender problem in Buddhism at all.

Fourth, some people may trivialize the problem and say, for example, "I am not interested in status, position, or fame. If someone is interested in becoming fully ordained, that is fine, but I am only interested in achieving *nirvāṇa*. If monks are regarded more highly than nuns, that is not a problem for me. Status is a worldly concern and has nothing to do with Dharma." This attitude can be misleading and dangerous for women. Not only does it ignore gender discrimination, but it also distorts the issue by suggesting that gender equality is a worldly concern and has no significance for Buddhism. Moreover, this attitude casts aspersions on the sincerity and motivation of those who voice concerns about gender inequalities.

A fifth related attitude is to belittle the problem of gender imbalance in Buddhism in an attempt to silence dissent. Advocates of equal opportunities for women may be intimidated or discouraged from raising gender issues. Some segments of traditional societies are resistant to change and prefer to maintain the status quo, an attitude that cannot help but perceive advocates of social change as threatening, simply because they challenge the prevailing social norms. The changes that feminists propose, for example, threaten people in positions of power. When women call for change, many elites begin to cling to their power and advantages. These very obvious reasons are why there is often enormous inertia and resistance to social change.

Women who seek changes in the status quo or want to move beyond their allotted social sphere often find obstacles placed in their way. For example, many women who seek higher education or ordination may be discouraged from pursuing their aims. In one case in the 1980s, about a dozen Tibetan nuns sought the advice of a highly respected male teacher about applying for admission to the Institute of Higher Tibetan Studies in Sarnath. All of these nuns were told that they would face "obstacles" if they applied and should stay in the monastery instead. Three other nuns went to different teachers with the same question and were all told that it would be very beneficial for them to apply for higher studies. One nun in the latter group eventually earned a Master's degree in Buddhist Studies and became qualified as a teacher.

When nuns approach their teachers for advice about receiving higher ordination, they are often told, "It is difficult enough to keep the ten precepts purely. Are you able to keep the ten precepts perfectly? Imagine how difficult it would be to keep more than three hundred precepts!" I have personally heard this response many times from different teachers. I have also heard many people, including monks, nuns, and laypeople, repeat it to novice nuns: "It is hard enough to keep the ten precepts. Why in the world would anyone want to take *bhikṣuṇī* ordination? Ten precepts are enough for nuns." Such remarks discourage nuns, and not only erode their self-confidence, but also dissuade them from seeking full ordination, even when they are qualified and have the opportunity to do so. Such remarks also prevent Buddhist women from standing up for their rights. When women repeat these intimidating remarks to others without having critiqued their value, they disempower themselves and each other.

Occasionally women encounter outright denigration and humiliation. When I was studying in India, I often heard disparaging remarks about nuns. A classmate of mine, a monk ten years my junior, told me, in all seriousness, "Women are inferior to men in every way. Women are smaller and less capable. They are physically, mentally, and emotionally inferior to men." It was quite shocking to encounter such an attitude, especially among young people. The case of this monk was particularly astonishing since he owed everything—his education and his very existence—to the kindness of women. We were studying logic at the time and learning to apply critical analysis to a wide range of Buddhist topics, but he seemed unable to apply logical reasoning to real life situations. Finally I presented him with the articles published in the

Times of India, with titles such as "Girls Score High in National Exam Results" and "Girls Outshine Boys Again," which indicate that girl students consistently achieve higher marks than boy students. I argued that girls, when given equal educational opportunities, often do better than boys, but I remained unable to shake his conviction that women were innately inferior to men. The playing field is still not level, even in the United States, even in the twenty-first century. Although some biases are culture specific, gender bias seems to extend beyond cultural boundaries.

CHALLENGING AND CHANGING THE SYSTEM

His Holiness the Dalai Lama, one of Buddhism's most highly respected leaders, frequently mentions the importance of challenging outmoded attitudes toward women. He repeatedly challenges women to correct the prevailing misconceptions about their abilities by striving for higher education and professional advancement, especially when it is for the service of society. He recommends that women set aside counterproductive emotions such as anger and resentment, and strive toward their goals with determination and perseverance.

According to the Buddha, all sentient beings have equal potential for enlightenment. The Buddha also taught his followers to use logical reasoning to test his teachings, just as they would test gold before purchasing it. Extending this logic to social analysis, it therefore stands to reason that the Buddhist teachings are inclusive in scope, and thus should be equally accessible to women and men. In my opinion, it is therefore the duty of thoughtful Buddhists to question the inequalities women have faced for centuries and to work to remove any limitations women face today in gaining access to their religious heritage.

Pointing out injustices in society has always carried risks, especially for disadvantaged sectors of society. Not only do social critics upset traditional apple carts, but women who seek changes may be disparaged or criticized for seeking their own advantage. In cultures where humility and self-effacement are highly valued—especially for women—speaking out takes courage. The situation of women in Buddhism is not unique, however, since anyone who works for social justice risks public censure. Fortunately, women in Buddhist cultures enjoy the freedom to express their views.

Education for women is essential to this process because educationally disadvantaged women lack the tools necessary to work for improvements for themselves and their families. Buddhist women in developing countries often lack adequate education, so the first step is to insist on equal educational opportunities for girls from a young age. As women gain confidence and skills, they can more effectively express their needs and hopes.

Equal opportunities for education, ordination, and economic development will naturally bring many changes for women, including changes in Buddhist institutions. The same skills that are used to debate Buddhist philosophy can be used to press for social change. When nuns are told that ten precepts are enough for women, they can counter by asking why ten precepts are not enough for monks. They can reason that, if full ordination is meritorious for monks, it must be similarly meritorious for nuns. A friendly debate along these lines is a good way to bring gender issues into the open. Debates will encourage nuns, monks, and laypeople alike to think more critically about women's capabilities.

In addition to educational disparities, there is also a gap between generations that disproportionately affects Buddhist women. For example, women of different generations approach problems from vastly different perspectives, and today, due to the process of rapid social change occurring in societies around the world, the generation gap is widening. Differences of psychology, values, and life experiences remain greatest in developing countries, where large segments of the population are left behind by economic changes. While members of the younger generation are caught up in new technologies and values, members of the older generation struggle to preserve their traditional cultures. Since women are the most likely ones to be left behind during rapid economic changes, the gender imbalance in human society is paralleled by an ever-increasing communication gap between generations.

Redressing the gender imbalance requires skill and tenacity, especially in Asian societies, where direct confrontation is often the least effective tactic. Perhaps a more effective tactic is to respectfully ask questions to gain a clearer understanding of different viewpoints, to subtly open up new avenues of inquiry, and gradually explain why educated women are an asset to Buddhism, not a threat. Most dialogue partners are quick to recognize that, if Buddhist practice is beneficial for men, it must be equally beneficial for women. And, if Buddhist practice is beneficial, women deserve to have equal access to it.

Working with the Buddhist women's movement has been very refreshing. Because Buddhist traditions are founded on logical reasoning and common sense, it is possible to engage in constructive dialogue and reach a deeper level of understanding, even about difficult issues. Over the past fifteen years, I have discussed gender issues with Burmese, Cambodian, Chinese, Japanese, Korean, Thai, Tibetan, and Vietnamese monks, nuns, and laypeople. These discussions have educated me, not only about monastic discipline and Buddhist philosophy, but also about how Buddhism can be adapted and applied in contemporary society. All parties to the discussion seem to come away with both a greater tolerance and awareness of Buddhism's usefulness, and a greater understanding about the importance of equal access for women within the tradition.

There are a number of reasons why I believe that attitudes toward gender can change in Buddhist cultures. First, Buddhist practice is concerned with the transformation of consciousness, and consciousness has no gender. Second, the Buddha affirmed that women are as capable of achieving enlightenment as are men, so discrimination against women is inconsistent with a fundamental Buddhist principle. Third, Buddhists, especially monks, want to make Buddhist practice accessible and they realize that gender discrimination is unacceptable in the modern world. If Buddhists are true to their stated principle of having compassion for all sentient beings, they must stand up for gender justice.

WOMEN AND ENDANGERED BUDDHIST CULTURES

When discussing the issue of women in Buddhism, it is also important to recognize that Buddhist cultures in general, and the Dharma teachings in particular, are in danger. Over the past fifty years, Buddhism has been nearly obliterated in Cambodia, China, Laos, Mongolia, Russia, Tibet, and Vietnam. It is also perilously close to extinction in regions of Bangladesh, Hong Kong, India, Indonesia, Korea, and Nepal due to politics, war, and increasing secularization. Buddhists are often among the poorest and most disadvantaged, and consequently are also often the most vulnerable to the aggressive conversion efforts of other religions. With so many ancient Buddhist cultures endangered, providing women with the resources they need to study and practice Buddhism will allow them to counter these destructive trends and share this traditional knowledge with others.

The benefits that Buddhist women can bring to society are obvious to anyone who visits Taiwan or Korea, two countries where Buddhist women and men have nearly equal opportunities to education, ordination, and facilities for religious practice. Although Buddhist women in Vietnam still face many difficulties by living in a communist regime, their courage and resoluteness in the face of adversity are also inspiring. To visit these countries and see thousands of well-educated, well-disciplined Buddhist women totally committed to working for the welfare of society makes it easy to understand the benefits that are derived from having a strong order of nuns (Bhikṣuṇī Saṅgha) to teach and serve as spiritual guides, especially to women. In these countries, nuns are supported in their study and practice primarily by laywomen. With this support, they are then able share the benefits of their knowledge and encourage others. This sharing of knowledge and experience with others creates patterns of mutual benefit. For example, when monks realize the benefits that committed women practitioners can have for society, they generally become women's allies in the struggle for equal opportunities. And as stated before, in Buddhist societies, women are generally trained to be humble and self-effacing, but monks have the power and freedom to speak out and therefore can be great advocates on behalf of equal opportunities for them. While women must gain their own voices, monks can also be tremendously helpful in transforming societal attitudes toward women.

Among the greatest obstacles Buddhist women face today is their limited access to qualified teachers and adequate educational facilities. There are several reasons that help explain this limited access. First, there is a critical shortage of fully qualified Buddhist teachers in almost every tradition, often due to wars and Buddhist persecutions during the last fifty years. Second, male teachers who teach nuns may be suspected of having ulterior motives, so many male teachers hesitate to teach nuns for fear of gossip in the community. Since most qualified Buddhist teachers are male, women are at a disadvantage in getting a Buddhist education. Other practical considerations also work against women. Sometimes women's monasteries are situated in remote areas, far from teachers and facilities. In developing countries, women's monasteries are poorly supported and nuns may be expected to earn donations by doing time-consuming prayers and rituals. Monks are regarded as a superior "field of merit" and their needs are given priority over the needs of women. Finally, there are many men and women who believe that women are incapable of and uninterested in higher studies. These combined obstacles put nuns at a serious disadvantage in gaining religious education.

While working to establish study programs for women in India over the past fifteen years, I have encountered all of these obstacles. It has been extremely difficult to find qualified teachers who are willing to teach women, especially in remote locations with poor living conditions. In one case, after searching for several years to find teachers for Himalayan nuns, I learned about a monk who had been meditating in a cave for many years, supported by the impoverished community nearby. After much persuasion, this humble monk agreed to teach the nuns. For a year, under this teacher's guidance, the nuns progressed steadily in their studies. Then, suddenly, one day a group of monks from his monastery appeared and insisted that he leave. These monks were not interested in studying themselves, but they insisted that he discontinue teaching the nuns. The teacher returned after several months, but again the monks from his monastery arrived in a jeep and insisted he leave. Finally the teacher made the decision to resign from his monastery and returned to teach the nuns, which he has kindly continued to do ever since. This incident is the most overt case of gender discrimination I have faced during twenty years of living in Buddhist societies.

Another similar incident occurred a few years later. At one of our projects, we were able to find a saintly, compassionate, and extremely knowledgeable teacher for the nuns. Similarly, in this case, the teacher was a humble, gentle monk who dedicated himself sincerely to teaching the nuns. The nuns progressed wonderfully under his tutelage. One day he received a letter from his home monastery that insisted that he leave the nuns' study program and go abroad. Feeling indebted to his monastery for his education there, he had no choice but to sadly agree. Fortunately, the teacher was able to find a temporary replacement, but the nuns miss their kind teacher and pray for his return.

Obtaining fully qualified teachers is the most serious challenge faced by women in many of the Buddhist traditions. To nurture a generation of fully qualified female Buddhist teachers, a systematic study program under qualified guidance is essential, and until women become qualified as teachers, they are dependent on the kindness of male teachers, when they can get them. The importance of women receiving equal educational opportunities cannot be overemphasized.

GENDER JUSTICE AS A PREREQUISITE TO PEACE

It is my belief that gender justice—social justice for all human beings, regardless of gender—is necessary if there is to be a genuine, lasting peace in human society. At first glance, it would appear that Buddhist societies belie this contention. With a few glaring exceptions, Buddhist societies have enjoyed more peace and suffered fewer armed conflicts than other societies, even though their social structures are patriarchal. But a peaceful veneer sometimes conceals underlying tensions and hypocrisies that are in urgent need of attention. Peace in any family requires effort, skill, and concessions, and peace in Buddhist societies has long rested on the efforts, skills, and concessions of women. The contributions of Buddhist women—whether subtle or exemplary—have largely gone unnoticed and unacknowledged, if not thwarted altogether. As long as women are excluded at any level of society, claims of justice and equality ring hollow.

All Buddhists need to take responsibility for achieving gender justice in Buddhism, but monastics have a special responsibility because of their expressed commitment to the spiritual pursuit. It could even be argued that monks have a greater responsibility than nuns to work for gender equity, since they have far more power within Buddhist institutions. Unfortunately, many monks feel that the welfare of Buddhist laywomen and nuns is not their responsibility.

Although the Buddhist women's movement is still very young, it enjoys several advantages. First, Buddhist feminist efforts rest on foundations of gender equality expressed by the Buddha himself. Second, these efforts profit from the experience of the broader feminist movement in terms of organization, communication, strategy, and networking. In just fifteen years, Buddhist women have joined forces and are becoming adept at shared decision making and at achieving consensus. Lay and ordained Buddhist women are collaborating with more experienced global women's networks in their struggle for gender justice.

As reflected in this book, the global Buddhist women's movement is an alliance of representatives from a remarkable variety of cultures, disciplines, and endeavors. In the first part of this volume, contributors explore the philosophical foundations for Buddhist women's empowerment or disempowerment, examining the ways in which feminist and Buddhist thought have become intertwined, and exploring the implications of these connections. Anne Carolyn Klein explores the topics of subjectivity and embodiedness from Buddhist and Western perspectives as a philosophical basis for constructive social engagement in "Buddhist Understandings of Subjectivity." In "Reflections on Buddhism, Gender, and Human Rights," Lin Chew applies a Buddhist analysis to the universal principles of respect and dignity for all life, and relates them to constructions of gender identity as well as legal reforms, self-determination, and economic opportunity. Taking a textual approach, in "Is the Bhikṣuṇī Vinaya Sexist?" I investigate the codes of monastic conduct to see whether gender bias in Buddhist societies can be traced to gender inequalities in these ancient texts.

The next few chapters apply Buddhist psychology and social theory to explore Buddhist interpretations of nonviolence and ways in which this ideal can help uproot or alleviate the sufferings of social injustice. In "Transforming Conflict, Transforming Ourselves: Buddhism and Social Liberation," Paula Green investigates the roots of conflict and how Buddhist teachings on mindfulness, wisdom, and compassion can help relieve human suffering through creative methods of peacebuilding. Meenakshi Chhabra, in her chapter "Redefining and Expanding the Self in Conflict Resolution," takes an alternative approach to peacebuilding by examining Buddhist theories of the self in the *Lotus Sūtra* and relating them to the politics of identity. In "Integrating Feminist Theory and Engaged Buddhism: Counseling Women Survivors of Gender-based Violence," Kathryn L. Norsworthy draws from both Buddhist and feminist psychological theory to discover practical means of healing the trauma of violence.

The most exhilarating way to document Buddhist women's history is to record it as it unfolds. In "Reclaiming the Robe: Reviving the Bhikkhunī Order in Sri Lanka," Ranjani de Silva tells the story of how the lineage of full ordination for women, lost for nearly a thousand years, is being recovered and revitalized in contemporary Sri Lanka. Sarah LeVine tells the equally compelling story of the resurgence of Theravāda Buddhist nuns in "Dharma Education for Women in the Theravāda Buddhist Community of Nepal." The extent to which social structures affect the lives of women in Nepal is the theme of the next two chapters: David N. Gellner's "Buddhism, Women, and Caste: The Case of the Newar Buddhists of the Kathmandu Valley," and Khandu Lama's "Trafficking in Buddhist Girls: Empowerment through Prevention." Next, in "Khunying Kanitha: Thailand's Advocate for Women," I document the life of Khunying Kanitha and her struggle to provide shelters for abused and abandoned women and to achieve educational opportunities and legal rights for Thailand's long-neglected nuns.

Shifting to a vastly different cultural and geographical setting, we find nuns in the Himalayas similarly struggling to gain equal educational opportunities. That story is told by Margaret Coberly in "Crisis as Opportunity: Nuns and Cultural Change in the Spiti Valley." Exploding the myth of Japanese Buddhist women's passivity and social irrelevance, Diana E. Wright documents the active roles that nuns played in the "divorce temples" of the Tokugawa Era in "Spiritual Piety, Social Activism, and Economic Realities: The Nuns of Mantokuji." In "The Infinite Worlds of Taiwan's Buddhist Nuns," Elise Anne DeVido tells the story of nuns in Taiwan, often considered the ultimate success story of Buddhist women. To conclude the volume, Caren I. Ohlson documents the international movement that has emerged to challenge male domination of Buddhist institutions in "Resistance without Borders: An Exploration of Buddhist Nuns across Cultures."

In a time of environmental and moral crisis, the world community needs to optimize all its human resources to ensure the survival of the species. Buddhists feel a special responsibility to promote peace, compassion, enlightenment, and justice for all living beings, regardless of gender. Consonant with the Buddhist concern for alleviating suffering and in view of the enormous suffering women often experience, the heroic stories of women's struggles in the face of adversity deserve to be told. Thus, it is imperative to document the lives of Buddhist women, whether ordinary or exemplary, before these stories are lost forever.

These stories could not have been told without the inspiration and sustained efforts of numerous mentors and friends. I am deeply grateful to the contributors for their commendable scholarship, amiable collaboration, and boundless patience. In equal measure, I offer heartfelt appreciation to Margaret Coberly, Jennifer Lane, Ellie Mennim, Rebecca Paxton, and Emily Mariko Sanders for their thoughtful reflections, challenging comments, and keen editorial vision. And for the cover artwork, which poignantly captures the paradox of Buddhist women and social justice, *me ke aloha* to Daphne Chu.

NOTE

1. Riane Eisler, *The Chalice and the Blade: Our History, Our Future* (San Francisco: Harper & Row, 1987).

Part One:

Theoretical Foundations for Buddhist Social Action

Chapter 1

Buddhist Understandings of Subjectivity

ANNE CAROLYN KLEIN

Buddhist materials speak of a subjective intelligence other than reason, for example, one that is associated with intense mindfulness, one that is not a matter of information accretion, but which focuses on another area of subjectivity altogether. The mind-body paradigm has governed much of Western philosophy to date and Western feminism continues to be subject to it, even though it objects to the way this paradigm figures women as "merely" body. The body is considered lesser than the mind for many reasons, but above all, in the post-Enlightenment era, for its apparent lack of rational intelligence. This nonrational capacity is, in turn, sustained by a certain type of steadying of the bodily energies (Sanskrit: *prāna*, Tibetan: *rlung*). The mind-body and the Buddhist paradigms taken together offer an alternative to the mind-body dyad. I will be taking material from Buddhist discussions of mindfulness and concentration, as well as from the Tibetan medical tradition, to develop a fuller description of the kinds of embodied processes—that is, the kinesthetic or energetic dimension—which are involved. I will address the recent work of Martha Nussbaum, *Upheavels of Thought*,[1] which, although not strictly a feminist work, is in fact addressing some of the concerns that feminists address. I argue, however, that she is caught in the very dyad that she seeks to open up.

I am especially interested in how Buddhist understandings of subjectivity and embodiment, and the relation between the two, can contribute to Western philosophical and religious reflection in general, and to feminist perspectives in particular. My initial attempt in this regard was to discuss, in *Meeting the Great Bliss Queen*[2] and various articles,[3] Buddhist views of mindfulness, and to suggest the possibility of a conversation about subjectivity that fits into neither of what then were fairly well-established, moderately antagonistic camps: the essentialists versus the postmodernists.

Most significantly, for our consideration here, mindfulness is valued *not* for specific content or "information" or conceptual understanding of any sort. It is significant for the ability of a person, a subject, to remain focused and increasingly aware of the *depth, strength, intensity, clarity,* and/or the *openness* of her own mind. This is amply clear from any number of texts across the Buddhist traditions, from the Theravāda *Foundations of Mindfulness Sūtra,* to Mahāyāna discussions of the calm state, to Dogen's descriptions of quiet sitting, to the most profound discussions in Tantra and Dzogchen. Western readers tend to hear such discussions primarily in terms of mind, as if the body were unimportant (though many of the same Buddhist texts just mentioned make clear that it is, with their focus on posture, breath, or a full-scale reimaging of the body as divine).

Thus, it is important to note that descriptions of "unmarked subjectivity" are not unmoored from the body. Indeed, when it comes to describing more subtle states of consciousness, including but not limited to those often called mystical, it is especially important to note what is occurring in the body. The Hindu and Buddhist tantric traditions are well aware of this; indeed, at least in Buddhism, one might say that the more esoteric and sublime the method, the more concretely linked to physiological processes it will be. In other words, subjectivity can be rarified without being actually disembodied. By contrast, in Western discourse, the more objective and rational, the more abstract and disembodied subjectivity tends to be. The ability to connect one's cultivation of insight, calming, or compassion with an embodied awareness is, it seems to me, a crucial element in ensuring that one's insights—Buddhist or non-Buddhist, contemplative or administrative—are, in fact, concretely directed at the well-being of other embodied beings. Imagine if the planners at the Pentagon, at the highest levels of Medicare or the social services systems, were actually in profound bodily awareness as they created their policy. Would it not make a difference? To genuinely understand subjectivity, moreover, is to profoundly see its interconnectedness with the body. Recent studies in phenomenology, of which Merleau-Ponty's are an outstanding example, have also emphasized such interconnectedness. In his last work in particular, he emphasized not only the interrelatedness that permeates the mind-body complex, but also what he called the "crisscrossing" of subject and object, seer and seen. This kind of inviolate connectedness to the "other" is, once fully digested, truly compatible only with supportive, positive interactions with or on behalf of those "others" so intermingled with ourselves. This of course is also a theme in Buddhist discussions of compassion. Social organization today increasingly mirrors this pattern as well.

The Dalai Lama recently observed that while in the past a nation or tribe could potentially gain something by destroying a neighborhood at some distance from itself, today, all of us are so interdependent that to harm another is, truly, to harm oneself. In fact, it is precisely this awareness that has kept us, so far, from going forward with nuclear and other holocaustal forms of mass destruction. Much of this is common knowledge. My intention is to show that recognizing such mutuality is rooted in reexamining our own subjectivity. That is, the clearer we are about the linked processes of our own and others' minds, perceptions, and energies, the more able we may be to extend benevolence socially, politically, and legally. Therefore, to reorient our understanding of subjectivity has both profound personal meaning and potentially great social consequences.

Thus, the question of subjectivity to me seems to be a major, often overlooked, area for fruitful reflection on how we understand others, including the human need for well-being and the circumstances that will provide it. (I am not eager to use the term "justice" in this context, since it often implies the opposite of mutuality, and tends toward a disembodied, administrative oversight that is a type of subjectivity quite different from what I am discussing here.)

In order to further this conversation, however, there is still the need to make the case to feminist and gender studies scholars overall that the study of religion is crucial to the project of plumbing the depths of female, male, and human disposition across cultures. The suspicion that all religions are unrelentingly patriarchal and therefore undeserving of attention has hampered the development of feminist studies in religion. My own sense is that even the most patriarchal of religions contains traditions that open new windows onto the old questions of self, spirit, and community that women and men everywhere continue to investigate (for example, in Christianity, the gnostics; in Islam, the Sufis; and in Judaism, certain readings of the Bible).

There are two elements I would like to call attention to here: first, the importance of including the body in any in-depth exploration of subjectivity; and second, the narrative strategies that literally incorporate the embodied state, in contrast to more abstract kinds of reflection. Both speak to the need for an epistemology of the body, and thereby for addressing the mind-body problem that is so popular in contemporary discussions. Both elements are also—and this is my emphasis here—useful for dismantling, or at least better understanding, the impulse toward oppositionality and dualism that has been widely observed to provide the formative structure on which Western juxtapositions of mind/body and subject/object discourse have traditionally been based. I will be lightly alluding to some of the formative moments that set such discourse in motion. I believe that Buddhist discussions of subjectivity will contribute to contemporary discussion in and out of feminism. I see as especially useful its detailed description of subjective states that are not easily assimilated into widely received categories. For example, such states are neither essentialist nor constructed, and some do not even bear the marks of personal, gendered, or cultural history, as many feminists and others claim every consciousness must.

It is common to understand the functions of mind and body as categorically different—minds know, bodies do. And yet, everyday speech suggests otherwise. When asked how we know something, we may say, "I feel it in my bones." We say, "That gives me goose bumps," or "That makes my skin crawl." This raises the important question of whether our bodies have, or significantly participate in, valid ways of knowing. Certainly there seem to be vestiges in our language of a time when people felt that their bodies did indeed know, or that people knew through the medium of their bodies, and that this knowledge was legitimate (i.e., their bodies gave them access to legitimate forms of knowledge). Adrienne Rich, in *Of Woman Born: Motherhood as Experience and Institution*, calls us to recapture some aspect of this ancient voice when she urges that we "think through the body." She writes this, she says, out a conviction that there are ways of thinking we have not yet learned about.[4] Clearly, the body knows many objects through the senses—through seeing, hearing, tasting, smelling, and touching.

Buddhist discussions of subjectivity and its relation to the body suggest important alternatives to the mind-body structures so deeply embedded in our worldview. In the process we can consider some of the components that support that structure. For example, in most Asian systems and especially those emphasized in Buddhism, the breath is a mediating element between the mind and body. The mind rides on subtle energy currents (*prāna*, *rlung*) of the body; because of this, the body and its energies are obviously affected by thought and, of course, meditation.

Body is both subject and object of meditation—and subject and object of experience in general. The body also becomes transformed in the process of meditation. The body itself can be the point of focus, and changes in bodily experience are classic outcomes of meditative endeavor. This is a well-known fact that has not been adequately incorporated into our understanding of body, either by scholars, feminists, or ordinary women and men who walk around, lo and behold, embodied.

The famous *Foundations of Mindfulness Sūtra*[5] enjoins the practitioner to watch the breath, as do countless other traditions. Mindfulness of breathing is a classic method for cultivating a calm state of mind. In Tibetan traditions, the achievement of the calm state famously yields an experience of the body being "light, like bubbles"—a feeling that the distance between subject and object has melted away, even, according to some writers, of being able to walk through walls. This phrase is said to describe the subjective and perhaps actual experience of those who attain high stages of concentration.[6] Je Mipham Rinpoche praises a way of developing stability that may also include watching the breath, but more significantly takes the mind itself as an object of stabilizing. This practice, too, eventually dissolves our sense of solidity, not only of the body, but also of any sense that the mind, identity, self, or anything the senses may contact is real.

There are more contemplative connections into the body. If I sit quietly for a time and allow my attention to rest, let us say, at my heart, I can gradually notice that my heart feels more or less open—that there are structures around it which, to my own mind, have a certain shape, consistency, and are often intimately linked with the kinds of self-narratives with which I construct my own identity. Being aware of my heart area actually helps to identify inner blocks to compassion, and clues me to when something is shifting. Both the mindfulness classically taught in Buddhism and simply processing one's life as one moves through it, are crucial aspects of self-awareness. Even a cursory glance at traditional human cultures in Asia and elsewhere can give us a vantage point on the premises of individualism. This is significant, for many of the critiques of mind-body dualisms take for granted the ethos of post-seventeenth-century individualism in the West, despite these two perspectives being utterly intertwined. It is very useful to note and analyze connections between the rise of individualism (with its consequent affect on the ideas of individual rights, justice, and social obligations, or the lack of them) and a tendency to disembodiment, also aided and abetted by a valorizing of intellect and abstract thought.

If this is so, then why is it that reflection, emotional or cognitive, seems in the West to take us out of the body, or at least to ignore it? There is not space here to go into this, but it has much, of course, to do with Descartes. The whole point of what Charles Taylor calls the "reflexive turn" in Western thought is to achieve a quite self-sufficient "certainty," a crucial component of individualism.[7] Taylor was continuing the trend toward interiority that had been set in motion by Augustine. Augustine wanted to go within, in order to ascend. In that rarified state of ascension to the divine there is, of course, no body. By contrast, post-Cartesian-style contemplation was "no longer a way to experience everything in God, rather, what I now meet is myself."[8] And that self was, increasingly after Descartes, bodiless. Disembodiment, the rise of individualism, and the relinquishment of a sense of the sacred—all of these seem to have contributed to the already incipient mind-body divide in Western thought. To the extent that the worthiness of the body, such as it was, derived in good measure from the sense that the body was God-made and God-given, it is perhaps not surprising that such a sense of "worthiness" has eroded as the body, like the world itself, became disenchanted, or secularized. For, in the West, reverence for one's own body, as a gift of God, or for the earth, as part of His creation, was tied up with a sense of worth that could not survive the disappearance of God from culturally prominent articulations of the nature of physical reality.

In Buddhist traditions, and especially emphasized in the Tibetan ones, the human body is an object of enormous and cultivated gratitude, not because God or Buddha made it, but precisely because it is the hard-won fruit of one's own prior good actions. The body is the fruit of good actions rare enough that one cannot be sure how many aeons it might be before we gain another one. The value of the body, however, is not its rarity, but that it places one in an excellent situation to disconnect from delusions, especially the delusions of self-representation and identity—including identification with either mind or body—and find complete freedom.

So there is an important connection between the desacralization of the world, the narrowing of "self" to the thinking mind of Descartes, the small point of consciousness of Locke that Taylor calls the "punctual self," and the discarding of the body as an axis of knowing. The freedom the Buddhist traditions seek, it is worth noting, is not a freedom from embodiment in general, such as Descartes seems to have entertained in his *Meditations*; it is a freedom from enslaved or random embodiment. One now has the freedom and wherewithal to select one's future incarnation, which is what enlightened beings, or even highly developed beings (such as bodhisattvas) are said to do. This choice is motivated solely by compassionate responsiveness to others.

Even feminists who wish to reclaim the body tend not to see the body as intimately participating in what, since Descartes, we have called the life of the mind. The cultural idealization of objective thought remains a perspective to be dealt with in contemporary sensibilities regarding the respective worth of subjective versus objective knowing. In the early phase of second-wave feminism, when Adrienne Rich exhorted women to think through the body, her instinct was right on, but the West does not really give us the resources with which to do this. This is all the more reason to look elsewhere for those resources.

We can see how difficult this is to do by considering, for a moment, how an exemplary philosopher, Martha Nussbaum, develops her theory of intelligent emotions. Nussbaum describes emotional knowing in terms of its physicality and motion. Yet she denies, or at least does not assert, that the body itself has real knowing, partly because the body does not consistently produce any specific physiological experiences in the event of any given emotion. Its palpitations do not help her philosophically in naming the identity of a particular emotion. In her view, the body is unimportant, cognitively, and therefore, however potent subjectively, it is essentially irrelevant to the identity and meaning of emotions. Her focus is determined by her self-given mandate, namely, to reveal that emotions deserve more philosophical respect than they have garnered in Western traditions, largely because of their supposed opposition to reason.[9]

Nussbaum is relatively atypical among classically trained philosophers for the degree to which she acknowledges the importance of the body and the challenge of adequately incorporating it into classic argumentation. In the context of exploring the identity of emotions, she observes that, "We should certainly grant that all human experiences are embodied, and thus realized in some kind of material process. In that sense, human emotions are all bodily processes. But the question is, are there any bodily states or processes that are constantly correlated with our experiences of emotion, in such a way that we will want to put that particular bodily state into the definition of a given emotion-type."[10]

Still, partly because the center of gravity of her discussion is the emotions and their identity, she is prepared to pass over bodily interplay, except to the extent that she must consider whether or not it actually constitutes the distinct identity of an emotion. Since it does not, she need not investigate what it does constitute, or know, or facilitate. This, however, is most worthy of consideration, for in the Buddhist traditions, if meditation is subtle enough, it is possible to gain direct insight into the connection that links the processes of body and mind.

At the same time, it is significant that Nussbaum honors the issue of embodiedness with more than usual respect. Asking whether, in the absence of certain physical symptoms, it would be possible to identify grief as grief, she notes that, "This is an extremely difficult question, about which we should be open-minded and humble, and prepared to change our minds."[11] Here I address the very potential for conceptual change that she invites. In these and other ways, we are inspired to pay attention to the body as a source of information, knowing, and even wisdom.

There is a closer connection between subject-object dualism and mind-body dualism than has perhaps been adequately explored. The emphasis on objectivity and individuality is part of a nexus of assumptions that make it difficult to reconfigure how we view these connections. Genuine learning can come through the body as well as the mind, and there is an intimate connection between energetic sensibilities and the religious as well as literary imagination. This type of imagination is not directly about the body, but uses the directness of myth, which is very much an embodied form of writing. As a case in point, the practice of visualization in the Tibetan Buddhist tradition presents, rather than represents. The religious imagery of Samantabhadra and other enlightened figures combines subjective and objective stances—subjectivity as embodied.

For example, a ninth-century Tibetan text known as the *Authenticity of Open Awareness* (*gTan tshig gal mdo rig pa'i tshad ma*)[12] is a series of debates that unfold as reflections on what it considers to be the ultimate subject, an intrinsically authentic state of self-risen wisdom. How can one use the dualistic language of logic to talk about a subject that admits of no dualism? What can this have to do with the apparently "objective" language of debate? The text can hold both such a subject *and* such arguments because ultimately the debates undo dualism, and leave the figure, the body—the ultimate body of everything—sublimated in the form of Samantabhadra. Experiences like that of *vipassanā* meditation effect something similar, minus visualization and imagery.

It can hardly be overemphasized that in the cultural life of which this text is a part, philosophical and what might be called mythic perspectives are profoundly interfused. Mythic dimensions, syllogistic logic, and an epic sense of history are matrixes in and through which *Authenticity* emerges. Thus, even while giving pride of place to the philosophical concerns of *Authenticity*, we also pay attention to the contextualizing narratives from Bön histories, such as the early dissemination of Bön throughout the heavenly realms, or *Authenticity*'s author, Lishu Daring, transporting thousands of texts on the backs of birds in flight from Zhang Zhung to Tibet. To understand the world of *Authenticity* is to recognize that the philosophizing mind behind it is in no way alienated from these other kinds of narratives.

Authenticity displays, with particular flourish, a feature found to some degree in many ancient Buddhist works. Traditional scholars of Indian and Tibetan Buddhism, who spent years debating Nāgārjunian logic, also have a strong imprint of how, a thousand years or so before *Authenticity*, Nāgārjunā discovered the philosophical matrix of Madhyamika beneath the ocean. Commentators on his work, revered to the present day for their reasoning and intellect, are admired in traditional circles for other things as well—often connected with what they did with their bodies. Candrakīrti is remembered for milking the image of a cow, and Tsongkhapa for his direct encounter with

Mañjuśrī.[13] Joza Bonmo is revered for twisting a sword into knots, and Lishu Daring for traversing the distance between Kailash and Lhasa in the time between lunch and dinner. The list is long and the events recounted are well known.

Western scholarship on the Buddhist philosopher Nāgārjuna, and on virtually every other exponent of Buddhist logic, focuses lucidly on their logic—on the disembodied. This, too, is a cultural marker. Aristotle's logic rejected myth,[14] and, in an important sense, the bodily activities extolled in myth, which sets the course for Western philosophy as a genre. Traditional readers of Buddhist materials, by contrast, are as comfortable with rigorous logic as they are with the mythic-fantastic elements in the background of that logic. These readers can show us the way to a rhetorical style that is both embodied *and* articulated with intelligence and distinction. This is especially relevant, because the text in question, *Authenticity,* is in part a story of language and its relationship to the non-conceptual, and also an exploration of the relationship between logic and concepts that are not formally logical.

The principle of unbounded wholeness (*thig le nyag gcig*)[15] reigns over the entire work. This wholeness is present—not merely represented—in *Authenticity*, especially through the figure, voice, and presence of Samantabhadra, represented throughout Buddhist and Bön iconography as a body seated in a lotus, clear and luminous, without the clothing of conceptuality. The text moves between taking unbounded wholeness as an object of logical inquiry and allowing Samantabhadra's sheer presence to counter such objectification.

Whereas, as has often been noted, Greek philosophy grew out of a mythical structure which it then increasingly rejected, in the Tibet of *Authenticity*, the respect for reasoning which began to take hold in the eighth century did not result in a rejection of mythic ways of thinking or of the religious reflections borne by it. Among other things, this suggests that, in the Tibetan and indeed larger Asian context in which Buddhist traditions participate, knowledge is not strictly localized within an individual mind forever divided from what it knows—a view strongly held in the post-Cartesian and post-Lockean West. On the contrary, in Tibetan culture, there is a sense that bodies, and the environment itself, hold and respond to wisdom. Knowing and the objects of knowing are thus not necessarily utterly discrete categories, at least not in the way modernity takes them to be, nor are knowing and bodies.

NOTES

1. Martha C. Nussbaum, *Upheavals of Thought* (Cambridge: Cambridge University Press, 2001).

2. Anne Carolyn Klein, *Meeting the Great Bliss Queen: Buddhists, Feminists, and the Art of the Self.* (Boston: Beacon Press, 1994).

3. Some previous articles include: "Grounding and Opening: Cross Cultural View of the Body," in *Being Bodies: Buddhist Women on the Paradox of Embodiment*, Lenore Friedman and Susan Moon, eds. (Boston: Shambhala, 1997); "Presence with a Difference: Buddhists and Feminists on Subjectivity," *Hypatia* 9:4 (Fall 1994); "Finding a Self: Buddhist and Feminist Perspectives," in *Sharing New Vision: Gender and Values in American Culture*, Clarissa W. Atkinson et al., eds. (Ann Arbor: UMI Research Press, 1987), pp. 191–218; "Nondualism and the Great Bliss Queen: A Study in Tibetan Buddhist Ontology and Symbolism," *Journal of Feminist Studies in Religion* 1:1 (1985): 73–98; and "Primordial Purity and Everyday Life: Exalted Female Symbols and the Women of Tibet," in *Immaculate and Powerful: The Female in Sacred Image and Social Reality*, Clarissa W. Atkinson et al., eds. (Boston: Beacon Press, 1985), pp. 111–38.

4. Adrienne Cecile Rich, *Of Woman Born: Motherhood as Experience and Institution* (New York: W. W. Norton, 1986), pp. 283–84.

5. *Satipatthana Sutra,* in *Teachings of the Buddha: The Long Discourses of the Buddha, a Translation of the* Digha Nikāya, Maurice Walshe, trans. (Boston: Wisdom Publications, 1987).

6. See Geshe Gendun Lodro, *Walking Through Walls: A Presentation of Tibetan Meditation* Jeffrey Hopkins, trans., and Leah Zahler, ed. (Ithaca, N.Y.: Snow Lion, 1992).

7. Charles Taylor, *Sources of the Self* (Cambridge: Harvard University Press, 1989), p. 136.

8. Ibid., p. 157.

9. I discuss this matter in relation to Buddhist cultivation of compassion in *Meeting the Great Bliss Queen*, pp. 110–11.

10. Nussbaum, *Upheavals of Thought*, p. 58.

11. Ibid., p. 57.

12. A crucial scholarly Dzogchen text from the Bon tradition. Listed under the category of "Philosophy and Logic," in Samten Karmay, *Catalogue of Bonpo Publications* (Tokyo: Toyo Bunko, 1977), p. 102. It is listed as No.

73, *gTan tshigs gal mdo rig pa'i tshad ma*, the same title given in the edition published by Lopon Tenzin Namdak. It is also listed under No. 54, *rDzogs chen bsgrags pa skor gsum* (this work is listed as *gTan tshigs nges pa'i gal mdo,* and, more fully, as *Sems nyid rdzogs chen gyis tshad ma gtan tshigs sgra don gtan la dbab pa*). A book-length analysis and translation of this text by Anne Klein and Geshe Tenzin Wangyal Rinpoche will be published by Oxford University Press in 2005. The Tibetan version can be viewed at: http://antioch.rice.edu/digproj/bonpo.

13. Nor is this a feature of Asia alone. Descartes, for example, for all his emphasis on objective reasoning, took a perfect God and the soul's immortality as his ultimate reference points.

14. This is all the more interesting because, as has often been observed, the love of wisdom, *philosophia*, which Plato and Socrates enjoined in Greece, was an outgrowth of mythmaking. However, as Judith Berling points out, this account of the rise of philosophy can itself be called a myth for two reasons: "It simplifies and reconstructs reality to make a particular point which denies . . . [and] it has been a powerful story that functioned to define and justify certain cultural divisions without submitting them to the scrutiny of rational argument." See Judith Berling, "Embodying Philosophy," in *Discourse and Practice*, Frank Reynolds and David Tracy, eds. (Albany, N.Y.: State University of New York Press, 1992), p. 34.

15. This is a crucial term in both Buddhist and Bon Dzogchen *(rtdzogs chen)* traditions; it is a term for the nature of reality recognized as the nature of authentic open awareness.

Chapter 2

Reflections on Buddhism, Gender, and Human Rights

LIN CHEW

From 1999 to 2002, I worked at the Asian Human Rights Commission (AHRC), based in Hong Kong, as the program officer for human rights education. AHRC is a nongovernmental organization that has historical links with the Christian Conference of Asia, but has been developing independently since 1994. The mission of AHRC is to protect, defend, and promote human rights in Asia. The organization is particularly concerned about those groups of people who have been excluded from participating in the development, benefits, and social and political processes of their societies.

The programs and activities of AHRC are as varied as the forms of human rights violations occurring in Asia. AHRC primarily focuses on:

1. Facilitating and supporting professionals and activists who are working to bring about the legal reform that is necessary for the long-term and systematic protection and promotion of human rights for all the people in their countries;
2. Drawing attention to and advocating action to stop the most acute situations of conflict and violence in Asian countries, and supporting the victims of these violations. Such violations, often at the hands of the police, include the rape and assault of women, and their torture, starvation, and "disappearance," to name only a few;

3. Analyzing and finding ways to end all forms of discrimination (class, caste, sex, sexual orientation, religion, ethnicity, etc.) against specific groups, discrimination that is preventing them from living freely and securely in their own communities;
4. Developing human rights education programs that will reflect these practical concerns while informing and enabling more people to work toward the removal of those obstacles that prevent the enjoyment of human rights by all, without exception. This particular task is my focus.

RELIGION AND HUMAN RIGHTS

One of our programs, initiated several years ago, is called, "Religious Perspectives on Human Rights." This program is aimed at collaborating with religious groups and individuals to work toward promoting human rights. The program was created because AHRC recognizes the important role that religious values and practice continue to play in the social and political consciousness of people in Asia. Religious moral values still permeate the political and social institutions of Asia and can have positive (liberating) effects as well as negative (discriminating, isolating) effects in society.

The question of whether Buddhism offers a concept of human rights has been the topic of some debate. Among the questions that have been raised are: Is there sufficient justification for a Buddhist theory of human rights? Is the concept of human rights compatible with the Buddhist concept of selflessness? Are Buddhist values compatible with the values of the contemporary human rights movement? Can human rights concepts be authentically conveyed in Buddhist language? The debate seems to turn on theories of what constitutes a "right," and whether the various categories of rights enunciated in the Universal Declaration of Human Rights are inherent to human subjects (which is problematic from a Buddhist perspective since nothing is inherent) or simply pertain to them. Viewed from an Asian perspective, one might also question how human rights apply in societies that are structured more in terms of human relationships than in terms of individuals.

Although a fully developed theory of human rights has yet to be articulated in Buddhism, on the basis of Damien Keown's definition of a right as being "a benefit which confers on its holder either a claim or a liberty,"[1] a strong case can be made for the Buddha's concept of human rights. The freedom to act and guidelines for reciprocal social duties are explicit in the early Buddhist texts. Human beings are equal in their most fundamental nature (no-self, *anatman*) and in their equal potential to be free from suffering. Keown argues for a Buddhist doctrine of human rights that is not grounded in the doctrine of dependent arising, the desire for self-preservation, or the responsibility for self-government.[2] Instead, he argues that human dignity, rights, and freedoms are grounded in the human potential for well-being, peace, and self-realization. The Buddhist teachings strongly validate the rights of individuals to freedom and opportunity, and prohibit cruel and unusual punishments or the death penalty. In addition to the moral commitments to preserve life and property, the teachings also suggest the overriding value of compassion as a justification for respecting human dignity.

Buddhism has more to say about human nature than it does about human rights. Like most religious traditions, Buddhism focuses more on the spiritual dimension of life than the social or political dimensions. It can be argued that the Buddhist concept of human nature as selfless and momentary contradicts the notion of human rights, yet a dynamic, mutable notion of personhood might also render the discussion of rights and their deprivation more rich than the notion of an eternal soul. As in contemporary discussions from other perspectives, the concept of human rights as a sense of personal benefit or entitlement naturally leads to a consideration of rights for other living beings.

AHRC has facilitated and participated in discussions to establish that there are close affinities between the original, universal elements in religious teachings and the principles underlying fundamental human rights encoded in international conventions and treaties. The moral values that are generally accepted as basic human rights are apparent in all religious traditions that support the dignity and equality of human beings—peace, tolerance, freedom of conscience, freedom from torture and inhumane treatment, and social justice. In addition, most religious traditions support advocacy for oppressed, marginalized, and excluded groups within society, including the poor, women, indigenous peoples, migrant workers, and children. These groups are also the concern of human rights advocates and activists. With these parallels and coincidences of concern, more and more strategies of solidarity action and practical engagement are being identified and created by both religious individuals and human rights groups.

BUDDHISM AND HUMAN RIGHTS

Using the "modern" way of investigation, the Internet, I found that there is already a wealth of information available, as well as a whole new world of Buddhist communities—communities that are developing a deeper understanding and insight into the Buddhist teachings and earnestly living the way of life exemplified by Śhākyamuni and many other Buddhas. The question of human rights in Buddhism has also engaged the attention of scholars such as Damien Keown and Craig K. Ihara.[3] Here, I would like to present the conclusions of the Consultation on Buddhism, Human Rights, and Social Renewal, which was organized by the AHRC and held at the Ecumenical Institute for Study and Dialogue, Colombo, in June 1999.

First, let us briefly consider the fundamental principles that underlie the body of "human rights" from which all concrete "rights" follow. Such rights form the basis for the protection, implementation, and promotion of human rights for all individuals and peoples.

1. The principle of nondiscrimination. Based on the acceptance of a common humanity—the principle of equality of all persons—the principle of nondiscrimination means that all persons, on the basis of their humanity, must be able to enjoy and exercise their human rights. These essential human rights include the right to have access to the economic and social resources necessary for human life, the right to live safely and with dignity, and the right to be free from torture and inhumane treatment and punishment.
2. The principle of participation. This principle refers to the right to participate in the community, society, and state affairs that govern the lives of men and women. It refers to the enjoyment of political, civil, economic, social, and cultural rights, and presumes that all men and women have access to all the different kinds of resources necessary to be able to participate in the decision-making and administrative procedures affecting their lives.

The Consultation on Buddhism, Human Rights, and Social Renewal further identified the essential teachings of the Buddha that are relevant and parallel to these human rights principles:

1. Regarding nondiscrimination. The Buddha's teachings on the biological unity of the human species denotes a common humanity that is the basis for nondiscrimination. "Culture" determines what a society regards as "nature;" thus social position is not determined by innate differences of nature. Gender and social identities are not the products of biology; rather, they are conceptualizations and reifications of repeated practices. The differences among human beings are cultural, not natural; thus what prevents people from changing their condition is not nature, but culture.[4]
2. Regarding participation. The Buddha's teachings on the principles of righteous governance demystify the sources of temporal power and authority. The Buddha rejected a belief in the divine origins of state or royal power. The social contract between rulers and their subjects is the only legitimate form of authority, which means that those in power are accountable for fulfilling their part of the contract and can be deposed if they break the contract or misuse their authority. This teaching provides the essential foundation for democratic practice. It anticipates both constitutional rule and the rule of law, both of which are necessary conditions for enforcing civil and political rights. This teaching further rejects the notion of impunity based on status; even the king is subject to the same Dharma as his subjects.[5]
3. Regarding justice. According to the Buddha, a good ruler "gives food to the poor" and ensures an equitable distribution of wealth in his kingdom. The Buddha's advice on the duties of the head of a household or employer sounds like a social charter on workers' rights. This advice is the basis for promoting the economic and social rights that are necessary conditions for social justice. These rights include: allocating work according to the strength and abilities of the employees, providing food and just wages to workers, providing health care to workers, cultivating close friendships with workers, not exploiting workers' labor, and recognizing workers' rights to periodic leisure and rest.[6]

HUMAN RIGHTS STRATEGY AND THE BUDDHIST WAY TO HUMAN LIBERATION

Strategies to ensure basic human rights have an empowering effect for all sectors of society. By providing human beings with their basic needs, each person becomes empowered, both as an individual and as a member of a community. Because members of the United Nations have agreed to recognize human rights, they are accountable for ensuring the protection and the enjoyment of these rights in their countries. At the same time, the human rights framework and strategy requires that each person become active in claiming and protecting these rights, because human rights, by their very nature, cannot be bestowed by religious benevolence or charity, social status or political favor. This strategy compels human beings to challenge unequal and unjust relations, to name causes and consequences, and to identify those who are responsible for violations. Such a strategy makes it possible to seek redress, to reconcile, and to create better conditions for the general good.

Social engagement is no longer based solely on charity, benevolence, or moral imperatives—motives that can, in some instances, create even more unequal relations between the bestower/benefactor and the recipient/grantee. The involvement of advocates and activists creates an authentic solidarity based on the conviction that, so long as everyone does not enjoy these rights, one's own enjoyment of these rights is based purely on good fortune, accident, or the privilege of descent or status—an unjust criterion.

The Consultation on Buddhism, Human Rights, and Social Renewal also concluded that the Buddhist way to achieve liberation from suffering can be seen as a strategy for change. The Buddha described the human condition during his time as "a sickness within and a sickness without."[7] This is a recognition that personal and social suffering are mutually conditioned factors. The diseased human condition is a product of human actions. Therefore, to bring about change in this situation, people must overcome their ignorance (*avidya*) about the real causes of their suffering and become aware of the dehumanizing character of the conditions in which they live. The Buddha declared that, in his new society, "there will be only one flavor, the flavor of freedom."[8] Constructive social change is twofold: personal change and a change of social conditions. In the Buddha's teachings, personal welfare and social welfare are not separate, but are two intrinsically interrelated aspects of the struggle for freedom from suffering: "In protecting oneself, one protects others; in protecting others, one protects oneself."[9]

Can we conclude, then, that, for a Buddhist, there can be no achievement of spiritual liberation (*nirvāna*) without actively working to achieve social justice? Are Buddhists obliged to work for changes in societies where rights are lacking, so that the "flavor of freedom" can be enjoyed by all? Can creating the conditions for a just society and ensuring basic freedoms in the society around us be seen as a means of achieving liberation?

THE NEGATIVE SIDE

Looking at present-day religious institutions and practices, one cannot ignore the negative developments that have crept into religious institutions. An essential aspect of human rights work is to examine the structures, procedures, and practices within institutions, organizations, and one's own home to bring these in line with human rights values. Without these correctives, religions can become causes of violence instead of peace.

Historically, there has been a direct connection between religion and violence. Religion is a potential source of conflict, as well as a potential tool that can be used by political leaders to create conflict in order to maintain domination and power. Religious institutions have colluded with forces of domination that have been responsible for systematic and extensive human rights violations, such as in the colonial periods of many societies and during the Apartheid regime in South Africa. Today, in many regions of the world, violence is committed or condoned in the name of religion. In addition to holy wars, we also find the inhumane and degrading punishment of women for transgressing religious codes of conduct, religious limitations on women's rights to express their sexuality, and religious injunctions preventing women from making their own reproductive health decisions.

Many Buddhist teachers and practitioners are surely already asking themselves questions such as: What aspects of Buddhist institutional and social practices contradict those elements of the Buddha's teachings that support human rights? Where have Buddhist teachings, organizations, and individuals taken part in the causes of violence, discrimination, and exclusionary policies and practices? Where has their inaction or non-involvement contributed or colluded with the condoning of violence, discrimination, and exclusion in society?

THE QUESTION OF GENDER

The women's human rights movement maintains that women's rights are no different than the rights that all human beings should enjoy. However, because these rights have been systematically withheld from women, the position and participation of women in relation to men within organizations, the community, and the society serve as a benchmark to determine the quantitative and qualitative measure of equality and democracy within that particular unit. The discrimination and oppression of women in human society is more serious and fundamental than forms of discrimination against so-called minority groups. Women have suffered discrimination throughout the world, in all historical periods, almost as if they were another category of the human species, subordinate to the male in the most critical and decisive aspects of life. Not only have the lives and work of women in society been rendered invisible, women have been systematically excluded from the enjoyment of basic human rights, albeit to different degrees and in different ways, in most societies. Special rules, spaces, and "protective" measures for women on the basis of their "special nature" are discriminatory, and usually treat women as if they are not able to understand and decide for themselves. They usually group women and children together; women are treated like children, denied responsibility and agency for determining what happens in their own lives and actions.

Religion has legitimized much of this on the basis of religious teaching. Religions have colluded with other authorities and agencies in maintaining discriminatory policies and practices against women. Many religious teachings on social/moral matters that intimately affect the lives of women—family relationships, reproduction, sexuality—have been the basis of infinite suffering for women, and have kept women in degrading and inhumane situations within religious and social institutions. Often, women are given a "special place" and "special rules" to follow; they are excluded from central/essential positions and direct lines of authority, and are limited to spaces and roles created especially for women.

CONCLUSIONS

The existence and growth of Sakyadhita is evidence that the situation of women within Buddhism is radically changing. Through conferences, newsletters, and the Internet, Buddhist women from many traditions and sectors of society are gathering to discuss a variety of questions that concern the lives and advancement of women everywhere. Increasingly, women are actively responding to social needs, and working to remove the obstacles women face, both within and outside Buddhist institutions. As more Buddhist women begin to work actively for social transformation, they are demonstrating that it is possible to build a world of *kalyāṇa mitta*, excellent friends.

NOTES

1. Damien Keown, "Are There Human Rights in Buddhism?" in *Buddhism and Human Rights*, Damien Keown, Charles Prebish, and Wayne Rollen Husted, eds. (Richmond, Surrey: Curzon Press, 1998), pp. 15–41.

2. Ibid., p. 29.

3. Notably, the essays in *Buddhism and Human Rights.*

4. "*Vāsettha Suṭṭa,* To Vāsettha" *in The Middle Length Discourses of the Buddha: A New Translation of the Majjhima Nikāya,* Bhikkhu Ñāṇamoli and Bhikkhu Bodi, trans. (Boston: Wisdom Publications 1995), pp. 798–807.

5. "*Aggañña Sutta,* On Knowledge of Beginnings," in *The Long Discourses of the Buddha: A translation of the Dīgha Nikāya,* Maurice Walshe, trans. (Boston: Wisdom Publications, 1995), pp. 407–15.

6. *Sigālaka Sutta,* To Sigālaka, Advice to Lay People," Ibid., pp. 461–69.

7. Hammalawa Saddhatissa, *The Sutta Nipata* (London: Curzon Press, 1985).

8. Bhikkhu Bodhi, *The Taste of Freedom* (Kandy: Buddhist Publication Society, 1976).

9. F. L. Woodward and C. A. F. Rhys Davids, trans., *The Book of Kindred Sayings* (Boston: Wisdom Publications, 1980).

Chapter 3

Is The Bhikṣuṇī Vinaya Sexist?

KARMA LEKSHE TSOMO

Feminists generally assume that Buddhism is detrimental to women. Despite the Buddha's spiritual egalitarianism, they cite certain Buddhists' claims that female rebirth is inferior to male rebirth and references to women as being inclined to lust, aversion, and craving like Mara's daughters.[1] They also refer to Buddhist texts that assert women's guilt by association with procreation and refer to women as fickle, sexually voracious, contentious, and evil. Sandra Wawrytko finds Buddhism "seething" with an old and deep-seated sexism.[2] Rita Gross asserts that "feminist analysis of any major world religion reveals massive undercurrents of sexism and prejudice against women, especially in realms of religious praxis."[3] Diana Paul seems to concur, stating, "Like Judaism and Christianity, Buddhism is an overwhelmingly male-created institution dominated by a patriarchal power structure. As a consequence of this male dominance, the feminine is frequently associated with the secular, powerless, profane, and imperfect."[4] To understand the roots of these contradictions, I maintain that it is necessary to examine the monastic texts upon which Buddhist institutions rest.

In Mahāyāna Buddhist texts, Paul notes, "One perceives a destructive, complex set of images preventing women from fulfillment within the Buddhist religion."[5] Liz Wilson questions "the received wisdom of the gradual disappearance of androcentrism and misogyny from Indian Buddhist texts and institutions," noting that even in the Nikāyas (early collections of the Buddha's teachings), "women are repeatedly blamed for the downfall of men and explicitly linked to the premature decline of the Buddha's teachings."[6] Kornvipa Boonsue, a Thai scholar, believes that Buddhism has been wielded as an instrument of manipulation to anesthetize women and to conceal gender oppression.[7]

Statements such as these raise an important question: Are these undercurrents fundamental to Buddhism itself or are they simply reflections of the cultural and social contexts within which Buddhism has evolved? Before concluding that Buddhism is fundamentally sexist and detrimental to women, we must consider the sources of gender inequality. Are most of these sources located in the words of the Buddha that were recorded after his death, therefore making them an integral part of Buddhist philosophical tenets, religious practices, and beliefs? Are they located in the monastic institutions charged with maintaining the purity of the Buddha's teachings? Or are they part of the cultural/social context within which Buddhism developed?

The Buddha purportedly recommended celibacy as the most efficient mode of practice, since it frees up time and energy for spiritual development. The monastic institutions that evolved to accommodate this practice have set the standard for the ideal way of life in Buddhist societies. These institutions have developed along patriarchal lines in all Buddhist cultures. Although the Buddha affirmed that all beings are capable of liberation and enlightenment, sexism and gender discrimination coexisted with this fundamental assertion long after Buddhism gained ascendancy and official dominance. The patriarchal archetype for Buddhist monastic institutions has continued over many centuries and has set a standard for other social institutions, albeit in stark contrast to Buddhism's egalitarian philosophical cornerstones.[8]

In all societies, strands of philosophy, religion, culture, literature, and the arts function simultaneously and become interwoven. These domains exist in symbiotic relationships and strongly influence one another. In Buddhist societies, numerous factors besides Buddhism affect people's values and perceptions. For centuries, non-Buddhist beliefs and social practices have operated simultaneously with Buddhist values and perceptions. When questioned by his cousin Ānanda, the Buddha asserted unequivocally that women are capable of liberation, yet gender inequalities have endured in Buddhist societies, hindering women's access to enlightenment and the practical benefits of Buddhist practice. This is still the case today.

The purpose of this study is to investigate specific aspects of the Bhikṣuṇī Vinaya, the monastic code for Buddhist nuns, to discover whether the foundations of monastic practice are discriminatory toward women and in what ways they may be responsible for the subordinate position nuns hold in Buddhist institutions. Using textual, comparative, and feminist methodologies, I consider the ordination procedures for fully ordained Buddhist nuns (*bhikṣuṇī*s), the eight special rules for nuns (*gurudharma*s), the precepts that the *bhikṣuṇī*s live by, and the methods prescribed for expiating transgressions of the precepts. In this way, I explore whether, and in what ways, patriarchal elements in Buddhist institutions and societies may be traced to gender-specific elements in the monastic codes, focusing specifically on the Bhikṣuṇī Vinaya.

RELEVANT RESEARCH

A number of previous studies on women in Buddhism are relevant to the research at hand. In an examination of early texts preserved in Pāli, Elizabeth J. Harris finds evidence of three attitudes toward women: pro, con, and neutral.[9] Diana Paul examines images of women in later Mahāyāna Buddhist texts and finds "the extreme views of misogynist attitudes, on the one hand, and the religious ideals of nondiscriminative wisdom, emptiness, and universal salvation, on the other."[10] Sandra A. Wawrytko finds sexism in the early Buddhist texts, but attributes it to "gynophobia" in Buddhism's historical context and goes on to say that sexism in the Saṅgha is "both philosophically groundless and pragmatically indefensible."[11] Rita Gross argues that some of the literature cited as evidence of misogyny has been misinterpreted and that elements thus interpreted should be ignored when reconstructing the tradition.[12] Cheng-Mei Ku's extensive philological analysis of the views of women in three Vinaya schools concludes that the different views of each are related to doctrinal differences.[13] Inyoung Chung compares the rules for nuns and monks in the Chinese Prtimoka and concludes that the Buddha's founding of the Bhikṣuṇī Saṅgha represents a social and spiritual advance for women.[14]

Drawing on the work of these scholars as well as my own comparative research on the Chinese and Tibetan *Prātimokṣa Sūtra*s,[15] this chapter examines monastic procedures and specific precepts for clues as to whether the formulation of these rules reflects: 1. social requirements of the era, such as the safety and protection of both the individual and the Saṅgha as a whole; 2. organizational needs for the efficient functioning of the Bhikṣu and Bhikṣuṇī Saṅghas in relationship to each other; 3. gender discrimination; and/or 4. sexism.

Buddhism began its development within the cultural setting of Indian Brahmanical society in the fifth century BCE, and records document the atmosphere that shaped the rules for regulating the Buddhist monastic orders. Women of that era were classified as dependents either under the protection of their father, their husband, or, upon a husband's death, their husband's brother. Women who lived under an unrecognizable agency were suspect and rejected—ostracized from their place of origin if suspected of an impropriety such as adultery or prostitution, or of being a demon in human form. In such a social milieu, to allow women to leave their families and enter the mendicant life was a radical departure from the norm. Under the circumstances, an order of monks was seen as providing protection for the nuns. Therefore it is necessary to evaluate issues of control, protection, gender discrimination, and sexism that are evident in these monastic codes and procedures. By investigating the special rules (*gurudharmas*) that are imposed on *bhikṣuṇīs*, and the probationary status (*śikṣamānā*) that is imposed on nuns but not monks, I will attempt to determine the assumptions that may have prompted these added requirements and the implications for women of living by an unequal monastic code. In addition, I will explore in what ways the additional rules are reflections of particular societal structures that are no longer relevant today.

THE EIGHT *GURUDHARMAS*

The first *bhikṣuṇī*, Mahāprajāpatī, was the Buddha's stepmother and aunt. According to Buddhist legend, Mahāprajāpatī agreed to abide by eight special rules (*gurudharmas*) in exchange for the admission of women to the monastic order—the Saṅgha. It is these eight rules that purportedly subordinate the *bhikṣuṇīs* to the *bhikṣus*. In his translation of Bhikṣuṇī Vinaya texts of the Mahāsāṃghika school, Akira Hirakawa explains the rationale behind the eight *gurudharmas* and contends that they originated at a later time:[16]

> The order of monks and order of nuns were basically independent of each other. They were self-governing institutions basing themselves on the *Prātimokṣa*. However, the two orders could not remain entirely separate. Since the men and women of the two orders were to live lives of abstinence, strict rules concerning the relations between the two orders were necessary. . . . According to the *Bhikkhunikkhandaka* [sic], when the Buddha, in response to Mahāprajāpatī's request, allowed women to become Bhikkhunī, he also set forth the eight *gurudharmas*. However, their contents indicate that they were actually formulated later.[17]

As Bhikkhunī Kusuma points out, these eight rules are not vows and their chronological origins are questionable.[18] Despite major inconsistencies, the eight *gurudharmas* have traditionally been accepted at face value for centuries and have had a significant impact on the history and status of nuns in Buddhist cultures.

Ann Heirman describes the eight *gurudharmas* found in the dominant school of Vinaya in China and the only extant lineage of full ordination for women, namely, the Dharamagupta.[19] Although the texts of six different schools of Bhikṣuṇī Vinaya survive, the Dharmagupta is the only school with a living *bhikṣuṇī* lineage. This lineage is still practiced today by nuns in China, Korea, Taiwan, and Vietnam. Increasingly, the *bhikṣuṇī* precepts of the Dharmagupta lineage are also being taken by Western Buddhist nuns.[20]

By the terms of the eight *gurudharmas*, the Bhikṣuṇī Saṅgha is dependent on the Bhikṣu Saṅgha in five ways: demonstration of respect, ordination, exhortation, residence during the rainy season retreat, and reinstatement.[21] *Bhikṣuṇīs* must pay respect to *bhikṣus*, seek ordination from both Bhikṣu and Bhikṣuṇī Saṅghas, invite a *bhikṣu* twice a month to give an exhortation, hold their rains retreat in a location where there is a *bhikṣu*, and, in case of a *sanghāveṣesa* offense, be reinstated by a *manātva* conducted before both Saṅghas. Because the eight *gurudharmas* stipulate the involvement of *bhikṣus* in these five activities, they have been criticized for institutionalizing nuns' dependence on and subordination to monks. For this reason, it is necessary to reexamine the eight *gurudhamas* to assess their origins and to evaluate the impact these eight special rules have had upon the survival and health of the Bhikṣuṇī Saṅgha.[22] A thorough examination of these rules deserves a separate study, but a few points are salient to the current discussion.

MANDATING RESPECT

By today's standards, one of the most obvious indications of women's subordination is the requirement that *bhikṣuṇīs* rise, greet respectfully, and bow at the feet of *bhikṣus*. This rule is the first of the *gurudharmas*, but also occurs elsewhere in the Vinaya. Mahāprajāpatī's morning-after efforts to coax the Buddha to overturn this rule were apparently to no avail. Although some have tried to justify this convention by citing the chronological seniority of the Bhikṣu Saṅgha, the fact that *bhikṣus* are not similarly required to pay respect to *bhikṣuṇīs* is clear evidence of inequality. Thus, it is crucial to assess whether the institution of gender hierarchy, as expressed through the custom of bowing, reflects a concern with propriety and protection, is modeled on societal norms, or is a deliberately constructed hierarchical structure of control. It should be noted that *bhikṣuṇīs* are required to express respect to *bhikṣus* (fully ordained monks), but not to *śrāmaṇeras* (novice monks), as is sometimes mistakenly presumed.

In a contemporary Western social lexicon, this dictate appears antiquated and degrading to women's dignity, but this assessment is based on a particular set of cultural assumptions. Whereas in Western cultures mannerisms such as curtsies, bows, handshakes, and the like signify courtesy and respect, in traditional South Asia bowing to a person's feet is standard practice. The custom of bowing at another's feet is widely used to express respect and to punctuate social distinctions; it is not seen as demeaning or lacking in dignity. On the contrary, the demonstration of humility and respect is valued and regarded as a positive indicator of character in both women and men. Gender is but one factor involved in the custom of bowing, which reflects other equally complex social factors.

The following passage, translated from the Pāli, explains the procedure for nuns to request a bimonthly exhortation from monks and illustrates the method of bowing:

> I allow, O Bhikkhus, two or three Bhikkhunis to go together to Exhortation; and let them go up to some one Bhikkhu, and arrange their robes over one shoulder, and sitting down on their heels, let them stretch forth their joined palms, and thus address him: "The Bhikkhuni-samgha salutes the feet of the Bhikkhu-samgha, and requests permission to come for the purpose of the Exhortation being held; may that be granted," they say, to the Bhikkhuni-samgha.[23]

Whether or not the *gurudharmas* were set forth at the time of Mahāprajāpatī's ordination, which is disputed,[24] passages elsewhere in the Vinaya give evidence that the *bhikṣuṇīs* were required to bow to *bhikṣus*. However, before concluding that this requirement is evidence of sexism in the Vinaya, it is necessary to carefully consider the cultural context within which the rules were formulated. The practice of demonstrating respect by bowing and touching the feet is ancient in South Asia. Thus, to "salute the feet" of another was in line with Indian social customs of the day. The fact that a *bhikṣuṇī* had to take two or three companions with her for protection when she went to the *bhikṣus'* residence to request the exhortation (*pravārana*) shows that the safety of the *bhikṣuṇīs* was an issue. The issue was not only the safety of the nuns, similar to having a female nurse present during a male doctor's examination, but also a concern for how the nuns' behavior was perceived by outsiders, and to prevent gossip. It may be inferred that paying respect to *bhikṣus* was not intended to compromise the *bhikṣuṇīs'* virtue in any way, but instead placed the nuns under the monks' protection.

The fact that the *bhikṣuṇīs* were required to pay respect to *bhikṣus* by bowing at their feet also involves factors other than gender discrimination, namely, social hierarchies based on age. The Bhikṣu Saṅgha was originally accorded seniority over the Bhikṣuṇī Saṅgha because it was founded five years earlier. By the time the first *bhikṣuṇīs* were ordained, the Bhikṣuṇī Saṅgha was already well-organized, so the first *bhikṣuṇīs* simply adopted the precepts and procedures that had already been established. From this point of view, we can understand that the practice of nuns bowing to monks reflects the customary practice of juniors paying respect to seniors, not necessarily inferiors paying respect to superiors. However, one could counter this by saying that the temporal seniority of the Bhikṣu Saṅgha is an inadequate justification for requiring all *bhikṣuṇīs* to pay respect to all *bhikṣus*, since over time there would be many *bhikṣuṇīs* who had been ordained longer, and were thus senior to many *bhikṣus*. This argument was actually raised by Mahāprajāpatī herself, not long after her ordination. When Mahāprajāpatī asked whether *bhikṣus* and *bhikṣuṇīs* might be allowed to pay respect to one another equally, according to seniority, Ānanda pleaded her case to the Buddha, who reportedly replied:

> This is impossible, Ānanda, and unallowable, that I should so order. Even those others, Ānanda, teachers of ill doctrine, allow not such

> conduct [i.e., bowing] toward women; how much less, then, can the Tathagata allow it?[25]

From the Buddha's response, it is clear that concern for social proprieties was foremost in his mind, not simply keeping women in their place. The fact that the Buddha agreed to allow women to abandon their families and lead the life of a renunciant, in defiance of societal norms, was a radical departure that already had incurred the laity's censure. To have allowed monks to bow publicly at the feet of nuns would have been far more controversial and possibly even disastrous to the new religious order. The Buddha therefore took steps to ensure that such social improprieties did not occur. Soon thereafter, having delivered a discourse to a group of *bhikṣus*, he announced:

> You are not, O Bhikkhus, to bow down before women, to rise up in their presence, to stretch out your joined hands towards them, nor to perform towards them those duties that are proper (from an inferior to a superior). Whosoever does so, shall be guilty of a dukkata.[26]

This pronouncement leaves no doubt that the Bhikṣu Saṅgha was to be regarded as higher ranking and senior to the Bhikṣuṇī Saṅgha in terms of monastic protocol. However, the practice was clearly a reflection of, and in defense of, societal norms.

Another of the *gurudharma*s is more obviously discriminatory: A *bhikṣuṇī* is forbidden to scold, slander, or admonish a *bhikṣu*, or to point out a *bhikṣu's* misconduct, even if he has transgressed the precepts or is teaching wrong views or behaviors. This is clearly problematic for women. Althouh the interactions between *bhikṣuṇī*s and *bhikṣu*s are clearly delineated in formal situations such as the ordination ceremony, disciplinary rites, the exhortation, and in less formal circumstances such as meals, at the time of the Buddha, nuns and monks were likely to meet at they went on their daily alms round to the surrounding neighborhoods and households. The bawdy behavior of certain monks (notoriously, the Licchavis) makes it apparent that not all who wore robes were saintly. For example, an incident involving a *bhikṣu* flasher occasioned an exception to the rule requiring nuns to bow to monks. But the Buddha could not be consulted on every single incident of a *bhikṣu's* inappropriate conduct. It is possible that instances of sexual harassment, or even sexual assault, occurred outside the Buddha's range of hearing, but in such cases, the *bhikṣuṇī*s would have been left with no enlightened court of appeal. Since *bhikṣuṇī*s were forbidden to admonish *bhikṣus* in the event of their misconduct, and were forbidden to speak of their faults, *bhikṣuṇī*s entered an institution that was ripe for abuse.

On the other hand, in the social context of the time, criticizing or accusing one's protectors publicly was viewed as unacceptable behavior for either a woman or a man. The public scandal of engaging in such behavior brought into question the virtue and credibility not only of a particular person, but the whole family, or in this case, the entire Saṅgha. Obviously a conflict of interest is apparent, which is not unfamiliar within many modern institutions. A whistle-blower affects not only the person accused, but also casts doubts upon the entire organization. If the criticism is leveled by a superior against an inferior, an entirely different attitude prevails and there is no public shame for the group as a whole. The problem, therefore, pertains to hierarchical structures and not necessarily gender differences, except insofar as gender differences are frozen into hierarchical differentials.

ORDINATION PROCEDURES

The process of becoming a nun begins with a rite that symbolizes renunciation of household life and culminates with the rite of *upasampadā*, full ordination as a *bhikṣuṇī*. The list of twenty-four qualifications for joining the Saṅgha is the same for women as for men.[27] A suitable candidate is a human being, of the proper gender (female for *bhikṣuṇī*s, male for *bhikṣus*) and age (twenty years or older, except for a woman who has been married, in which case she may be twelve),[28] free of disease and deformity, free of debts and the bonds of servitude, and equipped with robes and an alms bowl. Having these qualifications is just the beginning, however. A woman who wishes to become a *bhikṣuṇī* must pass through several more stages before being accepted into the order. After receiving the "going forth" (*pravrajya*), a candidate for full ordination receives the ten precepts of a novice nun (*śrāmaṇerikā*). She then receives the precepts of a probationary nun (*śikṣamānā*)[29] and must observe them purely for two years. After that she is eligible to receive full ordination (*upasampadā*).

The *upasampadā* for *bhikṣuṇī*s signals full admission into the order, and requires the presence of both *bhikṣuṇī*s and *bhikṣus*. This is one of the procedures that institutionalizes the dependence of the order of nuns on the order of monks.[30] The requirement that nuns must receive full ordination from both Bhikṣuṇī and Bhikṣu Saṅghas makes it at least twice as difficult for a woman to gain admission to the Saṅgha as for a man. The Vinaya stipulates that a *bhikṣuṇī* must be ordained by a "dual Saṅgha," that is, a full complement of ten *bhikṣuṇī*s (twelve in the Mūlāsarvāstivāda Vinaya[31]) and a full complement of ten *bhikṣus*. These requirements may be reduced by half in a "border area" (outside Magādha, or where fully ordained Saṅgha members are scarce). Even today, with the advantages of modern communication and transportation, it is not easy to gather twenty fully qualified *bhikṣuṇī* and *bhikṣu* preceptors and witnesses. Therefore it must have been extremely difficult to assemble such a group 2500 years ago. Originally the preceptors would have had to travel by foot to the site of the ordination—a difficult and dangerous journey, particularly for women. In that social context, without legal safeguards against the harassment and assault of women, and without a code of civil rights, assembling the requisite number of preceptors would have made receiving full ordination at least twice as difficult for women as for men.

There is a story in the Vinaya texts that explains the requirement that nuns be ordained by both Saṅghas. Originally, when the nuns were brought before the Bhikṣu Saṅgha for ordination, they were too shy in front of the monks to answer certain embarrassing questions that were among the list of twenty-four qualifications for joining the Sagha, namely, those pertaining to sexuality. The Buddha is said to have suggested that a *bhikṣuṇī* preceptor be appointed to pose these questions to new female candidates, and to explain the use of robes and other requisites. Because of problems that arose when "ignorant, inexperienced" preceptors were appointed to instruct new candidates, the *bhikṣuṇī* preceptor is required to have a minimum of twelve years of seniority.

These requirements give rise to several questions. First, and perhaps most importantly, this precept raises doubts about the historicity of the eight *gurudharma*s. What is the need for a precept prohibiting *bhikṣuṇī*s from ordaining new nuns without the approval of the *bhikṣus* if this requirement is already explicit in the eight *gurudharma*s? If the eight *gurudharma*s were in place from the time of Mahāprajāpatī and were meant to apply to all nuns, why formulate this precept? Second, the ordination procedure for *bhikṣuṇī*s requires that after a candidate satisfactorily answers the twenty-four questions regarding her qualifications and receives ordination before the Bhikṣuṇī Saṅgha, she must go before the Bhikṣu Saṅgha, answer the twenty-four questions again, and receive the precepts again. Why is a second ordination required? Why is ordination before the Bhikṣuṇī Saṅgha not sufficient? One answer may be that, according to the texts, certain *bhikṣuṇī*s were ordaining women indiscriminately, without properly checking their suitability for monastic life. Therefore, for quality control, a rule was created that required approval from the Bhikṣu Saṅgha. This rule implies that *bhikṣuṇī* are not considered qualified to assess the qualifications of new members of their communities, whereas monks are. Furthermore, if the reasoning behind appointing *bhikṣuṇī* preceptors is because female candidates are too embarrassed to answer certain of the questions in front of monks, then why are female candidates required to answer those same questions a second time in front of the monks?

To receive the *upasampadā* (full ordination) a candidate must be twenty years of age. For a man, there are three stages—*pravrajya*, *śrāmaṇera*, and *bhikṣu*—with no intermediary probationary period required. In the event that a man is twenty, he theoretically can receive the *pravrajya* (going forth), the ten precepts of a *śrāmaṇera*, and then ordination as a *bhikṣu* in quick succession, proceeding swiftly from the status of a layman to the status of a *bhikṣu* in a single day. In actual practice, this accelerated ordination procedure is quite common in both Theravāda and Mahāyāna countries.

For a woman, these same stages must be completed, plus one additional stage. After receiving the *pravrajya* and the ten precepts of a *śrāmaṇerikā*, and before receiving ordination as a *bhikṣuṇī* a woman must complete a two-year probationary period as a *śikṣamānā*. This requirement is enshrined in the *gurudharma*s and evident in the precepts related to ordination. For example, a *bhikṣuṇī* who takes a *śikṣamānā* (probationary nun) as a disciple must train her properly and ordain her as a *bhikṣuṇī*, as agreed, after two years. Although the two-year probationary period was apparently not always observed, even at the time of the Buddha, the additional requirement is nonetheless clearly discriminatory.[32] The rationale given for the intermediary period of training and probation was to ascertain whether or not a candidate was pregnant, but given that the rule was inconsistently applied and that gestation in human beings is only nine months in duration, not two years, this justification becomes suspect.

Two other rules related to ordination also suggest bias against women. First, for a *bhikṣuṇī* to confer ordination, she must have been ordained for at least twelve years; a monk, in constrast, need only have been ordained for ten. Second, a *bhikṣuṇī* is permitted to ordain only one disciple each year; if she ordains more than one, she commits an offense (*pātayantika*). Yet there is no such restriction on the number of disciples a *bhikṣu* is permitted to ordain. The fact that these two precepts have no corollary among the *bhikṣu* precepts raises questions. Stories narrating the origins of these precepts indicate that they were intended to ensure that *bhikṣuṇī* precept masters (*upādhyāyikā*) were fully qualified to train their disciples. These stories imply that a *bhikṣuṇī* with more than one new disciple per year lacks sufficient time and stamina to properly care for all of the new *bhikṣuṇī*s, even though the training of monk disciples would presumably require equal amounts of time and stamina. Overall, the more demanding regulations that govern the ordination of nuns have had the effect of limiting the number of women who join the order. The additional rules may indicate a fear that the female mendicants will become too numerous, compete for available resources, and perhaps come to outnumber the monks. Indeed, in contemporary Taiwan, where nuns have equal access to full ordination status and therefore obtain sufficient support from the laity, their numbers have grown far beyond those of the monks.

THE *BHIKṢUṆĪ* PRECEPTS

A glance at the precepts contained in the codes of conduct for fully ordained nuns and monks reveals obvious gender differences. The *bhikṣuṇī* and *bhikṣu* precepts are the moral and social guidelines that regulate Buddhist monastic life. These precepts are set forth in the *Bhikṣuṇī* and *Bhikṣus Prātimoka Sūtra*s, various renditions of which survive in Pāli, Chinese, Sanskrit, and Tibetan, and have also been translated into other languages. The precepts contained in the *Prātimoka Sūtra*s are described as having been formulated one by one in response to specific problematic situations that arose between individuals within the early Buddhist monastic communities, and between Buddhist monastics and the broader community. The texts narrate stories of incidents that served as precedents for the establishment of specific precepts. These stories relate an instance of misbehavior by a monk or nun, how the matter was reported to the Buddha, the

Buddha's investigation and adjudication of the incident, his formulation of a precept, and allowable exceptions to the precept. The precepts thus attributed to the Buddha gradually evolved into the monastic codes (*Prātimokṣa*) that have served as disciplinary guidelines for monastic life in Buddhist societies for centuries. These codes provide insights on ethical values, social conventions, and gender relations that were current in India during the time of the historical Buddha.

The precepts are organized into categories based on the seriousness of the offence. A transgression of a precept of the first category, a *pārājika* (defeat, or root downfall), is the most serious, and results in expulsion from the Saṅgha. A transgression of a precept of the second category, a *sanghāveṣesa* (remainder), is grounds for suspension; a transgression of a precept of the third category, a *nihsargika-pātayantika* (abandoning downfall), entails forfeiture of the item involved. Precepts of the fourth and fifth categories, *pātayantika* (propelling downfall) and *śaikṣa* (fault) are comparatively less serious.

In addition, there are two *aniyata-dharma* (individually confessed downfalls) for *bhikṣus*, eight *pratideśanīya* (offences requiring confession) for *bhikṣuṇī*s, and seven *adhikaraṇa-śamatha-dharma* (methods for pacifying disputes) for both. Although different numbers of precepts appear in the texts of the various Vinaya schools, these differences are often simply a matter of how the lists are organized, with certain precepts sometimes grouped together.

There are four *pārājika*s for *bhikṣu*s and eight for *bhikṣuṇī*s. Based on the fact that there are twice as many *pārājika*s for *bhikṣuṇī*s than *bhikṣus*, it may be assumed that a *bhikṣuṇī* is approximately twice as likely to be expelled from the Saṅgha as a *bhikṣu*. A thorough analysis of the precepts and the texts that explain them will help determine the extent to which factors of biology, society, religion, and cultural tradition are accountable for gender differences in the monastic codes. What is obviously discriminatory is that, whereas the *bhikṣuṇī*s were required to observe many precepts that were established on the basis of a monk's misconduct, the monks were not similarly required to observe the precepts that were subsequently established on the basis of a nun's misconduct. As in the case of requiring *bhikṣuṇī*s to pay respect to *bhikṣus*, but not the reverse, this has traditionally been justified by the chronological seniority of the Bhikṣu Saṅgha.

In each Vinaya tradition, there are approximately one hundred more precepts for nuns than there are for monks. The following chart facilitates a comparison of the precepts contained in the *Bhikṣus* and *Bhikṣuṇī Prātimoka Sūtra*s of the Theravādin, Dharmagupta, and Mūlāsarvāstivādin Vinaya traditions. These three Vinaya schools are of primary concern because they are still practiced today. The Dharmagupta tradition, which is practiced in China, Korea, Taiwan, and Vietnam, still has a living *bhikṣuṇī* lineage; the Theravādin and Mūlsarvāstivādin traditions do not, although there is an active movement to restore the lineage in these traditions.

	Bhikṣu Precepts	**Bhikṣuṇī Precepts**
Theravāda (Pāli)	227	311
Dharmagupta (Chinese)	250	348
Mūlāsarvāstivāda (Tibetan)	253	364

The fact that there are nearly one hundred more precepts for *bhikṣuṇī*s than for *bhikṣu*s is often cited as evidence that nuns are more apt to commit transgressions of moral and monastic discipline than monks. When the early order of nuns was established, the *bhikṣuṇī*s were expected to observe the precepts that had already been formulated on the basis of transgressions created by monks. That is, they not only inherited a body of precepts for which they were not personally responsible, but they also were expected to observe precepts established on the basis of subsequent transgressions committed by nuns.[33] These include the four root downfalls (*pārājika*s), created as a result of the major moral transgressions committed by monks, that are cause for dismissal from the Saṅgha. In itself, this does not necessarily imply gender discrimination, for newcomers can be expected to follow guidelines for conduct that are already in place, just as a new employee is expected to follow administrative procedures that are already in place when he or she joins a new firm. The larger number of precepts is not in itself necessarily evidence of gender discrimination either, for additional guidelines occasioned by specific misdemeanors could legitimately have occasioned the establishment of new precepts, regardless of the gender of the miscreant.

According to tradition, the *bhikṣu* precepts had already been in effect for five years by the time the order of *bhikṣuṇī*s was established. Although it is highly doubtful that the *bhikṣu* precepts were fully formulated at that early date, this five-year chronological lag between the establishment of the two orders is used as a reason to justify the senior status of the monks over the nuns and the nuns' obligation to observe the precepts that had already been formulated. The increasing size of the Saṅgha community alone, to say nothing of the new circumstance of male and female celibates interacting on a daily basis within the same support communities, presented circumstances that required additional monastic guidelines. The potential problems posed by close proximity between the two celibate orders was presumably one of the main reasons the Buddha hesitated to admit women to the order. Many of the additional precepts for *bhikṣuṇī*s were established specifically to ensure their physical safety and to prevent sexual liaisons between male and female monastics.

A large number of precepts added for nuns were created on the basis of the misconduct of a particular nun, Thullananda[34] Her role as the chief miscreant among the nuns is analogous to the role of Dabba the Mallian, the chief troublemaker among the monks. Thullananda is portrayed as very contentious and headstrong, yet charismatic enough to attract a large following of disciples. Her character, as described in the texts, is so complex that at least one writer has concluded that there may have existed two nuns by the same name.[35] Whether or not this portrayal is accurate, and whether Thullananda acted alone or was simply the scapegoat for a group of women with their own agendas, her eccentric behavior alone is not sufficient cause to conclude that women behave more poorly than men. On the contrary, almost twice as many precepts were created on the basis of monks' misbehavior as were created on the basis of nuns' misbehavior. At face value, this would indicate that men, or monks, are twice as rambunctious as women, or nuns.

To investigate whether the precepts are sexist, it is necessary to move beyond mere numbers and examine the nature of the precepts themselves. First, let us examine the *pārājika*s, the serious transgressions that are grounds for expulsion from the Saṅgha. There are four *pārājika*s for *bhikṣus*: 1. sexual activity, 2. stealing, 3. killing human beings, and 4. lying about one's spiritual attainments. These four are included among the eight *pārājika*s for *bhikṣuṇī*s and are considered censurable, regardless of gender. The four additional *pārājika*s for *bhikṣuṇī*s, all of which allude to sexual behavior, are less morally objectionable and more circumstantial. In the Dharmagupta version, the fifth *pārājika* reads:

> If a *bhikṣuṇī* with lustful mind has physical contact with a man with lustful mind in the area between the armpits and the knees, be it touching, holding, stroking, pulling, pushing, rubbing up or down, lifting, lowering, grasping, or pressing, that *bhikṣuṇī* commits a *pārājika* and is expelled.[36]

In the Mūlāsarvāstivādin version, the fifth *pārājika* is substantially the same:

> If a *bhikṣuṇī*, aroused by desire, comes into bodily contact with a man aroused by desire, such that they touch one another between the eyes and the knees, and should she accept having had the experience of fully touching him, then that *bhikṣuṇī* commits a *pārājika* and is expelled from the order.[3]

The main difference between the two versions is the area of contact: the Dharmagupta indicates the area between the armpits and the knees, whereas the Mūlāsarvāstivāda indicates the area between the eyes and the knees. The Dharmagupta is far more specific about the nature of the contact. The intent in both cases is clearly to prevent the *bhikṣuṇī*s from putting themselves in compromising situations with men, situations that might lead to a breach of the first *pārājika,* which prohibits sexual activity, resulting in expulsion from the monastic community.

The intent of the sixth *pārājika* is similar. In the Dharmagupta version, the precept reads:

> Suppose a *bhikṣuṇī* with lustful mind knows a man has a lustful mind, yet allows him to hold her hand, hold her clothes, and enter a secluded place where they stand together, talk together, walk together, lean on each other, and make an appointment to meet [to make love]. If a *bhikṣuṇī* transgresses these eight things, she commits a *pārājika* and is expelled.[38]

In the Mūlāsarvāstivādin version, the sixth *pārājika* is substantially the same:

> If a *bhikṣuṇī*, aroused by desire, together with a man aroused by desire, flirts, charms, behaves immodestly, enters a place together with him, makes coquettish gestures or inviting signs, allows him to approach her or goes with him, or lies down extending her limbs in a place suitable for relations between a man and a woman, then when a *bhikṣuṇī* engages in such actions as these eight, she commits a *pārājika* and is expelled from the order.[39]

Again, the intent of the rule is clearly to protect the *bhikṣuṇī*s from putting themselves into situations that might compromise their virtue.

The seventh and eighth *pārājika*s are almost identical in all extant versions of the Vinaya. The seventh *pārājika* prohibits concealing the serious transgression (*pārājika*) of another *bhikṣuṇī*. This *pārājika* is based on an event involving a *bhikṣuṇī* named Kali who concealed the serious transgression of another *bhikṣuṇī*. Kali was accused of misconduct because she concealed the fact that a *bhikṣuṇī* under her care secretly had sexual relations with "laymen and members of non-Buddhist religions, until finally she became pregnant." Although Kali was aware that the *bhikṣuṇī* was guilty of a *pārājika*, she did not reveal the fact; consequently, not only did the miscreant continue to live in the community and presumably bring discredit upon the Bhikṣuṇī Saṅgha, but she also continued to commit one *pārājika* after another.[40]

The eighth *pārājika* is incurred when a *bhikṣuṇī* follows a *bhikṣu* who has been expelled from the Saṅgha. This *pārājika* stems from the case of Chandrakamata who, despite three admonishments, refused to stop associating with her son Chandraka who had been suspended for not admitting or recanting his offenses. The story upon which this *pārājika* is based does not specify the nature of Chandraka's offenses, but implies that *bhikṣuṇī*s who refuse to dissociate themselves from suspended *bhikṣu*s put themselves at risk and set a bad example for others. The precept further suggests that *bhikṣuṇī*s who continue to associate with undisciplined monks who refuse to accept responsibility for their actions, may put themselves in danger of sexual assault.

The additional four *pārājika*s for *bhikṣuṇī*s thus all indirectly pertain to sexual activity. They describe conduct that is censurable because it might lead to the transgression of one of the four *pārājika*s that are grounds for expulsion from the Saṅgha. One of the main critiques of the Bhikṣuṇī Saṅgha was that it placed women beyond traditional systems of protection and in close contact with unrelated males. In sixth-century BCE India, sexual assault was not uncommon and there were no social services, safety nets, or alternatives for women who were victims of rape or other forms of sexual assault.[41] Especially if they became pregnant, such women were subject to public humiliation and had few resources for material or psychological support. The protection of women was therefore a major issue in Indian society of that day, and safeguards to protect them from assault were considered positive and necessary. In the view of Inyoung Chung, "It seems that Gautama Buddha put great emphasis on providing stronger guards for the life of chastity of *bhikṣuṇī*s than *bhikṣu*s, and strong guards against sexual behavior for *bhikṣuṇī*s because of their potential fertility."[42] She argues that the additional rules to protect the *bhikṣuṇī*s from sexual contact were not a result of women's unrestrained sexual desire; rather, they were imposed because sexual liaisons might result in pregnancy and were therefore far more problematic, not only for the nuns, but for the Buddhist monastic community as a whole.

The fact remains that the precepts designed to protect nuns were only imposed on nuns and not on monks. The men with whom *bhikṣuṇī*s may have been tempted to flirt ("make coquettish gestures") or have physical contact with were not necessarily *bhikṣu*s or novice monks (*śramaṇera*s); they may also have been laymen who were not bound by the proscriptions of the Vinaya. Since laymen were not restrained by the Vinaya regulations, it is perhaps understandable that the burden of responsibility for protecting the virtue of the *bhikṣuṇī*s was assigned to the *bhikṣuṇī*s themselves. If we presume that the hazards of close proximity between male and female celibates were factors in the Buddha's hesitancy to admit women to the order, we might surmise that the fifth and sixth *pārājika*s for *bhikṣuṇī*s were designed to prevent physical contact between the *bhikṣuṇī*s and the *bhikṣu*s. The texts do not support this conclusion, however; the alleged objects of attraction in the incidents that gave rise to these *pārājika*s were not monks, but laymen. The additional *pārājika*s therefore indicate that the *bhikṣuṇī*s were to be held responsible for guarding themselves against sexual involvement, especially with men who were not ordained and thus not subject to monastic supervision and discipline. It is therefore likely that these additional *pārājika*s were established to help the *bhikṣuṇī*s delineate boundaries in dealing with members of the opposite sex, especially since many had little practical experience in this area. In the absence of fathers, husbands, and sons, the precepts functioned to protect the *bhikṣuṇī*s from sexual assault, harassment, and entanglements.

The intent behind the establishment of the two other *pārājika*s is more difficult to assess. The seventh precept, which requires nuns to reveal a *pārājika* committed by another nun, has no parallel among the *bhikṣu* precepts in any Vinaya school. This lack of parity appears to reflect women's subordinate status in the social hierarchy and the attendant assumption that women need extra supervision and control. If revealing the major transgression of a fully ordained nun is considered constructive and necessary, then it should be equally constructive and necessary for monks to reveal the major transgressions of their fellow monks. This mutual reenforcing of discipline makes its appearance at several junctures in the Vinaya texts. Enforcing the standards of monastic discipline is the main rationale for holding the *pravārana* ("invitation"), a rite that concludes the rainy season retreat (*varsa*). The *pravārana* rite requires nuns and monks to reveal what they have seen, what they have heard, and what they have suspected regarding others' transgressions of monastic discipline. Revealing the major transgressions of Saṅgha members is a sanctioned way of ensuring the purity of the Saṅgha.

The reasons for enforcing standards of monastic discipline are not difficult to understand. Not only was monastic discipline a foundation for mindfulness and self-restraint, but support from the lay community for the Saṅgha was also linked with moral purity, and when standards of behavior slipped, so did respect and donations. Maintaining the purity of the Saṅgha, then, was clearly linked to survival. Continued support for the monks and nuns required them to behave in an exemplary fashion and the precepts served as guidelines for exemplary behavior. Enforcing careful observation of the precepts ensured that high standards of conduct were kept, which would inspire the laity and, consequentially, garner sufficient material support for the Saṅgha.

Ensuring exemplary behavior may also be the rationale behind the eighth *pārājika* for *bhikṣuṇīs*. This precept suggests that women were culturally and socially predisposed to follow men, in line with women's subordinate social status. It also suggests that women's tendency to be loyal to men despite moral laxity was potentially divisive and destructive to the monastic community. Systems were crafted to enforce the expulsion of wayward monks and nuns. If Buddhist mendicants could violate the precepts with impunity, flout monastic restraints, and continue to have a loyal following, the Saṅgha would lack the internal controls needed to maintain its moral purity and authority, safeguard its reputation, and retain its present and potential benefactors.

The additional *pārājikas* for *bhikṣuṇīs* raise questions of parity and also questions of a practical nature. If the nuns were required to keep the precepts that had been established for monks before the formation of the Bhikṣu Saṅgha, why were the monks not similarly enjoined to observe the precepts that were later established for the nuns? If the circumstances surrounding the four additional *pārājikas* were perilous enough to result in the expulsion of a *bhikṣuṇī* from the Saṅgha, presumably they would have been similarly deleterious for monks.

Gauging from the Buddha's cautions against contact with women, the monks were at least as vulnerable to the attractions of the opposite sex as were the nuns, so presumably the fifth and sixth *pārājika*s would provide desirable protection for *bhikṣu*s as well as *bhikṣuṇī*s. The circumstance of the seventh precept—concealing a grave transgression—seems equally as likely for a monk as for a nun. The circumstance of the eighth precept—following someone who has been expelled—could also involve a monk. The only viable explanation for why monks were not bound by the additional *pārājika*s, then, is that the body of *bhikṣu* precepts had already been fixed and could not be expanded. But textual evidence weighs in to the contrary. Extant renditions of the *bhikṣu* precepts show considerable variation; if the body of the precepts had been fixed within the first five years of the Buddha's *parinirvāna*, as the texts would have us believe, then these subsequent variations in the texts of the different Vinaya traditions would not have occurred. If, on the other hand, the precepts were a fluid, flexible body of guidelines subject to revision, then there is no reason why useful restraints like the additional *pārājika*s could not have been added for monks, creating an equitable monastic code.

SEXISM OR SOCIAL EXPEDIENT?

The aim of this study has been to evaluate whether, or in what way, the Bhikṣuṇī Vinaya can be identified as a cause for women's subordination in Buddhist societies. The essential elements of the study have been to examine the sociocultural context within which the order of Buddhist nuns arose, and to consider practical concerns: safeguarding the nuns' commitment to celibacy and protecting them from sexual harassment and abuse. Because elements of patriarchy and sexism are inextricably interwoven in the social fabric of Indian culture, it is difficult to distinguish patriarchy from sexism or patriarchy from other hierarchical social structures.

For example, because the practice of juniors paying respect to seniors was already in place, and because the nuns were regarded as juniors both chronologically and by virtue of their gender, the first *gurudharma* requires nuns to pay respect to monks. To have sanctioned the practice of Saṅgha members paying respect based on their individual ordination seniority, regardless of gender, would have constituted a major shift in social norms and practices. To require monks to bow at the feet of nuns would have been such a radical reversal of gender norms that it might even have led society to reject the Buddha's teachings.

Although the Buddha took certain steps to challenge gender and class hierarchies by ordaining women and members of the lowest castes, the role reversal of having monks bow to nuns would have been an extreme cultural inversion that might have caused widespread rejection of his message. Given the South Asian social context within which the Buddha was operating, he decided against this innovation, arguing that even non-Buddhists did not do so. The Buddha taught enlightenment for all, but he was not explicitly a social reformer or a feminist. Although his teachings were applicable to people of all social categories and have been interpreted by some as socially liberative, his intentions were soteriological, not political. Although feminists might hope and expect an enlightened being to speak out for gender justice, no religious leader thus far has been able to totally transform the norms of social behavior. The fact that the Buddha did not tackle the social inequities of his day more directly is open to critique, but teaching the path to spiritual liberation was clearly his priority and his greater contribution to society.

From the Buddhist texts, it is clear that the Buddha regarded celibacy as the most conducive circumstance for achieving enlightenment. Because sexual attraction is a great distraction, it poses a danger to the celibate lifestyle, and therefore the Buddha warned his ordained followers against close contact with members of the opposite sex. Numerous precepts in both the Bhikṣuṇī and Bhikṣu Prātimokṣa texts are designed to prevent physical contact, as physical contact may lead to attraction, sexual desire, and intimacy:

> Monks, I know of no physical appearance which reduces a man's mind to slavery as does that of women; the minds of men are completely obsessed with women's physical appearance. Monks, I know of no sound which reduces a man's mind to slavery as does the voice of women; the minds of men are completely obsessed with women's voices. I know of no scent which reduces a man's mind to slavery as does the scent of women; the minds of men are completely obsessed with women's scent . . . taste . . . caresses.[43]

As Mohan Wijayaratna points out, the *Bhikkhu-vibhaṅgha* (in the Pāli) devotes nearly forty pages to explaining the prohibition against sexual intercourse.[44] Whether female or male, a celibate practitioner filled with sexual desire will either be listless, distracted, or tempted to transgress the precepts and revert to lay life.

Although certain passages portray women as snares and liken them to monsters, demons, and venomous black snakes, the Buddha was well aware that women and men were equally vulnerable to sexual desire. Because the Buddha's audience often consisted solely of monks, the sexual allure and seductions of women were alluded to frequently in the texts, yet the same logic applies in reverse. The precepts that prohibit monks from propositioning women, touching them, or speaking obscenely or suggestively to them, indicate that such incidents did occur. It is likely that many of the additional precepts for *bhikṣuṇī*s were established to protect them against the advances of men and are not necessarily evidence of gender discrimination.

Possible reasons for the Buddha's hesitation to admit women to the Saṅgha—the sexist attitudes that were prevalent in Indian society, the dangers inherent in having male and female celibate orders living side-by-side, the difficulties of administering the two orders, and the potential competition for limited resources—have been considered elsewhere.[45] In addition, he presumably considered the dangers and difficulties women renunciants would face. In a passage that prophesizes the decline of the *sāsana* due to the admission of women, attributed to the Buddha, he gives two similes: a dam or dike that controls water in a field and a house that protects against theft. Like a dam or dike that is used to control water or a house that offers protection against thieves, the eight *pārājika*s are presumably set forth as a protection for women. Even though Buddhist monastics voluntarily take precepts to refrain from sexual activity, they are still sexual beings. Despite their vows of celibacy, they are still vulnerable to sexual attraction. Because uprooting desire is a major goal of Buddhist practice, sexual activity (heterosexual or homosexual) is classed as a *pārājika* and the additional precepts serve as further control mechanisms to protect the monastics from "losing their vocation."

The *gurudharma*s are not precepts and do not serve the same function. Instead, they seem designed to facilitate interactions between the Bhikṣuṇī and Bhikṣu Saṅghas. These dictates are sexist in that they discriminate against women, although their purpose may have been administrative. It was necessary to regulate the interactions between the two orders, which were growing quickly, and the only pattern the early founders had was the prevailing patriarchal social norm. Modeling the Saṅgha on conventional social patterns, the *gurudharma*s assigned to nuns a status that was dependent on and subordinate to monks. This patriarchal mode of functioning made sense in the social matrix of that day. The fact that it does not make sense in today's society necessitates a reexamination of these rules and their rationale. If Buddhist monastic institutions are to continue in the modern world, they must be based on gender equity. The Bhikṣu and Bhikṣunī Saṅghas must consider alternative ways of regulating their interactions.

Neither the Buddha, his followers, nor the Buddhist monastic codes can be extracted from their social context. Gender discrimination in the Vinaya mirrors widespread gender discrimination in South Asian society during the Buddha's time. The codes of Manu that date from before the Buddha's time decree women's dependence on men and their duty to worship as a god even the most vile of husbands. The climate for female renunciants may have been even less congenial than that for laywomen; the Vinaya texts record several instances when *brahmin*s castigated *bhikṣuṇī*s as harlots, whores, and shaven-headed strumpets.[46]

There are important ways in which the Bhikṣuṇī Vinaya texts depart from prevailing patterns of gender relations. They provide women with alternatives to domestic roles, establish the Bhikṣuṇī Saṅgha as a distinct monastic institution for women, and formulate guidelines for the relatively independent functioning of the *bhikṣuṇī* community. Against the patriarchal background of South Asian society and the textual evidence of gender inequalities at the time of the Buddha, these are significant departures from the status quo. Nevertheless, because the Buddhist monastic codes were undeniably shaped by patriarchal attitudes toward women, and future generations of women were similarly shaped by the patriarchal notions embedded in the literature, a fresh look at these early Buddhist texts becomes critical. What clues might they hold to help Buddhists model a truly equitable society? Now that gender equity has become part of a new global ethic, it is opportune to explore how Buddhism's egalitarian principles can be practically applied to social and religious institutions. Instead of masking gender injustice, the Buddhist ideal of women's equal spiritual potential can be actualized in social transformation.

NOTES

1. See Diana *Paul, Women in Buddhism: Images of the Feminine in Mahāyāna Traditions* (Berkeley: University of California Press, 1985), pp. 6–7.

2. Sandra A. Wawrytko, "Sexism in the Early Saṅgha: Its Social Basis and Philosophical Dissolution," in *Buddhist Behavioral Codes and the Modern World,* Charles Wei-hsun Fu and Sandra A. Wawrytko, eds. (Westport, Conn.: Greenwood Press, 1994), p. 277.

3. Rita M. Gross, *Buddhism After Patriarchy: A Feminist History, Analysis, and Reconstruction of Buddhism* (Albany, N.Y.: State University of New York Press, 1993), p. 4.

4. Paul, *Women in Buddhism,* p. xix.

5. Ibid.

6. Liz Wilson, *Charming Cadavers: Horrific Figurations of the Feminine in Indian Buddhist Hagiographic Literature* (Chicago: University of Chicago Press, 1996), pp. 192.

7. Kornvipa Boonsue, *Buddhism and Gender Bias: An Analysis of a Jataka Tale,* Paper No. 3 (Toronto: York University Thai Studies Project, 1989), p. 4.

8. Jens Peter Laut of the University of Freiburg has translated an Old Turkish text about the establishment of the order of nuns that gives us a very different picture than other texts:

> Near the monastery Nyagrodhārāma, Paṭṭiṇī, one of Gautamī's maidservants, is telling one of Buddha's female layfollowers that Gautamī wants to present the Blessed One with a homemade robe. This is out of gratitude for establishing an order of nuns. Paṭṭiṇī then goes on to tell how the order was established. This is quite unusual, as it is a report from the female side. According to her, some time ago Lord Buddha wanted to preach the Dharma to women. But at that time the Śākya princes passed a law forbidding women to attend the Dharma sermon. The angry women met and asked Gautamī to go to her husband Śuddhodana, Buddha's father, and intervene on their behalf. He finally gives them permission to attend and Gautamī and ten thousand women go to the monastery Nyagrodhārāma. On the way they are stopped by Śākya youths, who, as expressly stated, "have not yet attained the state of holiness and are dominated by *kleśas.*" They tell them that they are not allowed to attend Dharma teachings. In addition, they argue, "Our (caste) brother, Siddhārtha, speaks of your hundred-fold sins!" When asked which sins these are, the monks mention "five sins of women." "Each woman has five sins: 1. (Women) are hot-tempered and (at the same time) anxious, 2. they are jealous, 3. they are unreliable, 4. they are ungrateful and 5. they are possessed of a strong sexuality." The women defend themselves with considerable arguments: "It was a woman who carried Siddhārtha in her womb for 9 months and 10 days! Likewise it was a woman who bore him with great pains! It was a woman who took great pains to bring him up!" Finally the women managed to get to the monastery, where Buddha gave them and the monks a teaching on the "five virtues of women:" "The virtues of women, O monks, are fivefold: 1. They neglect neither (simple) houses nor palaces, 2. they are steadfast in keeping

together earned wealth, 3. in the case of sickness they take care of both their master (i.e., husband) and unrelated persons, 4. they can enjoy pleasures together with men, and 5. Buddhas, Pratyekabuddhas, Arhats, and all fortunate beings are born of women!" The women then accuse the youths of misrepresenting Buddha in his attitude towards women. At the end of the episode Buddha gives a discourse to the women, whereupon all 180,000 Śākya women attain the state of a *srotāpanna* (stream enterer), that is, they gain the first stage in the Buddhist monastic path to salvation. The order of nuns is established.

Jens Peter Laut, "Die Griindung des buddhistischen Nonnenordens in der alttürkischen Überlieferung," in *Türkische Sprachen und Literaturen: Materialien der ersten deutschen Turkologen-Konferenz,* Ingeborg Baldauf, Klaus Kreiser, and Semih Tezcan, eds. (Wiesbaden: Societas Uralo-Altaica 29, 1991), pp. 257–74. I am grateful to Jampa Tsedroen (Carola Roloff) for bringing this research to my attention and for her translation of the passage.

9. Elizabeth J. Harris, "The Female in Buddhism," *Buddhist Women Across Cultures: Realizations,* Karma Lekshe Tsomo, ed. (Albany, N.Y.: State University of New York Press, 1999), p. 49–65.

10. Paul, *Women in Buddhism, p.* 303.

11. Wawrythko, "Sexism in the Early *Saṅgha," pp.* 277–96.

12. Gross, *Buddhism After Patriarchy,* p. 41.

13. Cheng-Mei Ku, "The Mahāyānic View of Women: A Doctrinal Study," Ph.D dissertation, University of Wisconsin-Madison, 1983.

14. Inyoung Chung, "A Buddhist View of Women: A Comparative Study of the Rules for *Bhikṣus* and *Bhikṣuṇī*s based on the Chinese *Prātimokṣa,"* MA thesis, Graduate Theological Union, Berkeley, 1995.

15. Karma Lekshe Tsomo, *Sisters in Solitude: Two Traditions of Buddhist Monastic Ethics for Women, A Comparative Analysis of the Dharmagupta and Mūlāsarvāstivāda* Bhikṣuṇī Prātimokṣa Sūtras (Albany, N.Y.: State University of New York Press, 1996).

16. Akira Hirakawa, *Monastic Discipline for the Buddhist Nuns: An English Translation of the Chinese Text of the Mahāsāṃghika-Bhikṣuṇī-Vinaya* (Patna: Kashi Prasad Jayaswal Research Institute, 1982), pp. 47–98.

17. Ibid., p. 37.

18. Bhikkhuṅī Kusuma, "Innaccuracies in Buddhist Women's History," in *Swimming Against the Stream: Innovative Buddhist Women,* Karma Lekshe Tsomo, ed. (Richmond, Surrey: Curzon Press, 2000).

19. Ann Heirman, "Some Remarks on the Rise on the *bhikṣuṇīsaṃgha* and on the Ordination Ceremony for *bhikṣuṇī*s according to the

Dharmaguptaka *Vinaya,*" *Journal of the International Association of Buddhist Studies* 19:2 (1988) 33–85.

20. For example, see Thubten Chodron's *Blossoms of the Dharma: Living as a Buddhist Nun* (Berkeley: North Atlantic Books, 1999), and Karma Lekshe Tsomo, "Buddhist Nuns: Changes and Challenges," in *Westward Dharma: Buddhism Beyond Asia,* Martin Baumann and Charles Presbish, eds. (Berkeley: University of California Press, 2002).

21. There is one *gurudharma* that appears in the Mahāsāṃghika *Bhikṣuṇī Vibbhanga* that is blatantly sexist. This rule stipulates that a *bhikṣuṇī* is not allowed to receive donations before they have been presented to monks. When a *bhikṣuṇī* is offered something, she is required to repeat a formula requesting the donor to offer the food first to the worthy *bhikṣus*. This rule would certainly spell the doom of the *bhikṣuṇī*s in time of famine or scarcity. However, the fact that the rule appears only in the Mahāsāṃghika-Lokottaravādin Vinaya and not in any other version of the eight *gurudharmas* or *Bhikṣuṇī Prātimokṣa* suggests that it is a later accretion. It appears in place of the *gurudharma* prohibiting nuns from reproaching monks. Gustav Roth, *Bhikṣuṇī-Vinaya: Manual of Discipline for Buddhist Nuns* (Patna: K. P. Jayaswal Research Institute, 1970), pp. 61–62.

22. A brief comparison of the eight rules presented in the Dharmagupta and other Vinaya schools is found in Heirman, "Some Remarks," p. 35. An edited and annotated Sanskrit edition of the *gurudharmas* as found in the Arya-Mahāsāṃghika-Lokottaravādin school is available in Roth, *Bhikṣuṇī-Vinaya,* pp. 16–72. Also useful are I. B. Homer's *The Book of the Discipline* (London: Routledge & Kegan Paul, 1982), *Women under Primitive Buddhism* (London: George Routledge and Sons, 1930); and Chatsumarn Kabilsingh's A *Comparative Study of Bhikkhunī Paṭimokkha* (Varanasi: Chaukhambha Orientalia, 1984), and *The Bhikkhunī Paṭimokkha of the Six Schools* (Bangkok: Thammasat University Press, 1991).

23. T. W. Rhys Davids and Hermann Oldenberg, trans., *Vinaya Texts,* Part III (Delhi: Motilal Bamarsidass, 1984), p. 338.

24. See Bhikkhunī Kusuma, "Inaccuracies in Buddhist Women's History."

25. *Cullavagga* X.3, in Davids and Oldenberg, *Vinaya Texts,* p. 328.

26. Ibid.

27. In the Pāli canon, the qualifications for nuns are found in *Cullavagga* X. 17; those for monks are in *Mahavagga* I.63. Ibid., p. 349.

28. This reflects the South Asian custom of child marriage. A girl who has been married is assumed to be mature and strong enough to enter monastic life. She may leave the household life at the age of ten and, after a two-year probationary period *(śikṣamānā),* may receive full ordination (*upasampadā*) as a *bhikṣuṇī.*

29. The number and content of the *śikṣamānā* precepts differ in the various Vinaya schools. In the Theravādin and Dharmagupta schools there are six: to refrain from 1. taking life, 2. taking what is not given, 3. sexual activity, 4. telling lies, 5. taking intoxicants, and 6. taking untimely food. In the Sarvāstivādin school there are also six: 1 to 4 above, plus 5. touching a male with desire in one's mind; and 6. taking a man's hand, touching his clothes, talking with him, et cetera, with desire in one's mind. The twelve *śikṣamānā* precepts of the Mūlāsarvāstivādin school and the eighteen of the Mahāsāṃghika school do not duplicate the *śrāmaṇerikā* precepts; they are probably intended to be observed in addition to the *śrāmaṇerikā* precepts. A list of these precepts is found in Hirakawa, *Monastic Discipline*, pp. 52–55.

30. The ordination process and the precepts that pertain to it are discussed in detail in Heirman, "Some Remarks," pp. 51–77.

31. The stipulation that a women must be ordained by twelve *bhikṣu*s in addition to ten *bhikṣuṇī*s is found in both the Tibetan and Chinese translations of the Mūlāsarvāstivāda Vinaya.

32. Heirman cites as evidence the fact that a lactating woman was given ordination and therefore presumably became pregnant and gave birth beforehand instead of observing the *śikṣamānā* precepts. "Some Remarks," pp. 80–81.

33. For example, *Cullavaga* X.4, in Davids and Oldenberg, *Vinaya Texts*, Part III, pp. 328–29.

34. In the Pāli, 36 of the 118 additional precepts established for *bhikṣuṇī*s are formulated due to Thullananda's misbehavior.

35. Meena Talim, *Women in Early Buddhist Literature* (Bombay: University of Bombay, 1972), p. 53.

36. Tsomo, *Sisters in Solitude*, p. 28.

37. Ibid., p. 81–82.

38. Ibid., p. 29.

39. Ibid., p. 82.

40. Hirakawa, *Monastic Discipline, p.* 121–26. The precedent is related in similar terms in all extant versions.

41. The rape of six Śākyan girls by King Virhaka and subsequently by his officer-in-carge is a case in point. Related in Roth, *Bhikṣuṇī-Vinaya*, pp. xlix–li.

42. Chung, "A Buddhist View of Women," p. 14.

43. Ibid., p. 99.

44. Mohan Wijayaratna, *Buddhist Monastic Life: According to the Texts of the Theravāda Tradition,* Claude Granger and Steven Collins, trans. (Cambridge: Cambridge University Press, 1990), p. 94.

45. Tsomo, *Buddhist Women Across Cultures,* pp. 6–7.

46. *Sacred Books of the Buddhists,* Vol. 8, pp. 178, 257. Quoted in Chung, "A Buddhist View of Women,' pp. 23–24.

Chapter 4

Transforming Conflict, Transforming Ourselves: Buddhism and Social Liberation

PAULA GREEN

The world community has become increasingly interdependent. War in one region destabilizes not only neighbors, but the global commons as well. Problems of weapons proliferation, human trafficking, poverty, and disease know no boundaries. At the same time, concepts and practices of democracy, human rights, compassion, nonviolence, reconciliation, and sustainable peace also cross borders. Karuna Center for Peacebuilding is part of a worldwide movement educating for creative peace initiatives, tolerant intercommunal relations, cooperative responses to conflict, and engagement in the peacebuilding process. This kind of change, much less visible than that which destroys, requires visionary leadership, sustained commitment, and conscious community participation.

I founded Karuna Center for Peacebuilding in 1993 in response to the growing global need to develop innovative, sustainable strategies to address ethnic, religious, and sectarian conflict. Our core mission is to pioneer efforts to promote dialogue, reconciliation, cooperative problem solving, and nonviolent solutions to conflict in troubled and war-torn regions. Karuna Center works by invitation and in partnership with in-country nongovernmental organizations (NGOs), academics, community groups, educational and religious institutions, local governments, and community peacebuilders. Through these partnerships,

Karuna Center facilitates peacebuilding trainings and intercommunal dialogue workshops designed to foster trust and communication between conflicting parties, so that together these groups can effect positive social change. The core threads that I attempt to weave together in my work include psychological training, Buddhist meditation practice, and a long-standing passion for equality, social justice, and nonviolent solutions to conflict and competing interests.

My journey as a peacebuilder began in the United States in the 1960s, before I knew myself well or had been introduced to the Dharma, and long before the word "peacebuilder" had become part of my vocabulary and identity. In recent decades, Dharma teaching, humanistic psychology, the women's movement, international relations, and inner awareness, combined with the original impulses that drew me to the civil rights and antiwar movements, led me to the Buddhist Peace Fellowship, the International Network of Engaged Buddhists, and the formation of Karuna Center for Peacebuilding. Through Karuna Center and my work as a professor at the School for International Training, I am able to act on my concern for the world, my solidarity with oppressed and war-ravaged peoples, and my values of interdependence and mutuality.

Although I no longer work solely in societies that are specifically Buddhist, as I did when Karuna Center first developed, the Dharma continues to inform my work. The teachings of the Buddha provide guidance in many situations that arise as I teach in communities recovering from war and I use these understandings as I train practitioners of conflict transformation. Of special usefulness in my work is the concept of balancing wisdom with compassion, the deep recognition of interdependence, and the insight that conflict arises from greed, anger, and delusion. It is my experience that the teachings of Buddhism, introduced in secular language, can be applied in whatever religious or national tradition is struggling to transform conflict and rebuild community. In this chapter I will explore Buddhist teachings that particularly illuminate social action, and share examples of Buddhist perceptions applied to my work in conflict transformation and reconciliation.

COMPASSION, NONVIOLENCE, AND INTERDEPENDENCE

A disciple once asked the Buddha, "Would it be true to say that a part of our training is for the development of love and compassion?" The

Buddha replied, "No, it would not be true to say this. It would be true to say that the *whole* of our training is for the development of love and compassion."[1]

Each year I facilitate an international training program called CONTACT, or Conflict Transformation Across Cultures, at the School for International Training in Vermont. Participants come from all over the world, many carrying the wounds of war and the scars of hatred and separation. At the deepest level, the intention of our month together is experiential training in compassion and love. Along with the transmission of concepts, skills, and activities, we attempt to weave a global community, to rebuild understanding where ethnic and religious groups have violated each other, and to promote understanding where the human connection has failed. This program is compassion training in action, and it works. Interreligious and intercultural differences diminish, replaced by actual experiences with others that defy inherited stereotypes. I remember an Armenian man previously taught to hate Muslims finding that his best friend at CONTACT was a Muslim man from Bosnia. The Bosnian man had also arrived hating Serbs, until he connected very deeply with a lawyer from Serbia who has remained his close friend and ally. Compassion opens hearts and breaks down walls built for protection. Compassion alone does not put an end to war or suffering, but is the foundation upon which peacebuilders can encourage mutual exploration and joint problem solving. Without compassion, the work of restoring intercommunal relations and promoting tolerance has less chance of success, for it is human relationship that provides the bonds of peace.

In addition to rooting our work in the development and expression of compassion, we uphold a firm commitment to exploring nonviolent solutions to conflict. Nonviolence can be practiced as a strategic response to conflict and as a way of life, both of which we embrace. In the conflict resolution movement, we have come to see that communities engage in endless and ultimately futile cycles of revenge and counterviolence that lead to interminable instability and suffering. Encouraging nonviolent methods of replacing the cycles of revenge with cycles of reconciliation is a central element in our work. For me, the deep commitment to nonviolence is part of my attraction to Buddhism; this philosophy resonates with my own life experience and is consistently reinforced by my witness as a conflict resolution professional.

Buddhist thinking, from the beginning to the present day, has maintained a deep commitment to nonviolence and to caring for others. For followers of the Buddhist way, meditation is the foundational discipline through which the nature of suffering is perceived and understood. Practitioners come to understand that war does not end by war, nor can anger be overcome by anger. Nonviolent responses to violence hold the potential for true transformation, and kindness holds out the possibility of redemption and reconciliation. Recently the Dalai Lama responded to a question about basic Buddhist practice, saying, "My true religion is kindness."[2] The fullness of this belief was exemplified by the Dalai Lama's acceptance speech at the 1989 Nobel Peace Prize ceremony: "I speak not with a feeling of anger or hatred towards those who are responsible for the immense suffering of our people and the destruction of our land, homes, and culture. They too are human beings who struggle to find happiness and deserve our compassion."[3]

One of Buddhism's unique contributions to today's nonviolence and social change movement is its emphasis on spiritual training, which can develop the open heart, self-knowledge, and awareness that facilitate skillful responses in a violent world. Spiritual practice has an unseen beneficent influence on one's actions in the world. Buddhist practitioners who participate in social action come to understand that to heal self and society is one and the same, that inner and outer work are imperative and interrelated. As one engages in confronting society's violence, one must simultaneously acknowledge and tame the violence within oneself. Personal and world peace are linked by the thoughts and actions of every human being; in myriad ways, we each contribute daily to a violent or a peaceful world.

Violent and nonviolent behaviors arise according to the conditions of the mind and the society. Purifying and strengthening the mind, cultivating consciousness, acting from awareness, developing abundant compassion and loving kindness, and understanding the interdependent nature of being and acting in the world can all contribute to nonviolence within the self and in the global community. Perhaps the earliest spokesperson for this current fusion of Buddhism and activism was Venerable Thich Nhat Hanh, who coined the term "Engaged Buddhism" to describe social action based on Buddhist principles. His practices were developed by necessity in the heat of the Vietnam War, where, as a monk, he developed nonviolent social service derived from Buddhist philosophy. Thich Nhat Hanh observed that meditation leads to insight, and insight leads to skillful behavior and action that can help liberate everyone involved in the war or conflict. In the past several decades, the movement of Engaged Buddhists has grown significantly and worldwide, with leading spokespersons in Asia, Europe, and North America.[4]

In the heat of confrontation between opposing ideologies or behaviors, nonviolent behavior requires discipline. Several years ago I participated in a women's march for peace in New York State led by a Buddhist nun. As our nonviolent peace walk approached the military base to express our opposition to their preparations for war, we were met with jeering neighborhood residents expressing particularly hurtful obscenities about our group. It took great presence of mind to respond with kindness, and we were grateful for the exemplary behavior of our leader, the nun Jun Yasuda, who bowed and smiled to each jeering citizen. Whatever the onlookers learned from this, at least they observed our nonviolent behavior and our refusal to turn them into enemies.

For Engaged Buddhists, perhaps the most central insight that arises in meditation practice is the realization of the interconnectedness of all life. As in meditation, the concept of a strong, separate self-identity becomes more permeable. In Karuna Center's intercommunal dialogue groups, a breakthrough to empathy and forgiveness becomes possible when adversaries are able to imagine the conditions of their opponent's lives and to understand that, under those conditions, they might well have acted the same way. A clear awareness of interconnection may develop, in which everything is seen as mutually influenced and dependent upon everything else. Through this experience of interconnection, the practitioner may realize that violent behavior produces harm to the self as well as to others. According to Buddhist scholar Joanna Macy, "This law of dependent co-arising is such that every action we take, every word we speak, every thought we think is not only affected by the other elements in the vast web of being in which all things take part, but also has results so far-reaching that we cannot see or imagine them. We simply proceed with the act for its own worth, our sense of responsibility arising from our co-participation in all existence."[5] We understand that each ripple in the pond sends changes in all directions. If the intention of our words, deeds, and thoughts are benevolent, compassionate, and clear, we have faith that the reverberations of this consciousness will add positively to the vast web of interconnection, beyond our ability to discern or control.

UPROOTING POISONS IN THE MIND

The Buddha devoted his life to the problems of the human mind. Through his own direct experience, he came to see both the causes of suffering and the path to end suffering. He identified three root causes of suffering and saw that, through meditation and principled conduct, the practitioner could develop behaviors to counterbalance each of them. The three root causes are greed, hatred, and delusion, and the antidotes for these poisons are generosity, loving-kindness, and wisdom. Wholesome and unwholesome conditions of mind exist in all of us, and that which is unwholesome can be transformed through diligent practice and awareness.

From my years of experience studying and teaching conflict analysis and the causes of interpersonal and intercommunal conflict, I have not yet found any paradigm that describes the causes of conflict more succinctly and accurately. Professionals in the fields of mental health, conflict resolution, and political science have made many attempts to probe the unseen and largely inexplicable rise to violence that seems to live so closely below the surface in human beings. Through the lens of greed, anger, and delusion, and the fear that accompanies and fuels these three toxic conditions, the violence that erupts seems explicable. Thus, for me, these clear and direct Buddhist teachings on the causes of suffering, unhappiness, and violence are of great benefit, and useful to all people whatever their spiritual or political orientation.

Greed, the first of the toxic mind states, can also be described as desire, selfishness, or clinging. We have only to look at our imbalanced world to see the effects of greed on our economic, political, social, and environmental decisions. The deleterious effects of self-interest are evident in our impoverished inner cities and the countries of the global South. Unfortunately, capitalism thrives on stimulating desire and continually increasing the appetite for more goods and services, and the capitalist system dominates the world. The Buddhist monk with his begging bowl contradicts the harmful economic misdeed of hoarding. In traditional Asian Buddhist society, the monk goes forth each morning with an empty bowl, making his alms rounds, trusting the people for his sustenance, and hoarding nothing for the next day. Whatever greed and fear arises in his mind must be managed and disciplined.

Whether in gross or subtle forms, most of us are addicted to our desires and preferences, which, with commodities such as oil, may lead to war and domination. Greed becomes a spiritual prison and ultimately a cause of misery in both individual and communal life. Uprooting greed and selfishness stands at the very heart of Buddhism; through practice and insight, we can put an end to the sufferings of unending desire, clinging, and craving. Transforming greed would radically alter our priorities, reduce our selfishness, and ultimately set the world on a much more peaceful course. Communities engaged in peacebuilding are often startled to experience the mirroring of needs on both sides. In my work, as people explore the roots of conflict and come to understand the needs of those with whom they are at war, it becomes clear that desire, greed, and hoarding have been connected with the struggle, and that more equitable distribution of resources such as land, water, and economic opportunity will help ameliorate the difficulties.

Loosening the grip of greed within the mind allows for generosity on an individual and communal level. Generosity can be consciously cultivated. Its practice can lead to an increasingly nonviolent way of life, a reduction in greed, and a greater sense of satisfaction and happiness. Meditation teacher Joseph Goldstein speaks frequently about the fruits of generosity and writes: "The karmic results of generosity are abundance and deep harmonious relationships with other people."[6] Some years ago I observed a monk who appeared to be completely and spontaneously generous. Whatever was given to him he immediately offered to someone else. I decided to follow this practice and for a number of years consciously practiced generosity as fully as I could, both materially and in terms of the spirit behind the act. I found it true that the fruits of that practice of generosity included internal happiness and harmonious relationships.

In the peacebuilding field I am frequently privileged to meet people with great spiritual generosity, sometimes risking their lives to save others in an ultimate gift of generosity. To protest war, protect the environment, and rescue those in danger, activists frequently relinquish comfort and safety, or risk arrest or death. A Bosnian colleague, who could have emigrated during the war, chose to stay in Sarajevo during the more than three years that Sarajevo was under siege, where he opened soup kitchens and established free pharmacies, distributing the only medicines available in that besieged city. When I asked Yakob why he took such a risk, he replied that five hundred years before, his people had been saved by the citizens of Sarajevo. He believed he owed them the same response. His generosity brought great happiness to many and an undoubted sense of satisfaction to his own life.

Hatred and anger are difficult mind states that frequently give rise to thoughts of violence and revenge. The Buddha likened anger to a burning coal; in the process of picking it up to throw at another, anger burns one's own hand. In anger, the mind is contracted and tight, so that a person experiencing anger is already suffering very deeply. In the peace movement, righteous indignation and anger are often used to energize and propel action. Buddhists believe that this tempting reflex creates separation. An "us/them" mentality must be avoided, because it is a form of violence that, in the end, only begets more violence. "Anger cannot be overcome with anger," wrote the Dalai Lama, "and world problems cannot be challenged by anger or hatred. They must be faced with compassion, love, and true kindness."[7]

In my rural New England town, the Japanese monks of Nipponzan Myohoji were given land to build a peace pagoda—a Buddhist stupa or shrine. At a traditional town meeting, many residents expressed strong opposition, which was likely based on their fear of difference, their lack of knowledge about Buddhism and monks, and, perhaps, veiled racism. The head monk, Venerable Kato Shonin, stood in front of the townspeople, and after each vitriolic comment, offered a long, silent, respectful bow, nothing more—no words, no anger, no justification, or explanation. For me, this was a beautiful display of dignity, discipline, and management of whatever hurt or anger may have arisen in his mind. Through his many years of practice, he was free of vengeance or unskillful and angry retorts.

Compassion (*karuna*) and loving-kindness (*metta*), the sweet fruits of meditation practice, are the antidotes to anger and hatred. Thich Nhat Hanh believes that anger has far-reaching social effects and that we should apply an antidote in the form of compensating behavior as soon as anger arises. Clearly, unskillfully expressed anger and hatred becloud the mind, poison the heart, and destroy relationships. On the world stage, intercommunal and international relations deteriorate through the hatred of prejudices and intolerance as well as through greed and selfishness. Uprooting these behaviors on a massive scale is extremely difficult and indeed has never succeeded, but we have reached a point in history where new approaches to survival must be tried. Applying the antidote of compassion to these toxic thought forms as they arise would, at the least, create a much safer and kinder world, one in which emotions could be tamed and hatreds disciplined. The Sri Lankan monk/activist Dr. Rewata Dhamma writes, "The cultivation of universal compassion by every possible means is essential, a compassion that has immediate, practical, and sustainable results in the alleviation of suffering."[8] Taking responsibility for one's anger and the harm that it causes and developing compassionate and calm mind states serves the individual, the family, the community, and society.

The third and last toxic mind state is delusion, or ignorance. This arises and is maintained by an untrained, undisciplined mind that has not been penetrated by its "user," one who has not directly experienced interdependence, the consequences of harm and anger, or the roots of alienation and violence within the self. Delusion is the state of mind that most human beings live with: confused, restless, and unhappy. Ignorance or delusion is based on a failure to penetrate the truth of *anatta*, the theory that there is no separate self. Ignorance is thus the foundation of the poisonous delusions that we have something to protect from others, that we are apart.

Through practicing one of the various forms of meditation, insight into the nature of reality can gradually replace ignorance. With devoted practice comes purification, which makes the mind less violent on increasingly subtle levels. Gross harm is avoided; awareness and self-control are increased; and, with time, wisdom develops. Ethical conduct, which is the foundation of Buddhist practice, becomes internalized, so that behavioral choices are made with great care and personal responsibility.

APPLICATIONS OF DHARMA PRINCIPLES TO PEACEBUILDING

For Buddhists involved in active nonviolence, Buddhism begins, but does not end, on the meditation cushion. The notion that Buddhism is passive is misinformed. As the Thai scholar/activist Sulak Sivaraksa writes, "Many people, particularly in the West, think that Buddhism is only for deep meditation and personal transformation, that it has nothing to do with society. This is not true. Particularly in South and Southeast Asia, for many centuries Buddhism has been a great strength for society."[9] In Tibet as well, a unique and highly principled society arose from centuries of devotion to the Buddhist path. For Engaged Buddhists, responding to the needs of others comes out of the practice and *becomes* the practice. One does not wait until personal enlightenment, or even full moral development, is attained before embarking on the path of Engaged Buddhism. Rather, one sees the reciprocal nature of practice in the meditation hall and service in the world.

In the past decade, I have had the privilege and challenge of serving as a peacebuilder in war-ravaged societies and in communities seeking to prevent the recurrence of violence. The Dharma travels with me, serving as a guide for the interventions I might suggest, the words I choose, and the particular ways that I respond as a facilitator of interethnic dialogue. Early on, I selected the term "Conflict Transformation" for my work rather than "Conflict Resolution," based on a belief, developed through meditation practice, that we must transform ourselves as we simultaneously set about transforming the unjust structures and violent behaviors in our society.

Thich Nhat Hanh's poem, "Please Call Me by My True Names," repeatedly comes to mind when I engage with war victims and transgressors, reminding me that we are all capable of extremes of innocence and treachery, kindness and cruelty. One verse from his poem is especially illustrative of the illusion of blame and separation:

> I am the 12-year-old girl, refugee on a small boat,
> who throws herself into the ocean
> after being raped by a sea pirate,
> and I am the pirate,
> my heart not yet capable of seeing and loving.[10]

The knowledge that we are all capable of inflicting great harm helps me monitor self-righteousness and separation. The Buddhist insight that, at the deepest level, there is no separation between self and other is crucial, albeit difficult to experience. Groups in conflict instinctively separate and sort, identifying themselves as fully good and others as completely evil. Utilizing these Buddhist teachings about interdependence and nonseparation helps me stay related to all sides and guides my encouragement of community rebuilding after war.

Postconflict dialogue groups attempt to cut through this separation and identification. Working with the same people over many years, I can observe the gradual relinquishment of separateness and the acknowledgment of commonality and binding ties. Participants come to recognize and own the tendency toward violence inside themselves, as well as the gifts of altruism and compassion that exist among their opponents. I have seen this occur among group members in Bosnia and Rwanda who have been wrenched apart by ethnic warfare and now face the task of rebuilding their communities. Difficult as this task is, they are able to retract their projections of evil, own their own aggression, and rehumanize the other.

When I express my compassion, group members experience my care for them, which acts as a model and also gives them psychological permission to express their own compassion and loving-kindness. Through this process of opening to others, group members often discover their mutual needs and interests, which serve as an important bridge in resolving the underlying conflicts causing the violence. In the process of postconflict reconciliation, it is essential to recognize that all sides suffer during and after conflict, and that all parties have unmet needs. In the end, there are no winners in these wars, only damaged and hurting communities and individuals.

Although I do not talk about Buddhism or give Dharma talks during international workshops, the Buddhist concepts and beliefs that I have been taught are apparent to participants in my workshops and classes. In times of anxiety or danger, I remember to breathe and smile. I encourage silence and self-reflection, attention to thought processes, and deep listening. When we hear the stories of suffering, I invite participants to take in the pain of the speaker and then breathe it out. I may speak about impermanence and about the great turning of the wheel that carries all of us through time and brings us measures of both joy and suffering, which reminds those suffering from the wounds of war that joy will again be possible. In non-Buddhist regions, such as Africa, the Middle East, and the Balkans, we avoid specifically Buddhist language, but workshop participants recognize the value of interdependence and the need for compassionate social engagement.

WOMEN'S LEADERSHIP IN SOCIAL TRANSFORMATION

Women in the Buddhist community and beyond have a decisive role to play in the immense tasks of personal and social transformation. Sidelined from the halls of power for too long, women manage interpersonal and familial peacemaking, but rarely serve as policy makers. While we cannot assume that all women in powerful positions will advocate nonviolent conflict resolution, we can hypothesize that sufficient numbers of female decision makers will change the worldwide culture of war and edge humanity closer to a global culture of peace. Thus women must become educated and empowered visionaries, full partners in creating a new political paradigm based on women's strengths of connection, collaboration, and interdependence.

In Buddhist contexts in North America, Europe, and Asia, many accomplished women are engaged as intellectual, spiritual, moral, and social leaders within the Saṅgha and the academy. The authors represented in this volume are among them. Their influence on the future of Buddhism is not in doubt. Hopefully, gender struggles in the Buddhist community will eventually move forward to allow full ordination, equality for nuns, and equivalent educational opportunities for women. The gradual resolution of these issues will influence laywomen in Asia and the West, who will be taught the Dharma by ordained women who value their contributions and are sensitive to their priorities, fears, and cultural restrictions.

Women in leadership roles within and beyond Buddhist circles are challenged by the difficulties of maintaining core values of connection and relationship while negotiating in the halls of power, whether academic, political, corporate, or religious. Dharma inculcates an understanding of interdependence and mutuality, and there is much in women's lived experiences that echoes this theme. Contemporary life pulls in the other direction, toward individualism, self-centered fulfillment of one's personal needs, and competition for power and privilege. How women negotiate these opposing poles may determine the depth of women's abilities to change society and to nurture nonviolent responses to the conflicts that inevitably arise in human interaction.

Women have always been the indirect victims of war. In current warfare, women and children are direct victims, with extremely high casualty and refugee rates. In World War I, 10 percent of war casualties occurred among civilian populations; in the 1990s, that figure has jumped to 90 percent of war casualties occurring among civilian populations, most of them women and children. While many women perceive that cycles of revenge and retaliation only create more suffering, women in most circumstances have little control over their situations. Women are often pressured by their own desperation and destitution to support violence in a futile effort to restore stability to their lives. Offered skillful leadership, however, most women in war zones would opt for negotiation over more warfare, and for just distribution of resources over greed. How to mobilize these voices, silenced by deprivation, isolation, guns, tribal loyalties, and fear, remains a challenge for women in leadership generally, and for Buddhist women committed to nonviolent social liberation.

Within and beyond Buddhism, women have the power to put forward an alternative vision, mobilize their allies, and use their skills to change the course of history. Or, on the contrary, women can be seduced by the mind-numbing lures of contemporary life, lose the threads of connection, and imitate the worst of our social norms. The choices are clear. Without the moderating voices of women and women's values of connection and mutuality worldwide, the global community will likely slide into further conflict and chaos. As natural resources become progressively scarcer, as nations vie for power and supremacy, as populations increase and migrate, humanity will need wise and visionary leaders with a deep understanding of interconnection and dependent co-arising. To manage these multiple crises and prevent catastrophe from consuming the global commons, the relational and nonviolent values traditionally held by women in most parts of the world will be needed by both men and women to solve global problems and ensure human survival. Women trained in the Dharma have much to contribute to this necessary change of direction. It is of critical importance that their voices become part of a new paradigm of gender-inclusive, spiritually based social activism.

BUDDHISM AND SOCIAL LIBERATION: THE CHALLENGES BEFORE US

Buddhism rests on the two foundations of wisdom and compassion. Without wisdom and insight, human beings cannot know how to act skillfully, and our behavior may be unwholesome. Without compassion, our actions may be dry and distant, lacking sufficient heart. One puzzling aspect of applying Buddhism to social transformation is the understanding that wisdom and compassion arise from long years of disciplined practice and cannot be instantly attained, simply taught through texts, or transmitted through Dharma talks. Wisdom and compassion are the fruits of great effort. We see the results of great effort and discipline exemplified in such leaders as the Dalai Lama of Tibet and Aung San Suu Kyi from Burma, and we are automatically drawn to their light. We recognize the benefits of enlightened leadership in its service to all humanity, and we know its depth and solidity.

Although most beings do not, will not, and often cannot engage in such a profound commitment to developing realization, their efforts must be harnessed in the service of planetary change. Thus, questions abound. If there is no instant access to wisdom and compassion, and if the world is in as precarious a moment as it appears to be, how do we utilize Dharma wisdom in global change? How do we increase the capacity for enlightened leadership? Can the voices of highly developed spiritual leaders be suitably amplified to lead countries and communities toward peace and reconciliation? Can such voices of wisdom arise in the United States, currently a source of so much suffering for many of the world's peoples? Without the personal experiences of transformational insight on the part of community members, is skillful leadership sufficient?

One small answer emerges from our experiments in dialogue between people caught in extremities of conflict and stress. When the facilitators are able to create a safe environment, the highest wisdom and compassion can emerge, wounds will heal and individuals engaged in this healing process can bring along their communities. People and communities can and do change, frequently for the better. These changes can be maximized and amplified with cooperation from the world's media and political bodies. Even without ultimate wisdom, much can be preserved and much violence can be prevented. The nascent movements of Engaged Buddhism and conflict transformation are worthy of more investment, as are other burgeoning nongovernmental organizations (NGOs) whose rapid rise is indeed transforming societies.

For people familiar with Buddhism and searching for peaceful conflict resolution, these questions are the puzzles and perhaps the koans for our time. Despite the spread of Dharma study and practice in the United States, for example, we do not find Buddhists at the forefront of movements that oppose war. Nor do we find a flowering of generosity, compassion, and nonviolence in countries with predominately Buddhist populations. We have only to look at the repressive government of Burma, the autogenocide in Cambodia, or the role of the Buddhist clergy in opposing the Sri Lankan peace process to remember that Buddhist countries also experience communal violence and a lack of compassion. We might wonder whether the nature of Buddhism or the particular style of teaching Dharma creates a quiescent population focused on inner change and personal relations. Can the teachings of Buddhism be made more relevant to social, economic, and political concerns, given the level of suffering they cause? Would such an effort weaken Dharma, as some may fear, or would it extend the gifts of insight and compassion to more populations and conditions, thus serving the whole even more fully?

The teachings of mindfulness and skillful means, of kindness and compassion, of change and impermanence, of silence and stillness, are taught with great richness and depth in Buddhism. Young people raised with peace, altruism, and compassion are shaped by ideals that seem especially relevant for our scattered, high-speed, overstimulated, and self-absorbed modern societies. When leaders value and model generosity and concern, people modify their behavior and inculcate ethics that are less opportunistic and self-serving. The clear and forthright practice of generosity, loving-kindness, and wisdom—the antidotes for greed, anger, and delusion—would have a healing effect globally. Daily reports of altruistic behavior and attitudes coming from political, religious, social, or academic leaders could stimulate our imagination and encourage new methods for responding to conflict and differences.

Engaged Buddhist leader Joanna Macy wrote: "It is my experience that the world itself has a role to play in our liberation. Its very pressures, pains, and risks can wake us up, release us from the bonds of ego and guide us home to our vast true nature."[11] Through engagement with the world and its concerns, we practice generosity, increase wisdom, deepen our understanding of suffering, and experience our interconnection. Whether as women, Buddhists, leaders, followers, or simply citizens of this planet, we are bound together in what the people of South African call *ubuntu*, described by Archbishop Desmond Tutu: "We belong in a bundle of life. My humanity is caught up, is inextricably bound up, with others."[12] For Buddhists, this is what Thich Nhat Hanh refers to as "interbeing."

Interbeing, or *ubuntu*, is the human condition. How we use this profound insight to guide our actions, shape our decisions, influence our steps toward relieving human oppression and pursuing a nonviolent path of peacebuilding is up to us. The way seems clear when we remember again the wisdom of the Buddha that the whole of our training is for the development of love and compassion.

NOTES

1. Fred Eppsteiner, ed., *The Path of Compassion* (Berkeley, CA: Parallax Press, 1985), p. 19.

2. *Reconciliation International* 7:1 (1992), p. 19.

3. Sidney Piburn, ed., *A Policy of Kindness: An Anthology of Writings by and About the Dalai Lama* (Ithaca, N.Y.: Snow Lion, 1990), p. 16.

4. For more information on Engaged Buddhism, see Christopher S. Queen and Sallie B. King, eds., *Engaged Buddhism: Buddhist Liberation Movements in Asia* (Albany, N.Y.: State University of New York Press, 1996); and Christopher S. Queen, ed., *Engaged Buddhism in the West* (Boston: Wisdom Publications, 2000).

5. Joanna Macy in Eppsteiner, p. 172.

6. Joseph Goldstein, *Experience of Insight* (Boston: Shambhala Publications, 1976), p. 74.

7. Piburn, ed., *A Policy of Kindness*, pp. 54–55.

8. *World Council on Religion and Peace Newsletter* 1991, p. 1.

9. Sulak Sivaraksa in Eppsteiner, p. 12.

10. Ibid., p. 31. Also see Thich Nhat Hanh, *Please Call Me by My True Names* (Berkeley, CA: Parallax Press, 1993).

11. Joanna Macy, *World as Lover, World as Self* (Berkeley, CA: Parallax Press, 1991), p. 8.

12. Desmond Tutu, *No Future Without Forgiveness* (London: Random House, 1999), p. 35.

Chapter 5

Redefining and Expanding the Self in Conflict Resolution

MEENAKSHI CHHABRA

In the seventh chapter of the *Lotus Sūtra*, The Parable of the Phantom City, the Buddha narrates a story to his disciples about a leader who guides a group of people along a difficult and treacherous path toward a place full of rare treasures. After journeying part of the way, the group becomes disheartened and addresses the leader, "We are utterly exhausted and fearful as well. We cannot go any farther. Since there is still such a long distance to go, we would like to turn around now and go back." At this point, the leader conjures up a phantom city so that the group can rest there. Once they have rested, the leader erases the phantom city so that the group can continue on their journey to the place of rare treasures. Like the phantom city in this parable, images of world peace and social harmony give hope and encouragement to those engaged in the work of conflict resolution.

APPROACHES TO CONFLICT RESOLUTION

A wide spectrum of conflict resolution approaches have emerged in the last century, ranging from "hard power" (the use of force), to adjudication, arbitration, negotiation and mediation, interactive problem solving, and reconciliation. As seen in the case of Bosnia, forcibly imposed "hard power" solutions are not real solutions at all, since they usually leave wounds that continue to fester, leading to an intractable cycle of conflict and revenge. Although adjudication, arbitration, negotiation, and mediation have quelled the conflict, they have failed to deal with its causes. As a result, the solutions that have emerged out of the conflict have been difficult to sustain.

The interactive problem solving approach has a sociopsychological basis. It focuses on resistance to change, a resistance that is typically rooted in psychological needs and pervasive fears. The psychological needs that can be identified include cultural identity, security, recognition, participation, dignity, and justice. The fears that can be identified are often rooted in being deprived of these needs. Interactive problem solving seeks to understand the impact these needs and fears have on people's perceptions and beliefs.

Thus far, the field of conflict resolution has focused on either the political or the social-psychological dimension of human experience. Like an ancient three-legged kettle that struggles to balance on two legs, conflict resolution strategies that have been grounded on political and sociopsychological theories are missing a vital component. Until reconciliation work began in South Africa, an entire dimension of human experience was left out of the field of conflict resolution—the dimension of spiritual experience. It is this third dimension of experience, the missing third leg of the kettle, that can bring balance to the field of conflict resolution. This is the challenge for the twenty-first century.

In this chapter I attempt to respond to this challenge. The two lenses that I bring to this challenge are my practice of Buddhism, as taught by Nichiren Daishonin and practiced in Soka Gakkai International (SGI), and my experience with the interactive problem solving approach as a student in the field of conflict resolution.

THE WIDELY ACCEPTED CONCEPT OF SELF

Why have contemporary theories of conflict resolution focused on the political and psychological dimensions of human experience and neglected the spiritual dimension? This has not been a deliberate oversight, but instead appears to be dictated by widely accepted conceptualizations of the "self." According to Mead's theory, there are two aspects of this self: the "I" and the "Me."[1] The I is the core identity—

that which one cannot change. The second aspect, the Me, is that part of the self that is socially constructed—that which evolves as a consequence of our interactions with the world.

We use these interactions with the world to construct our own reality and end up with a set of beliefs about the self, others, and the world. Along with the beliefs that we establish comes a degree of certainty about those beliefs, a strong desire to be "right," and a strong aversion to being "wrong." These beliefs create a sense of inner coherence and also provide us with a set of expectations about the world. A major challenge to this process is being able to maintain this coherence while integrating new information from the outside world. When we are in a learning mode, in the best case scenario, we are in a mode to assimilate information from the outside and accommodate to it. We can tolerate some uncertainty about our beliefs, accepting that these beliefs may change after learning more from our experiences of others and the world, or may even have been "wrong" from the beginning.[2]

THE SELF IN CONFLICT

As individuals, even under the best of circumstances, there are limits to how much new learning we can tolerate. We know when we have reached the limits of our tolerance, because we feel it or experience it as an overload. We begin to psychologically "disintegrate." This is experienced as fear, anxiety, anger, exhaustion, and a general psychological destabilization. At these times, an automatic, self-preserving homeostatic process is activated that shuts down the learning channels. As a consequence, the capacity to take in information about others and the world becomes frozen, as do our existing beliefs about the self, others, and the world. As a result of this "shut down," beliefs crystalize and we become resistant to change. Certainty about our assessment of what is "right" arises, and feelings of ambivalence about what we "know" are lost. Our capacity to accommodate and to assimilate new information are lost in the service of self-protection.[3]

This same psychology becomes activated in conflicts. The conflicting parties feel destabilized by the threatening event, which creates fear, anger, anxiety, and a strong sense of self-protection. There is a communication breakdown between the parties, which further exacerbates the frozen images of the other. The communication void becomes filled with more negativity and hostility, giving rise to a number of cognitive distortions about the other.[4] In turn, these developments further limit our chances for new learning.

Along with the frozen beliefs and the shut down comes an intensive need to be "right" and to place the blame for what has happened on an "evil aggressor." There is rarely any self-reflection about our own contribution to the conflict. The threat at this point is not to the individual, but rather to the way we are able to maintain our coherence or stability. The threat is to our beliefs and the "rightness" of those beliefs. In the face of the fear of the other, it becomes threatening to let go of those beliefs that have so long stabilized us. It becomes difficult, almost impossible, for people to disengage themselves from that mode of being.[5] When this happens, any attempt at conflict resolution reaches a deadlock. The challenge then becomes how to open up the learning process so that an individual can reflect on his or her own role in the perpetuation and escalation of the conflict and take responsibility for the stalemate. What solutions can Buddhism offer to this impasse?

BUDDHIST CONCEPT OF SELF

In the Yogacāra school of Buddhism, the concept of self is anchored in the concept of nine consciousnesses. The first five consciousnesses correspond to conventional notions of the five senses—sight, hearing, smell, taste, and touch—that arise as a result of the contact of the five sensory organs—eyes, ears, nose, tongue, and skin—with their respective objects. The sixth consciousness integrates information gathered by our five senses to form coherent images and distinguish among objects. For example, this mental consciousness distinguishes, "This is a chair, it is hard;" "This is an apple, it is edible;" and so on. These six consciousnesses function in response to everyday external objects and are entirely influenced by phenomenal notions of time and space. They operate on the outer surface of the mind, that is, in the conscious realm. These six consciousnesses correspond to the concept of "I" in relation to "others," rooted in the belief of an unchanging self or permanent self.

Buddhism teaches that reason, logic, or judgments based on the sixth type of consciousness can easily be overrun by impulses from a deeper level of the mind. Intelligence is often powerless when confronted by self-centered egoism or distorted perception. What is the root of such impulses? Yogacāra Buddhism explains that there is a part of our mind, called the seventh level of consciousness, or *mano* consciousness, which operates independently of any external circumstances. It relates to the unseen or to abstract thought, and enables one to make moral value judgments, for example, "It is wrong to kill," "Beethoven was a great composer," and so on. Worldly desires and attachments are also said to arise from this level of consciousness. Thus, although the seventh consciousness can be a locus of reason, it is simultaneously a reflection of one's attachment to self or ego, tempting one into arrogance and egoism. In a state of egoism, the self looks down on others and does not hesitate to sacrifice them out of self-interest. It is this function of the seventh consciousness that confines us within the framework of our own ego and gets us excessively activated in situations of conflict. Due to the inherently unstable nature of the *mano* consciousness, one is urged to go beyond this level of consciousness.

The eighth consciousness taught in the Yogacāra school is the *ālaya* consciousness, from the Sanskrit term for storehouse, or receptacle, of all karma. In Buddhism, karma refers to actions, including thoughts, words, and deeds. All actions, positive and negative, in the present and past lives, are imprinted as latent tendencies, or "seeds" in the *ālaya* consciousness. When activated by an external stimulus, the karmic imprints stored in the *ālaya* consciousness produce corresponding effects on the functioning of the first seven consciousnesses. The *ālaya* consciousness thus continues to flow like a "life flow," reflecting the law of cause and effect throughout the three times—past, present, and future. It is a continuity of intense karmic energy that flows through life and death and changes from moment to moment.

This *ālaya* consciousness goes beyond the individual. It contains not only the individual's karma, but also the karma common to one's family, ethnic heritage, and even to humanity as a whole. The culture or nationality of a people is thought to derive directly from their shared karma. This is not fixed, eternal, or unchanging, but is relative, contingent, and evolving. The realm of *ālaya* consciousness broadly links all living beings; in this sense, it can be correlated to the notion of the collective unconscious proposed by C. G. Jung.

Some Yogacāra Buddhist scholars posit the existence of a ninth consciousness, the *amala* consciousness, which is a level of awareness deeper than the *ālaya* consciousness. The Sanskrit word *amala* means "pure." The *amala* consciousness remains untainted by karmic accretions; it is eternal, immutable, and one with the life of the cosmos. In this system of Buddhist thought, the *amala* consciousness is regarded as a life force or greater self. It is not a fixed entity and does not negate the sense of self that appears to the six consciousnesses; rather, the ninth consciousness manifests itself through the self in the six consciousnesses. However, in contrast to the widely accepted notion of a self that is caught up in self-seeking behavior, this greater self, which is sometimes called "no-self" (*anatman*) in Buddhism, is not caught up in the snares of egoism. The fundamental identification of oneself with the entire living universe, one's true self, is *amala* consciousness.

Central to this greater self are the concepts of dependent arising and the Treasure Tower. The Treasure Tower is depicted in the *Lotus Sūtra* as symbolic of universal life and the Buddha nature that exists within all human beings. The concept of dependent arising (*pratityasamutpāda*) explains the coexistence and interconnectedness of all things in the universe, including human beings and nature. It denotes that all things exist in interdependent, mutually supportive relationships—what modern philosophers might call "a semantic whole." These two concepts—the Treasure Tower and dependent arising—confirm the Buddhist ideals of respect for life and the right of all living beings to exist. These two principles lie at the core of the greater self.

BUDDHIST CONCEPTS OF SELF AND CONFLICT

What implications does this concept of self have for conflict resolution? Buddhism regards the three poisons—greed, anger, and ignorance—as the underlying causes of conflict. Issues at stake in a conflict include land, power, respect, and so on. Desire for these things and resistance to change are functions of greed. In a conflict, greed is often magnified, as two or more parties seek their own gain at the expense of the other. The conflicts that result further compound the feelings of greed and anger, and thought patterns become hardened into attitudes of fear, hostility, and resentment. Conflicts also involve absolute and unchanging images of self. The illusion of the self leads all parties to cling to images of "self" and "enemy," which also become hardened into fixed attitudes.

In the Buddhist view, to bring peace and security we must transform these three poisons of greed, anger, and ignorance into the three virtues of responsibility, compassion, and wisdom. How can one effect the transformation of unwholesome attitudes to wholesome ones? This transformation cannot be effected merely through intelligence, judgment, or reason. Nichiren Daishonin states, "Base your heart on the ninth consciousness and your practice on the six consciousnesses."[6] This implies that by awakening the ninth consciousness and developing it, this fundamental pure consciousness will awaken the power and wisdom of all the other consciousnesses. In other words, tapping into the *amala* consciousness enables us to develop a wisdom that perceives the world without distortions. We become able to perceive the fundamental nature common to all, without discrimination, and to overcome the fervent attachment to ego. As a result of this self-transformation, we take actions that are rooted in a sense of responsibility and compassion, and therefore benefit ourselves and others. Awakening to this expanded concept of self is the answer to the self deadlocked in conflict.

IMPLICATIONS FOR CONFLICT RESOLUTION

How does one awaken to this expanded concept of self? Daisaku Ikeda's interpretation of Nichiren Daishonin's Buddhism gives concrete expression to the ninth consciousness, *amala*, in the phrase "*Nam Myoho Renge Kyo*," a homage to the *Lotus Sūtra*.[7] It is given physical form in the *mandala*, or *gohonzon*, the shrine or altar which is the object of worship in the homes of SGI (Soka Gakkai International) members and in SGI community centers. When members of SGI practice every morning and evening, they recite the second and sixteenth chapters of the *Lotus Sūtra* and chant "*Nam Myoho Renge Kyo*" before the *gohonzon*. The significance of this practice is that, by offering prayers to the *gohonzon*, which is the embodiment of the *amala* consciousness, practitioners tap into the *amala* consciousness—the life force or Buddha nature within their own lives. This experience of connecting with the *amala* consciousness then influences and permeates all the other eight consciousnesses—the realms of thought and action.

In Nichiren Daishonin's view, Buddhism also expounds the principle of oneness of life and environment. He writes, "Environment is like the shadow, and life is like the body. Without the body, there can be no shadow."[8] "Life" here refers to the subjective self and "environment" refers to the world around us. In other words, there is a symbiotic relationship between our subjective self and our surroundings. This also suggests that individuals can influence and reform their environments through inner change. This is the theme that resonates in the words of Daisaku Ikeda, President of SGI: "A great human revolution in just a single individual will help achieve a change in the destiny of a nation and further will enable a change in the destiny of all humankind."[9]

How does this "human revolution" play out practically in conflict resolution? Applying the principle of oneness of life and environment to situations of conflict, the discordant parties will uphold the principle of dialogue as central to the process of conflict resolution. Dialogue is not simply an assertion of our own beliefs, it is rooted in a conscious effort by both parties to mutually understand the other. For a third party, dialogue implies bringing one's presence to the table and indirectly influencing the process of conflict resolution. Practical guidelines for the process are found in the *Lotus Sūtra*: "To open, show, awaken, and cause all living beings to enter the way." "To open" signifies opening the way to deliberate engagement and dialogue between people and cultures in conflict. "To show" means to help participants see the prejudices about others they hold in their hearts and minds, and see their potential to bring about change. Through this process, it is possible to awaken them to the numerous possibilities and dynamic nature of human relationships. Finally, the process can "cause them to enter" into a new mode of relationship, free from fears about the differences between self and others, with respect and the courage to learn from others.

For a third party, an awareness of the nine consciousnesses would also have implications for the process of conflict resolution, especially for the politics of identity. During the process of conflict resolution, rather than perceiving moments of identity crisis as moments of deadlock, these moments can instead be viewed as opportunities to push the dialogue forward in new directions and toward new understandings of self and identity, especially toward a greater sense of human beings' common humanity. Interactive problem solving workshops require building trust between two parties. Building trust does not necessarily signal a shift in identity, however. It does not necessarily lead to the understanding that, "I share your suffering as a human being." A shift toward this more expansive notion of self would contribute greatly to closing the gap between the two sides, establishing fresh perceptions of self and other.

As a practical strategy in the process of conflict resolution, this kind of identity expansion can be used to design interventions that create a sense of shared suffering and trauma. Throughout human history, practically all religions and cultures share concepts that can be used as the underpinnings for dialogue. These shared concepts, traditions, and beliefs can be employed to develop appropriate methods of acknowledging the past, validating the sufferings of both parties, and developing a sense of shared humanity.

The concept of nine consciousnesses can also be applied to address the tension that exists between conflict resolution and issues of justice and human rights, which may seem to be at opposite ends of the peacebuilding continuum. Buddhism upholds the ideals of respect for life and the rights of all living beings to exist. From this perspective, both conflict resolution and issues of justice and human rights are central to the process of peacebuilding. Drawing from the *Nirvāna Sūtra*, Nichiren Daishonin writes, "One who rids the offender of evil is acting as a parent." An offense here means any act that tramples human dignity and disrespects others. To "rid the offender of evil" requires commitments from both sides, the offender and the victim. The offender must take responsibility for the offense and make a commitment not to repeat the offense against anyone in the future. The victim must take responsibility for letting go and make a commitment to transform feelings of anger and hatred into feelings of compassion toward the offender. Both take responsibility to ensure that justice will not be guided by feelings of ill will and revenge.

From this, it follows that issues of human rights and justice are addressed as part of the conflict resolution process. It also follows that these issues are not addressed from a self-righteous or self-centered perspective on the part of the victim or a sense of guilt on the part of the offender. Instead, both parties must accept shared responsibility for future outcomes, acting so that human beings will not experience these sufferings again. In a sense, each self experiences an identity shift or, more appropriately, an expanded sense of identity, as explained before. Since justice and human rights are integral to the conflict resolution process, building peace in this way will be more sustainable. In practical terms, interventions that facilitate identity expansion should occur prior to the process of conflict resolution and prior to dealing with issues of justice and rights. Further research, workshops, and interpersonal applications will be necessary to assess the effectiveness of these interventions.

BUDDHIST WOMEN AND CONFLICT RESOLUTION

What is the role of Buddhist women in peacebuilding? What can Buddhist women bring to the process of conflict resolution? According to the United Nations, women and their families fleeing from conflicts make up 80 percent of the world's refugees. Throughout the last century, a clear trend emerged toward greater civilian participation in wars and conflicts. This was the case in the two World Wars, in the ethnic conflicts in Rwanda and Bosnia, and many other areas of the world. Women and their families suffered disproportionately in these conflicts. The inconceivable sufferings that women have experienced have caused them to envision societies without war. Even if they are called "naïve idealists" for their beliefs, women persist in their idealism, which, they say, is simply common sense. The unconditional compassion and optimism of these women lend conviction to their beliefs.

The *Lotus Sūtra* refers to the dragon king's daughter as one whose "eloquence knows no hindrance" and who "thinks of all living beings with compassion, as though they were her own children." Women who have the conviction to articulate their ideals and the ability to speak out with all-embracing compassion can greatly enhance the process of peacebuilding and create a future filled with hope. My personal reflection expresses this hope:

> Why do we bring life into the world, my friends?
> Not to lose it to hate and anger,
> But to experience the joy of life.
> One step at a time,
> We will build phantom cities
> Of peace along the way.
> Together we create a future time
> When we triumphantly declare
> The joy of life itself.

NOTES

1. Mead, George Herbert, *Mind, Self and Society from the Standpoint of a Social Behaviorist* (Chicago: University of Chicago Press, 1967), pp. 209–10.

2. Jean Piaget, *The Construction of Reality in the Child* (New York: Basic Books, 1954), pp. 361–62.

3. Donna Hicks, "How Functional Aspects of Identity become Dysfunctional in Protracted Conflict" (paper presented at the Twelfth Conference of the International Association for Conflict Management in San Sebastian-Donostia, Spain on June 22, 1999).

4. See Herbert C. Kelman, "Social Psychological Dimensions of International Conflict," in *Peacemaking in International Contflict: Methods & Techniques,* I. W. Zartman and J. L. Rasmussen, eds. (Washington, D.C.: United States Institute of Peace, 1997); and R. Holt and B. Silverstein, "On the Psychology of Enemy Images: Introduction and Overview," Journal *of Social Issues* 45:2 (1989) 1–11.

5. Hicks, "How Functional Aspects of Identity become Dysfunctional."

6. "Hell in the Land of Tranquil Light," in *The Writings of Nichiren Daishonin,* ed. and trans. by The Gosho Translation Committee (Tokyo: Soka Gakkai, 1999), p. 458.

7. Further explanation of Daisaku Ikeda's interpretation of the Buddhist concept of self can be found in, "Nine Consciousnesses—Probing the Depths of Life," in *Unlocking the Mysteries of Birth and Death: Buddhism in the Contemporary World* (London: Warner Book, 1994).

8. "On Omens," *The Writings of Nichiren Daishonin,* p. 644.

9. Daisaku Ikeda, *The Human Revolution, Vol. I* (Taplow, U.K.: Soka Gakkai Intemational, 1994), p. v.

Chapter 6

Integrating Feminist Theory and Engaged Buddhism: Counseling Women Survivors of Gender-Based Violence

KATHRYN L. NORSWORTHY

In 1995, along with over 30,000 women and a few men from more than 180 countries, I attended the NGO (Nongovernmental Organization) Forum on Women, in Beijing, China. The Forum was held concurrently with the United Nation's more official End-of-the-Decade Conference on Women. Both meetings were meant to provide opportunities for participants to discuss the most pressing issues and concerns for women and girls around the globe. As the meetings progressed, it became increasingly clear that gender-based violence is one of the most serious threats to the physical and emotional health and well-being of women and girls worldwide, demanding the attention of countries and communities on every continent. While the forms and contexts may vary from culture to culture, the impact of gender-based violence is devastating—to the victims/survivors, their families and communities, and to the very fabric of their societies.

For over twenty years I have worked with children, women, and men who have survived violence. The early years of my practice involved individual, group, and family therapy aimed at helping children (mainly girls) who were physically, emotionally, and/or sexually abused, whereas now I work almost exclusively with women who are survivors of trauma. In this work, I have been struck by the fact that, when a woman seeks therapy, some form of trauma usually enters the picture. Because gender is an organizing principle that underlies or interacts with other aspects of women's identity and experience, I use the term "gender-based trauma" throughout this discussion to reflect the important role gender plays in understanding sources and types of traumatic experience and how these affect women and girls. Gender is not always the most salient issue for a woman in explaining or understanding her trauma or in the larger schema of its meaning within the traumatic event; the term simply reminds us of the ways that gender can interact with and influence other aspects of a woman's or girl's identity and experience.

Feminist perspectives are useful for understanding the social and political factors that support and promote the maltreatment of women and girls.[1] These theories describe the roles of male supremacy, patriarchy, power, and privilege in the abuse of women, and extend the responsibility for change to society at large. Principles of Engaged Buddhism, especially as discussed in the mindfulness trainings of the Order of Interbeing led by Thich Nhat Hanh, emphasize the responsibility that we, as a society, share for the existence and elimination of all forms of oppression and domination, including gender-based oppression.[2]

Both feminist and Engaged-Buddhist psychology provide important practices and perspectives relevant in the recovery and healing of trauma survivors. These principles can be integrated with a range of other psychological theories and practices already documented as effective in counseling women survivors of trauma to provide a more complete and holistic counseling process. Although there has not yet been much discussion of counseling and psychotherapy from a Buddhist-feminist perspective, several useful volumes have been written proposing integrations of Buddhist psychology and psychoanalytic theory,[3] as well as Zen Buddhism and humanistic psychological theory.[4]

This chapter is an effort to break new ground by examining intersections and commonalities between Buddhist and feminist psychologies in understanding gender-based trauma. Sources and types of trauma and the social and political systems that reinforce and justify the oppression of women are discussed. A range of psychological effects that result from traumatic experiences are explored and the typical components of post-traumatic stress reaction are reviewed. Efforts will be made to weave together feminist and Buddhist theories and practices that can be useful in the process of healing and recovery.

In keeping with feminist values, I must note that the perspectives represented in this chapter are based on my understanding of the research and how I have applied what I have learned from others, as well as my own clinical, personal, and academic experiences. It should be recognized that I am both informed and limited by my knowledge and experience as a white, middle-class (with a working-class upbringing), United States citizen, Buddhist (with a Christian childhood), feminist, academic and practicing psychologist, woman. I trust that each reader's identity and experiences, together with the cultural, social, and political contexts of her or his life, will influence how this material is interpreted. Thus, this chapter is *not* an effort to represent the lives and experiences of all women everywhere. Readers are challenged to question, expand, and reformulate these ideas, since this chapter is best described as a starting point in exploring the connections of Buddhist and feminist psychology in understanding and supporting women survivors of gender-based violence.

CONTEXTS OF VIOLENCE AGAINST WOMEN

At the global level, women and girls remain vulnerable to exploitation and violence, in large part because of gender. Patriarchal systems, in which groups of individuals have power over others, form the foundation of most societies. For example, in the dominant U.S. narrative, feminine, "nonwhite," and "not middle- or upper-class" characteristics, as well as women and people of color, have been relegated to a less powerful position in society. They have generally been defined as weak, inferior, and in many cases, pathological. For example, a woman who is assertive and direct is often viewed as pushy and demanding; a woman who is passive or indirect is not taken seriously; a woman who cries or shows "too much feeling" is considered hysterical.

Of critical importance, from a feminist perspective, is that this patriarchal structure, where masculinity, whiteness, heterosexuality, economic/class advantage, and the male gender are dominant and privileged has deep *his*torical roots. Buddhist teachers and scholars have only recently begun to address these important elements of experience directly. For example, when we examine popular accounts of Buddhist history, we find evidence of discrimination against women early on. Most Buddhist practitioners are aware of the stories of the Buddha leaving his wife and child so that he could be free to pursue his spiritual path, and of his early reluctance to accept women into the Saṅgha. Less known and emphasized, except by feminist Buddhist practitioners, researchers, and historians, are the accounts of a strong Bhikkhunī Saṅgha during the time of the Buddha, and the Buddha's efforts to support and nurture women on their spiritual paths in a context of a sexist, oppressive Indian society.[5] Rita Gross notes the androcentrism (the concept that masculine equals human) in Buddhist literature.[6] Chatsumarn Kabilsingh points out that the Buddhist texts appear to have been "recorded by monks, in the interest of monks" over three hundred years after the *parinirvāna* (passing away) of the Buddha.[7]

From a legal perspective, we know that, until this century, women and children were defined as property in the United States. This attitude continues to pervade modern society. Violence and aggression have historically been sanctioned by society as viable options for men when their "property" has been threatened or when women do not meet their expectations. Our contemporary legal system and prevailing community attitudes make it clear that women are not necessarily protected from violence and assault and may be held responsible for their traumatic experiences, especially if the abuse is perpetrated by a male partner. This trend is reflected by the grossly underreported incidences of physical and sexual assault of women and girls in the United States, and the low prosecution rates of assailants. Therefore, an attempt to understand issues of women and girls who have survived gender-based trauma must necessarily broaden its scope beyond the individual woman and her emotional and psychological wounds. The personal is both social and political. The Buddha's encouragement to look deeply and with insight into the nature of things "as they are" is critically relevant in deconstructing culturally, socially, and politically defined realities of the oppression of women and girls.

THE PSYCHOLOGY OF TRAUMA

Feminist psychologists often describe traumatic experiences as the shattering of the belief in the world as a safe and just place.[8] Trauma can result from betrayal by a trusted individual, as in the case of child sexual abuse by a parent, and the denial of the abuse by the offending parent of an adult incest survivor.[9] Traumatic experiences can involve a single experience, such as an assault, or may be as continuous as a beach being worn away by the waves. Many women experience chronic exposure to traumatic situations, such as ongoing sexual harassment or regular beatings by their spouse or partner. Secondary trauma, resulting from witnessing or supporting someone else who has experienced traumatic events, is a common hazard for women and girls since gender-based oppression is common across cultures and communities.

It is important to note that all forms of oppression, including racism, sexism, ageism, classism, homophobia, poverty, spiritual oppression, and oppression of people with disabilities, are all sources of trauma for women. When women experience gender-based trauma in conjunction with other forms of oppression, the impact of the traumatic experiences are exponentially complicated.

Marilyn Frye discusses the "birdcage model" with regard to the issue of multiple oppressions.[10] When we conceptualize each form of oppression (e.g., racism, sexism, homophobia, etc.) as one individual wire of the cage, a close-up view of an individual wire prevents a perspective of the total predicament of the "caged." As one focuses on a single wire, the other wires blur and it appears that the imprisoned could simply fly around it and be free. As the observer steps back and gets a more complete picture, however, it is easy to see how the multiple wires of oppression serve to keep the "bird" trapped, thus preventing self-determination. Depending on where in the cage one stands, one or two wires may seem more significant than the others. Therein lies the importance of recognizing how critical the survivor's standpoint is in understanding the meaning and effects of the trauma(s). The interrelationships among a woman's various identities and how these identities converge to organize traumatic events must be taken into account to appreciate her experience of violence and how she is affected by it and able to cope with it in the aftermath. For example, consider a professional Muslim woman who is a political refugee from Algeria living in the United States and now doing unskilled labor for a living. If she is raped by a white man in her new country, the interplay between her identities (woman, Muslim) and identity shifts (professional to laborer, ethnic majority member to ethnic minority) will likely influence how she interprets the event and her ability to cope during and following the traumatic event.

ECOLOGICAL VARIABLES INFLUENCING TRAUMA RESPONSE

It is easy to assume that traumatic experiences have predictable effects on the human psyche. However, multiple factors influence how each survivor is affected. Mary Harvey offers a useful ecological model for understanding the variables involved in the impact of traumatic events and the recovery process.[11] She discusses the three factors—person, event, and environment—that interact in influencing trauma response. As might be expected, the personal variables include age, physical health, intellectual capacity, personality characteristics, coping strategies prior to the trauma, and other individual identity factors. Other personal variables are the nature of the relationship between victim and perpetrator and prior traumatic experiences.

Variables of the event, such as frequency, duration, severity, degree of physical violence or other violation, and degree of fear and humiliation endured, also affect the extent of the adverse impact. Other important variables are the idiosyncratic or specific events that occur during the traumatic experience(s) that may hold special meaning for the survivor. For example, a woman survivor may be especially troubled because she was sexually assaulted on her way to church on an important religious holiday.

Environmental variables, meaning the response of the environment to a survivor of trauma, are critical factors in determining the impact of the traumatic event and the quality of the recovery. The initial responses of individuals from whom a trauma survivor seeks help are critical. Offering support, facilitating constructive coping, and providing sanctuary and affirmation minimize the possibility of the further trauma that can be caused by counter-productive reactions to a woman who seeks help. When a community is validating and supportive, and offers safety and control, the survivor is better able to integrate the experience(s) and move on with her life. Conversely, when a community invalidates the woman's experience, denies the traumatic events, or responds with rejection, the effects are detrimental and can complicate healing. Additional environmental variables include community attitudes and values, and cultural and sociopolitical factors such as economics, gender constructs, race, class, and other aspects of identity, as well as the availability and relevance of community resources for women survivors.

In examining these ecological factors from an Engaged Buddhist perspective, the Saṅgha, or spiritual community, a fundamental component of the Buddhist practitioner's life, can be instrumental in supporting the survivor post-trauma or in further contributing to the trauma response. Ideally, the Saṅgha would be educated, informed, empathetic, and supportive in response to the woman or girl survivor of trauma. This means understanding the ways in which gender-based oppression occurs in our social and political systems, and striving to examine the Saṅgha to determine how to enact systems that are based on gender equity, free of male supremacy, sexism, and misogyny. For the Saṅgha to do this work effectively, leaders and other members need to recognize that the Saṅgha is situated in a culture of structural oppression and that sexism is an integral element of such structures.

I have noticed that it can be very difficult for members of a community, even a Buddhist community, to be willing to "see clearly" and assume responsibility for taking constructive actions to remedy problematic gender relations. To free ourselves from oppressive attitudes regarding gender and other aspects of identity such as race, class, and sexual orientation that we inevitably internalize from society, involves taking responsibility for doing our own consciousness-raising in regard to issues of oppression and their manifestation in our personal lives and in our communities. It is impossible to live in a society full of sexism and other forms of oppression without internalizing oppressive values and participating at the individual, institutional, and structural levels. The work of liberating ourselves entails a lifelong commitment to ending these oppressive conditions and mind-states, and creating wholesome community environments that can respond effectively to a woman or girl who has experienced gender-based violence.

PSYCHOLOGICAL EFFECTS OF TRAUMA

Women's responses to trauma are complex and often involve many phases. When a woman experiences prolonged feelings of helplessness and fear, various psychological symptoms inevitably result.[12] With good environmental support, symptoms may abate and recovery occurs spontaneously. Other women, especially those who do not get positive responses from their environment, may endure chronic and persistent trauma and may develop post-traumatic stress reaction (PTSR), a condition that persists long after the identifiable traumatic experience. Post-traumatic stress reaction involves three broad categories of symptoms: numbing responses, reexperiencing symptoms, and hyperarousal. Women trauma survivors with PTSR may vacillate between shutting down their emotions and feeling nothing (numbing), and feeling irritable, angry, or seeing threats and danger everywhere (hyperarousal). Any reminder of the original trauma may trigger flashbacks and nightmares of the experiences (reexperiencing). Along with the cognitive, somatic, and affective elements of each category of symptoms come associated behavior patterns. Many of the symptoms of posttraumatic stress reaction originally developed as coping strategies for dealing with the traumatic situation, for example, avoidance of places in the environment that remind the woman of the assault. Therefore, it is very important for the helper to recognize the integrity of the symptoms when initiating the helping/counseling process.

Two other important factors in understanding symptomatology and trauma response of women survivors are somaticization and dissociation.[13] For a variety of reasons—developmental, physiological, and cultural—physical symptoms (somaticization) are common forms of expression for women and girl trauma survivors. Because traumatic events seem to be encoded differently than other experiences in the brain, there may be a lack of cognitive and semantic integration that often leads to bodily expressions of distress.[14] When a culture silences the victims of violence and holds a shaming, "blame the victim," perspective, there is a greater likelihood that physical symptoms of trauma will emerge. Thus, self-medication, through the use of alcohol and prescription and nonprescription drugs, is a common coping strategy for trauma survivors with PTSR.

For many women and girls, dissociation, or mental escape from the traumatic event when other exits are unavailable, is an integral part of surviving and may be a continuing symptom post-trauma. Although this response can be useful during a traumatic situation, significant dissociation can limit access to other useful coping strategies as well as impair judgment. A continual disconnect between emotional responses and ongoing life events after a trauma becomes part of a problematic coping style that can prevent holistic integration of experience.

UNDERSTANDING THE TRAUMA RESPONSE FROM A BUDDHIST PERSPECTIVE

Elements of Buddhist psychology can be useful in understanding the trauma response. The Buddha's teachings about the ways in which the mind responds to painful events and develops reactive habits is a useful paradigm for making sense out of some elements of the suffering that follows traumatic experiences. It is understandable that a woman who has experienced a serious violation of her physical and/or psychological boundaries might attempt to regain some sense of integrity and control. Some survivors develop self-blaming explanations for the traumatic events. This kind of meaning making may allow the woman to believe that she can control or avoid future violations. Other trauma survivors will disconnect from difficult emotions or generalize fear and mistrust to a wide range of situations or people in order to feel safer and in charge. Thus, the original difficult and painful feelings and thoughts become shrouded in an ever-expanding veil of protective mind-states. These strategies help prevent the traumatic events and attendant thoughts, feelings, and/or physical sensations from overwhelming her capacity for holding and experiencing that which is too much to bear. It is likely that a woman trauma survivor is not only coping with the difficult emotional and sometimes physical consequences of one or more traumatic experiences, but also is attempting to do so within a social, political, and cultural context of sexism, misogyny, and a "blame the victim" mentality. In the absence of appropriate social and cultural support for a trauma that occurs within a context of structural, institutional, and individual gender-based violence, it is understandable that these protective mind-states may be keys to survival or continued functioning for the woman trauma survivor. Thus, the habit energies that develop can be compassionately viewed as efforts to cope with and manage the aftermath of the trauma as well as the sociopolitical context of continued gender-based oppression.

COUNSELING WOMEN SURVIVORS OF GENDER-BASED TRAUMA

The conjoining of feminist and other Western psychological models of counseling with Buddhist principles can offer a useful framework for helping the woman trauma survivor navigate the healing process. Western researchers and mental health practitioners have documented a number of steps and phases of recovery.[15] First and foremost, it is critical that the woman be assisted in finding a safe environment to support her efforts to do the necessary therapeutic work. A functional and educated Saṅgha or group of spiritual friends (*kalyana mitra*) can be critical in this process. The woman needs many opportunities to be with friends who can offer her what Thich Nhat Hanh describes as "deep listening."[16] Many women need to tell all or part of their story over and over in an atmosphere that is validating and nonjudgmental, full of empathy and stability. A supportive environment of safety and trust, with a Saṅgha of people who enact gender relationships that are nonsexist and empowering, particularly for women, is crucial for the survivor in rebuilding close relationships and reclaiming her sense of agency, authority, and competence.

It is also important that the woman learn positive coping strategies and methods of self-care and self-soothing that she can use when difficult memories and thoughts about the trauma arise in her mind. Buddhist meditation principles may be extremely useful in this process, especially in increasing psychological stability. The cultivation of calm abiding (*śamatha*) through traditional single-pointed meditation practice can help the woman to develop the steady mind needed to focus and work through the traumatic event(s). As with any difficult mindstate, there is a tendency for the survivor of violence to become absorbed in, or to feel engulfed by the painful memories and intrusive thoughts that are likely to arise post-trauma. Alternatively, a woman may consciously attempt to push these painful thoughts and memories out of her mind and repress them. Meditation methods such as *śamatha* and *vipassanā* can help develop mindfulness and moment-to-moment awareness and offer the survivor a mechanism for recognizing and dismantling the habit energies, or strong emotional charges associated with traumatic thoughts and images that arise in the mind. The systematic practice of "just noticing with bare attention," touching the experience and letting go, can help eliminate the habitual tendency to react automatically to painful thoughts, feelings, and body sensations. These practices also help the woman to see the impermanence of the difficult thoughts and emotions, and to notice the peaceful, calm spaces between them. As the practice continues, a sense of equanimity can extend for longer periods of time. Developing equanimity is an important, empowering aspect of the healing process for the woman trauma survivor.

Mindfulness and moment-to-moment awareness can be foundational ways of being as well as useful tools as the woman trauma survivor begins the work of integrating traumatic memories and emotions into a coherent narrative. For example, often, due to numbing responses, the survivor's feelings during the assault are moved out of conscious awareness as a protective mechanism. "Storying" her experiences, while expressing congruent affect within a therapeutic environment, facilitates the survivor's ability to make meaning of what has happened to her, and to integrate the experience into the bigger picture of her life, and move on. This kind of process also contributes to a continued diffusing of the emotional charge associated with the trauma experience.

A trauma experience also needs to be contextualized from a cultural, social, and political perspective so that the "problem" can be appropriately located. Engaged Buddhist perspectives are very helpful because they clearly acknowledge that oppression, including gender-based oppression, exists and is a serious problem in contemporary society.[17] When a spiritual community and its teachers name the existence of sexism and misogyny and the forms they take, women members of the community receive a message that their experiences are valid and that they are not responsible for the ways they may be exploited or oppressed in society. By writing into the precepts, or mindfulness trainings, that oppression exists in society and that all of us have the responsibility to work to end oppression, as in Thich Nhat Hanh's Order of Interbeing, there is an acknowledgment that the community of spiritual friends is committed to working together toward this common goal. This challenges the contemporary social prescriptions for blaming the victim and staying silent about various forms of violence against women, and helps the survivor to feel empowered to seek support and regain a sense of control in her life.

Of course, care should be taken in recommending or encouraging meditation practices. Some survivors immediately begin to reexperience the traumatic events or other difficult experiences when they attempt meditation, and may or may not recognize that they are not ready for formal meditation practices. A therapist or helper trained to work with trauma survivors, who is also an experienced meditator, can be an invaluable consultant in helping with the decision to engage in meditation and in assisting the survivor in processing confusing or difficult experiences that occur during meditation.

Both feminist therapy[18] and Engaged Buddhism[19] include an emphasis on activism as a source of growth and healing. Many trauma survivors find it beneficial to engage in activities geared toward social change, possibly in activities directly related to the source of the traumatic experiences. For example, Cambodian women have organized peace marches as a step toward ending violence in their own country and in other war-torn parts of the world. Many women survivors of partner abuse volunteer or engage in activist work in shelters or other community programs for women. Each survivor needs to assess whether participation in such activities will trigger further stress reactions or whether the activism will be a helpful path toward a restored sense of self-confidence.

Ultimately the goals of the recovery and healing process involve empowerment of the woman as the author of her own life narrative and liberation from the suffering brought on by the trauma and also sometimes by society's response to the survivor. In any case, each trauma survivor must be assessed individually in order to understand the best intervention process, and each survivor will have a unique resolution to the trauma experiences.

CULTURAL ISSUES

The cultural context of women trauma survivors must be considered in formulating the most efficacious and relevant strategies for support and helping. For example, in northern Thailand many women value the input of "sha-women" in addressing emotional distress. While a Vietnamese woman might be willing to consult with a nun after an incidence of rape, she would not be likely to seek out a psychologist or psychiatrist. In the United States, counselors and psychotherapists may be viewed as culturally appropriate helpers for many white middle- and upper-class women, whereas poor working women and women of color may be mistrustful of the predominately white, middle/upper-class mental health system and prefer to see a religious teacher or leader. A multitude of sociopolitical factors, for example, the race, ethnicity, and gender of both helper and survivor, along with cultural belief systems about helping, must be taken into account in developing meaningful counseling services. For Buddhist women, various types of meditation or familiar Buddhist rituals may serve as meaningful and useful pathways to liberation from trauma-related suffering.

As difficult as it may be, we must make every effort to help survivors identify and disentangle themselves from sexism, oppressive cultural practices, and other forms of oppression. It is challenging to renegotiate culturally supported, gendered power arrangements, such as, "The woman should always place herself last in the order of priorities in the family so that others can be happy, regardless of the impact on her well-being," "The man's job is to earn the money for the family, and not to be weak by showing tender emotions such as sadness, hurt, or vulnerability, while the woman takes care of the home and family, even if she holds a job outside the household," and "Ultimately the man is in charge, and can do what it takes to enforce this arrangement, including the use of violence and aggression." Generally speaking, every culture and community has its version of gender arrangements that can be examined and questioned in terms of who is advantaged and who is not. Just as the Buddha taught the practice of "looking deeply," deconstructing and challenging the ways in which cultures support and reinforce violence against women and girls is crucial to real liberation.

We must also examine the effects of sexism and misogyny on how Buddhism is taught and practiced in various cultures. This is critical in creating contexts that contribute to the empowerment or disempowerment of women. For example, within the Western Buddhist community, many meditation retreats include a time for retreatants to report their meditation experiences to the teacher, either individually or in a group. The teacher then offers the students advice about what they have experienced. This process implies that the teacher has the wisdom and authority to define and make meaning of the experiences of the student, rather than helping the student make sense of the experience herself with the support and facilitation of a caring teacher. The implication is that the transformation is one-sided rather than mutual. In line with feminist and Engaged-Buddhist values, learning involves a process of mutuality within the teacher-student relationship. Within a context of sharing, discussion, and collaboration, meaning and self-discovery are more likely to emerge for everyone involved. Teachers are respected for their knowledge and experience, students are acknowledged for the wisdom they have developed regarding their own lives, and both teacher and student benefit from the relationship.

While mutuality, respect, and empowerment in the teacher-student relationship are important Engaged-Buddhist and feminist values for any member of the Saṅgha, they are particularly relevant for the woman trauma survivor. Earlier discussions point out that gender-based violence perpetrated against women typically involves culturally supported actions that render women unable to have control and mastery over their own bodies, spirits, or minds. Clearly, power and control are the primary motivators for rape and wife- or partner-abuse. Accompanying cultural messages usually include, "Women do not know what is good for them," "Women need men or other authorities to make their lives meaningful," and "Men have a right to treat women as they wish and to use violence and aggression to force women to do their bidding." It is important to avoid replicating these patriarchal and male-supremicist values in settings that offer teaching, support, and assistance, especially within our spiritual communities. It is a great challenge to recognize oppression when we see it, whether externally or within ourselves, because we live in societies in which oppression is institutionalized and insidious. Examining and transforming the teacher-student relationship to one that is empowering and supportive of the agency and authority of the student, especially the woman survivor of trauma, requires our deepest connection with our Buddha nature.

SEEING CLEARLY, TAKING RESPONSIBILITY

Transforming society and providing meaningful support and assistance to women and girls who are victims of violence and other injurious experiences will vary from community to community, and culture to culture. We have much to learn from one another about this process and we need each other's support and encouragement along the way. Critical steps involve seeing clearly the structural, institutional, and individual gender-based oppression and violence that exist, taking responsibility for our own continued consciousness-raising and behavioral change, and working to end oppression of all forms in our families, communities, and societies.

These are great challenges. As Thich Nhat Hanh has said, "For my part, I have not practiced long enough or well enough to end this suffering and injustice." Through collaborative Engaged-Buddhist-feminist efforts, and earnest listening and learning, we can certainly develop creative, culturally relevant methods for understanding and caring for women and girls who have survived gender-based trauma and oppression.

NOTES

1. See Laura S. Brown, *Subversive Dialogues: Theory in Feminist Therapy* (New York: Basic Books, 1994), and Judith Lewis Herman, *Trauma and Recovery* (New York: Basic Books, 1992).

2. For example, see Thich Nhat Hanh, *Interbeing: Fourteen Guidelines for Engaged Buddhism* (Berkeley, Calif.: Parallax Press, 1998).

3. Mark Epstein, *Thoughts without a Thinker* (New York: Basic Books, 1995).

4. David Brazier, *Zen Therapy: Transcending the Sorrows of the Human Mind* (New York: John Wiley & Sons, 1995).

5. Chatsumarn Kabilsingh, *Thai Women in Buddhism* (Berkeley, Calif.: Parallax Press, 1991), p. 24.

6. Rita M. Gross, *Buddhism After Patriarchy: A Feminist History, Analysis, and Reconstruction of Buddhism* (Albany, N.Y.: State University of New York Press, 1993), p. 22.

7. Kabilingh, *Thai Women in Buddhism*, p. 25.

8. Ronnie Janoff-Bulman, *Shattered Assumptions: Toward a New Psychology of Trauma* (New York: Free Press, 1992).

9. Jennifer J. Freyd, *Betrayal Trauma: The Logic of Forgetting Childhood Abuse* (Cambridge: Harvard University Press, 1996).

10. Marilyn Frye, "Oppression," in *Race, Class, and Gender in the United States: An Integrated Study*, Paula S. Rothenberg, ed. (New York: St. Martin's Press, 1998).

11. Mary R. Harvey, "An Ecological View of Psychological Trauma and Trauma Recovery," *Journal of Traumatic Stress* 9 (1996): 3–24.

12. Maria P. P. Root, "Reconstructing the Impact of Trauma on Personality," in *Personality and Psychopathology: Feminist Reappraisals*, Laura S. Brown and Mary Ballou, eds. (New York: The Guilford Press, 1992);

Bessel A. van der Kolk, ed., *Psychological Trauma* (Washington, D.C.: American Psychiatric Press, 1987); and Lenore E. Walker, *Abused Women and Survivor Therapy: A Practical Guide for the Psychotherapist* (Washington, D.C.: American Psychological Association, 1994).

13. Herman, *Trauma and Recovery.*

14. van der Kolk, *Psychological Trauma.*

15. Herman, *Trauma and Recovery*; Mardi Jon Horowitz, *Stress Response Syndromes* (Northvale, N.J.: Jason Aronson, 1986); Anna C. Salter, *Transforming Trauma: A Guide to Understanding and Treating Adult Survivors of Child Sexual Abuse* (Thousand Oaks, CA: Sage, 1995); and Walker, *Abused Women and Survivor Therapy.*

16. Thich Nhat Hanh, *Teachings on Love* (Berkeley, CA: Parallax Press, 1997).

17. See Chatsumarn Kabilsingh, "Present Situation of Women in Buddhism," in *Women, Gender Relations and Development in Thai Society*, Vol. I, V. Somswaski and S. Theobald, eds. (Chiang Mai: Ming Muang Navarat, 1997); and Sulak Sivaraksa, *Global Healing: Essays and Interviews on Structural Violence, Social Development and Spiritual Transformation* (Bangkok: Thai Inter-Religious Commission for Development, 1999).

18. Brown, *Subversive Dialogues.*

19. Hahn, *Interbeing.*

Part Two:

Women Transforming Buddhist Societies

Chapter 7

Reclaiming the Robe: Reviving the Bhikkhunī Order in Sri Lanka

RANJANI DE SILVA

Śākyamuni Buddha first began ordaining women in India in the sixth century BCE. His foster mother, Queen Pajāpatī Gotamī, was the first woman he ordained. She became the first *bhikkhunī*.[1] The Bhikkhunī Saṅgha that developed after the ordination of Pajāpatī and her five hundred followers existed in India until at least the eleventh century. The Bhikkhunī Saṅgha produced many fully awakened women and *arahant*s who made significant contributions to the early Buddhist monastic order in India.

The Bhikkhunī Saṅgha began in Sri Lanka when Princess Sanghamitta, daughter of Emperor Asoka and sister of the *arahant* Mahinda, came to Sri Lanka in the third century BCE. According to Sri Lankan chronicles, she presided over the ordination of Queen Anula and five hundred women at King Devanampiyatissa's royal court. When Sanghamitta arrived in Sri Lanka for this historic ordination, she brought a sapling from the sacred *bodhi* tree in Bodhgaya with her. She planted this sapling in Anuradhapura, the capital of Sri Lanka. The descendent of this tree remains at that spot today and is regarded as the oldest tree in the world. The symbolic planting of the sapling firmly rooted Buddhism in Sri Lanka, and the ordination of nuns in that same place was a highly auspicious, legitimizing event.

The order of nuns thrived in Sri Lanka for many centuries but died out around the eleventh century, probably due to famine and the Chola invasions from the north. Until that time, laywomen and nuns were engaged in the study of the Buddha's teachings and social welfare work. The *bhikkhunīs* lived separate from the monks, in nunneries with their own independent administrative structures. The order of nuns flourished with the support of Buddhist kings, the Bhikkhunī Saṅgha, and the lay community. This early period of Sri Lankan Buddhist history, with Anuradhapura as its capital, was known as the Golden Age, a time when culture and the arts were at their peak. The country was said to be so peaceful that a beautiful woman could carry gems in her hand and journey by foot from the north to the south of the island without fear of attack. In this atmosphere, both the Bhikkhu and Bhikkhunī Saṅghas developed and flourished.

In the year 1017, Anuradhapura fell to the Chola invaders from South India. As a result, the orders of both nuns and monks disappeared. When King Vijayabahu (1010–1111 CE) finally defeated and expelled the Cholas in 1086, he discovered that some Sinhala monks had taken refuge in Burma.[2] He invited them to return to Sri Lanka, where they restored the Bhikkhu Saṅgha. Later, on two separate occasions when conflicts and natural disasters caused the demise of the monks' order, monks were again invited from Burma to revive the Bhikkhu Saṅgha in Sri Lanka. In 1753, when the monks' order had declined yet again, a retinue of monks headed by Upali Thera from Siam arrived in Sri Lanka and revived the order by conferring the higher ordination (*upasampadā*) to six male novices.

When reading these historical accounts, some questions come to mind: What happened to the nuns? The nuns disappeared along with the monks, so why was there no attempt to revive the order of nuns, either from within Sri Lanka, or from Burma or Thailand? Were there no living nuns from the Sri Lankan Bhikkhunī Saṅgha who survived alongside the fleeing monks? If the nuns did manage to escape to Burma along with the monks, what became of them? Was there an order of nuns in Burma in the eleventh century that could have sheltered the Sri Lankan *bhikkhunīs*? Why is there no documentation of a complementary group of nuns? If such a group did exist, why did King Vijayabahu not request their return to Sri Lanka? Alternatively, could it be that he asked them to return to Sri Lanka, but the surviving nuns chose not to? These are the intriguing questions for which there are few documented answers.

THE LEGITIMACY OF THE CHINESE BHIKKHUNĪ LINEAGE

Records exist to document that nuns from the Sinhala Bhikkhunī Saṅgha ventured out of Sri Lanka and offered ordination to women in China. According to the *Biographies of Buddhist Nuns*, a Chinese text compiled in 520 CE, two groups of Sinhala nuns traveled to China to introduce the lineage of *bhikkhunī* ordination. The first group, led by a nun named Devasara, arrived in China in 429 CE. In the year 433 C.E., at a monastery in Nanjing, Sinhalese *bhikkhunī*s ordained more than three hundred Chinese nuns who, until that time, had received ordination only from monks. The higher ordination that the Chinese nuns received was a highly significant form of empowerment. It enabled nuns to establish their own Vinaya tradition,[3] gather followers, gain support, and eventually transmit the tradition of full ordination to nuns in Korea and Vietnam.

As the Mahāyāna Buddhist teachings developed and flourished in China, the nuns adapted the precepts they received to the vastly different living conditions that prevailed in China. They practiced the Dharmagupta school of Vinaya, which enumerates 348 Pāṭimokkha precepts (rules of conduct) for *bhikkhunī*s, 37 more than the Theravāda tradition, which has 311.[4] The additional rules of the Dharmagupta restrict such actions as receiving alms at wealthy patrons' houses, overstaying invitations, and taking food in excess of what is permissible. Today, nuns around the world who trace their lineages to the Chinese Buddhist tradition still observe the Dharmagupta Vinaya. Because nuns of the Chinese tradition are fully ordained, they live by high standards of conduct, receive adequate education and training, and enjoy ample support from their followers, most of whom are women. In contrast, the Sri Lankan Bhikkhunī Saṅgha, which provided the *bhikkhunī* preceptors who began the *bhikkhunī* order in China, completely disappeared in Sri Lanka by the twelfth century—erased from Buddhist social history and memory. Only in recent years has a movement emerged to restore the *bhikkhunī* order in Sri Lanka. This is the story of that recovery and reawakening, a story that cries out to be told.

REAWAKENING

In 1903, a young Sri Lankan woman named Catherine Alwis Gunasekera met some Burmese nuns (*maeshila*s) at the Temple of the

Tooth in Kandy, Sri Lanka. She was so impressed by them that she decided to renounce the life of a layperson and become a ten-precept nun like these inspiring Burmese nuns. Being from a highly respected family, Catherine met with great difficulties when she told her family and the order of monks about her wish. At this time in Sri Lanka, there was no order of nuns, not even ten-precept nuns (*dasasilmātā*). Her family was embarrassed and enraged by her decision to become a nun. The monks in Sri Lanka refused to give her the ten precepts, so she went to Burma to fulfill her dream. She was ordained there and was given the ordination name of Sudharmacharini. Her preceptor was Daw Ni Chari, a venerated Burmese nun. There were no fully ordained *bhikkhunī*s in Burma during this time, and the ten-precept ordination was the only ordination possible.

Sudharmacharini returned to Sri Lanka and founded the order of *dasasilmātā*s, which still exists today. At this time in Sri Lanka, there were foreign colonials who, despite their faults and closed-mindedness, were quite open to the advancement of women. Henry Blake, the Governor of Sri Lanka under British rule, fully supported the work of Sudharmacharini. His wife, Lady Blake, supported the construction of a nunnery in Katukele, Kandy, which became known as the Lady Blake Aramaya Nunnery. This large institution, where many *dasasilmātā*s live even today, is still one of the most powerful and thriving nunneries in Sri Lanka.

Sudharmacharini's contribution to Sri Lanka's women is monumental. Not only did she provide the opportunity for women to more fully engage in the Dhamma, she also encouraged laywomen to participate with the Saṅgha in a more meaningful way. Women were able to study the Dhamma at this time, although this had been prohibited by earlier colonial rulers for over two hundred years, and women actively supported the nuns and monks by their almsgiving and charitable acts.

Today in Sri Lanka, there are over four thousand *dasasilmātā*s with shaven heads and saffron robes who have renounced lay life and practice as nuns. However, their lives are not easy. They are discriminated against by the government and by the order of monks. They are not even given the *sāmaṇerī* ordination, which is routinely given to novice monks. They follow the same precepts and live a life very similar to the monks, but the Sri Lankan government policies do not entitle them to receive the four basic requisites of a monk—food, shelter, clothing, and medicine. Therefore, they are dependent upon the kindness of the community—primarily their female followers—for the four requisites in order to live and practice.

In 1985, after years of struggle and protest, public attention was drawn to the plight of the nuns. The Department of Buddhist Affairs was forced to take some remedial measures to improve conditions for the nuns. The Department identified the nuns living in the various districts of the country and registered them in the Buddhist Affairs Registry. This enabled the nuns throughout the island to meet each other and organize themselves. They formed a national council of nuns and reestablished a code of conduct. Leaders emerged from each of the districts where nuns lived, and educational and social service centers were established to meet the needs of the nuns and the lay community. The educational centers began to offer Dhamma education to the community and to the nuns.

In 1993, when the third Sakyadhita Conference was held in Colombo, hundreds of *dasasilmātā*s participated.[5] Sri Lankan nuns met *bhikkhunī*s from many different traditions for the first time. They also met Buddhist women from all over the world. The nuns and laywomen present at the conference had a keen interest in solving women's problems in monastic life and in supporting the Sri Lankan women in their struggle. This made the Sri Lankan nuns aware of their potential and of the great backbone of support they could count on from other women. The Sakyadhita organization in Sri Lanka began to work with these women and to conduct workshops to raise awareness among the *dasasilmātā*s and the public regarding the situation of the Sri Lankan nuns. This work has resulted in a great rallying of support and recently led to a call for the revival of the lost order of *bhikkhunī*s. Not only have laywomen joined in this call, but a number of prominent and learned monks and professors from the major universities in Sri Lanka have voiced their support. Many progressive members of the community have publicly supported this revival but many conservative monks have protested and publicly opposed this move. There have been open debates, but most of the male Saṅgha members refuse to engage in these discussions. They staunchly refuse to address the issue at all.

THE BHIKKHUNĪ ORDINATION CONTROVERSY

Why is there so much controversy surrounding the reestablishment of the *bhikkhunī* order in Sri Lanka? Why does the Bhikkhu Saṅgha protest it? Why has the government been so hesitant to do anything about the problem? These are political questions and searching for answers can be complicated and even dangerous. According to representatives of the Bhikkhu Saṅgha, the main objection to the reestablishment of the *bhikkhunī* order is that the lineage of Theravāda *bhikkhunī*s has been broken and no Theravāda Bhikkhunī Saṅgha exists to confer full ordination on the nuns. These representatives argue that, until Maitreya is born to reestablish the order of *bhikkhunī*s, the lineage cannot be revived. In light of the fact that, according to the Theravāda tradition, Maitreya Buddha will not be born for another million years, this seems an untenable solution to the problem.

The lineage of fully ordained nuns (*bhikkhunī*s) no longer exists in any Theravāda country. The Theravāda countries include Sri Lanka, Thailand, Burma, Cambodia, and Laos, and among them, only Sri Lanka ever had a *bhikkhunī* order.[6] Unfortunately, the Theravāda order of fully ordained nuns died out in Sri Lanka around the eleventh century CE, and was never reintroduced. Only recently have progressive individuals in Sri Lanka begun to voice their aspirations and lend support to the reestablishment of the order.

According to the dominant interpretation of the Theravāda tradition (that is, the monks' interpretation), reestablishment of the Bhikkhunī Saṅgha will never be possible in Sri Lanka. The Supreme Advisory Council of the Ministry of Buddhist Affairs does not recommend a revival of the order. It is interesting to note that this Advisory Council is composed of the three heads, or prelates, of the three major monastic orders (*nikāya*s) of Sri Lankan Buddhism: Siam, Amarapura, and Ramanna. The situation is rather like the fox guarding the chicken coop. These prelates and their constituencies seem to believe that it is not in the best interests of the Bhikkhu Saṅgha to have a flourishing Bhikkhunī Saṅgha with whom they would have to share their wealth, power, and prestige.

The attitudes of the Advisory Council are well known. It was this same Council that made it difficult to gain the government's approval to hold the Sakyadhita Conference in Colombo in 1993. Before granting its approval, which was mandatory for holding the conference in Sri Lanka, the Council demanded that no mention of the *bhikkhunī* issue be raised during the conference. They claimed that it would be contrary to the Dhamma and the Vinaya to revive the Bhikkhunī Saṅgha in the Theravāda tradition. Therefore, if the *bhikkhunī* ordination issue was mentioned at the conference, it would create false hopes, since the *bhikkhunī* order could never be revived in Sri Lanka.

One monk, Talale Dhammaloka, who is the deputy chief prelate of the Amarapura sect, was supportive of the move to reestablish the Bhikkhunī Saṅgha. He even wrote an article stating his opinion, which appeared in both the English and Sinhalese newspapers. In the article, he requested that the prelates provide the references in the Vinaya and the *sutta*s that prohibit the reestablishment of the Bhikkhunī Saṅgha in Theravāda countries. He says that, to this day, he has received no response to his request. No reply can be expected either, since there is nothing in the texts to substantiate the detractors' claims. Talale Dhammaloka also headed the team of monks who administered the higher ordination to twenty-one *dasasilmātās* in Bodhgaya, India, in February 1998, as part of the International Ordination Ceremony sponsored by Foguangshan, a large monastery in Taiwan. These nuns had been interviewed and selected in Sri Lanka by senior *bhikkhunī*s from Foguangshan and had received fifty days of monastic training at Foguangshan Monastery in Taiwan prior to the ordination.

The major objections to the revival of the Bhikkhunī Saṅgha stem from the requirement that the higher ordination for nuns be conferred by ten *bhikkhunī*s, as well as ten *bhikkhu*s. This form of dual ordination was the practice when both orders were fully functioning, but is not possible in the absence of *bhikkhunī*s. The majority of monks are unwilling to challenge the dual ordination requirement or even to discuss challenging it. Although there are no *bhikkhunī*s in Theravāda countries, *bhikkhu*s can and do administer the ten precepts of a novice to women. In the same way, Theravāda monks could administer the higher ordination with the assistance of fully ordained *bhikkhunī*s from the Mahāyāna tradition, but they are unwilling to accept this as a viable alternative. There is another alternative, however. In the *Cullavagga Vinaya*, in the section entitled "Bhikkhunī Khandaka," the Buddha permitted the monks themselves to administer the higher ordination to women: "I permit you, monks, to confer the higher ordination on *bhikkhunī*s."[7]

It has been suggested that the practice of ordaining women by ten *bhikkhunī*s and then by ten *bhikkhu*s began because the nuns became shy when asked such questions as, "Are you pregnant?" or "Have you started menstruating yet?" To avoid this embarrassment, the Buddha instructed the *bhikkhunī*s to ask the twenty-four required questions and perform the ordination, then have it confirmed by the *bhikkhus*. This fact seems to have been forgotten by most monks. If this were all that prevented the reestablishment of the *bhikkhunī* ordination, it would be an easy thing to rectify. However, the matter is far more complicated. The fear and politics that are engendered by the discussion are difficult hurdles to overcome. Nonetheless, attempts are being made to eliminate these obstacles, and many women and men are gallantly striving to create a new reality.

A NEW REALITY

In October 1988, five Sri Lankan nuns were ordained in a dual ordination ceremony at Hsi Lai Temple in Hacienda Heights, California. Upon their return to Sri Lanka, however, they did not receive public recognition as *bhikkhunī*s. As a result, they have continued to live as *dasasilmātās* as they did before. This was a setback for the nuns who were waiting to see what response their sisters would receive. Despite their valiant efforts to receive the ordination, the silence of these nuns and their consequent marginalization caused other nuns to shrink back and consign themselves to living as subordinate members of the religious community.

Then, in 1996, a historic event took place that catapulted Sri Lankan Buddhist women and their cause onto the international stage. Mapalagama Vipulasara Mahathera, President of the Mahabodhi Society, took the bold step of arranging the higher ordination of ten Sri Lankan *dasasilmātā*s in India. Inspired by the writings of Anagarika Dharmapala, the founder of the Mahabodhi Society, Vipulasara noted that women should be fully ordained in order to promote Dhamma propagation activities. In openly declaring his support for the ordination, Vipulasara cited statements from the diaries of Dharmapala that said that the next step, after establishing the Mahabodhi Society and its charitable institutions, was to revive the Bhikkhunī Saṅgha. This ordination ceremony, presided over by Korean monks and nuns, and cosponsored by the Mahabodhi Society and the Korean Center of the World Buddhist Saṅgha Council, took place in Sarnath on December 8, 1996.

In the morning on the day of ordination, five Theravāda monks from Sri Lanka administered the *sāmaṇerī* (novice) ordination to the nuns, and in the afternoon, ten Korean *bhikkhus* administered the higher ordination (*upasampadā*) according to the Dharmagupta Vinaya. Hundreds of people witnessed the ordination, including two hundred Koreans representing many Buddhist societies in Korea, and fifty *bhikkhus* and *bhikkhunīs* from various other Buddhist traditions.

Kusuma Devendra was the first to receive the *upasampadā* ordination, creating history by becoming the first Sri Lankan *bhikkhunī* in about 1000 years. It is fitting that she was the first to receive ordination, because she had been instrumental in arranging the event. Already a well-known scholar who had done doctoral work in Buddhist philosophy and produced a dissertation on the Bhikkhunī Vinaya,[8] Kusuma had worked tirelessly to gain support for the revival of the Bhikkhunī Saṅgha for many years. The mother of five children, she had lived as an *anagārikā* (lay renunciant) for many years before becoming a *dasasilmātā*. Because Buddhists in Sri Lanka had been listening to her Dhamma talks on television and the radio for over fifteen years, they were greatly inspired by her ordination and received the news with great joy.

For many, the 1996 ordination of the ten Sri Lankan *dasasilmātās* marked the beginning of the revival of the Bhikkhunī Saṅgha. Leading newspapers in Sri Lanka and India carried many pictures and articles of the ceremony in Sarnath. The first news item on government television and radio programs that day stated, "The Bhikkhunī Saṅgha has been restored in Sri Lanka." This announcement was alarming to some *bhikkhus*, especially those conservatives and traditionalists who believed that the full ordination of women would not occur until the coming of Maitreya Buddha. Many senior monks of that persuasion wrote articles that appeared in the newspapers and on the news. They protested and repudiated the event, but their claims were countered by learned monks and professors of Pāli and Buddhism who publicly applauded and supported the ordination.

The revival of the Bhikkhunī Saṅgha is now a part of public discourse and it is up to individuals to accept or reject its validity. Many progressive and learned monks have started to train more *dasasilmātās* for higher ordination. One such monk, Inamaluwe Sri Sunmangala Thera, opened a training center for nuns in February 1997. He selected thirty-five nuns who had been *dasasilmātās* for over ten years. These nuns ranged in age from thirty to fifty-five years, and many had received higher education. He began teaching them the Vinaya, Abhidhamma, and the *suttas*, in addition to various methods of meditation practice.

Around this time, in May 1997, a seminar on monastic discipline was held at Foguangshan Monastery in Taiwan, which was attended by monks from many Buddhist traditions. Porowagama Somalankara represented Sri Lanka at this seminar and, upon his return to Sri Lanka, he selected twenty nuns to be trained to receive the higher ordination. Somalankara selected ten *dasasilmātā*s from his own training center and ten others from a pool of two hundred applicants. At the seminar in Taiwan, the attendees invited Xingyun, the abbot of Foguangshan, to arrange an international ordination for nuns and monks. This ceremony took place in February 1998 at the Chinese monastery in Bodhgaya, India, and the 21 *dasasilmātā*s who had been selected and trained by Somalankara were among the 132 nuns who received *bhikkhunī* ordination at that time.[9]

This ordination ceremony was conducted according to the procedures required by the Theravāda Vinaya. The *sāmaṇerī*s received their ordination first from the Chinese *bhikkhunī*s and then from Xingyun and other senior monks, including several from Sri Lanka. The ordination masters (*acharya upadaya*) included Talale Dhammaloka (Deputy Chief Prelate of the Amarapura sect), K. Dhammananda (Chief Sanghanayaka of Malaysia), Mapalagama Vipulasara (President of the Mahabodhi Society), Madagoda Vajiragnana (Chief Sanghanayake of Great Britain), Kamburugamuwe Vajira (Vice Chancellor of Pāli Buddhist University of Sri Lanka), Inamaluwe Sri Sumangala, Porowagama Somalankara, Kamburupitiye Nandaratna, Mahagalkadawala Punnasara, Waragoda Premaratana, and Kahavita Siriniwasa. Because Theravāda monks were among the precept masters who conferred the higher ordination and because the nuns received the traditional robes and bowls in the same manner as the *bhikkhus* in Sri Lanka, this ordination ceremony was accepted as legitimate by the Theravāda monks in attendance and many others in the Buddhist world.

A total of 132 nuns and 10 monks from 23 countries received the higher ordination in February 1998 in Bodhgaya. Sri Lanka had the largest number of nuns at the ordination and received special recognition at the ceremony because it was Sri Lankan *bhikkhunī*s who originally transmitted the lineage of full ordination to China in the fifth century CE. The Taiwanese organizers of the ordination ceremony claimed that one objective of the ordination was to restore the Bhikkhunī Saṅgha in Sri Lanka, to repay the debt of gratitude that Taiwanese *bhikkhunī*s owe to Sri Lankan progenitors of the lineage.

The Sri Lankan nuns who were ordained at the ceremony in Bodhgaya returned to Sri Lanka on February 26, 1998. Previously they had great trepidations about the reception that might await them in Sri Lanka, because of the controversy that swarmed around the *bhikkhunī* ordination issue. Their fears were unfounded; instead of bombs or protests, thousands of devotees lined up at the airport in Colombo to salute them and to make offerings to them. Receptions were held in their villages and they were taken in a procession with drummers, dancers, and Buddhist flags. Monks living in their village temples, other learned monks, and lay Buddhists all gathered in the *aramaya*s to congratulate the newly ordained nuns.

On March 14, 1998, soon after the *bhikkhunī*s returned from Bodhgaya, Inamaluwe Sumangala Thero organized and Chief Sanganayaka of Rangiri Dambulla Monastery administered ordination to twenty-two *dasasilmātā*s who had completed their training at his center. With the assistance of the *bhikkhunī*s who had been ordained in Bodhgaya, five senior monks conducted a *bhikkhunī* ordination at Rangiri Dambulla Monastery in the same hall where monks ordinarily receive their ordination. This *bhikkhunī* ordination was the first to be held on Sri Lankan soil in approximately a thousand years, adding another page to the history of the revival of the Bhikkhunī Saṅgha in the world. A further group of *dasasilmātā*s are currently being trained to receive the higher ordination in Sri Lanka.

The *bhikkhunī*s who were ordained in Sarnath, Bodhgaya, and Sri Lanka now perform the *uposatha* (the bimonthly recitation of the Bhikkhunī Pāṭimokkha)[10] and other Vinaya procedures (*karma*) under the guidance of senior monks from the Nayaka and the Anu Nayaka sects. They have begun observing the tradition of the three-month rainy season retreat, and are engaged in Dhamma propagation work and service to the community.

CREATING COMMUNITY

Currently in Sri Lanka, there are more than a thousand fully functioning nuns' communities, known as *aramaya*s. The majority are located in remote villages, although some newer nunneries are beginning to appear around the larger cities of Kandy and Colombo. Nuns generally prefer to live away from the cities, in quiet surroundings, and most *aramaya*s have only a few nuns living together. Only in the suburbs of Colombo, Kandy, and Anuradhapura are there nunneries with ten to fifteen nuns. These nunneries not only provide living quarters for nuns, but also serve as educational centers. Almost all *dasasilmātā*s in Sri Lanka have a place to live, whether they live on their own or with their teacher, and most enjoy the support of the community in which they live. Unlike the monks, the nuns are not funded by the government, but must rely on the lay community for their *dāna* (offerings). Their needs for medicine, travel, and education are also met by the community. Usually the nuns' donors (*dāyaka*s) are not rich, but they do provide meals for the nuns. The donors will either prepare the meals and bring them to the *aramaya*, or they provide the nuns with the provisions to prepare their own food.

Today younger nuns are realizing the need to study, not only the *sutta*s and Vinaya, but secular knowledge as well. Sometimes nuns attend classes jointly with monks or with lay boys and girls. Many of the nuns now hold Bachelor's degrees in Pāli or Buddhist studies from universities in Sri Lanka. A few have received advanced degrees (Masters and PhDs) in Buddhist philosophy.

RENEWING AND TRANSFORMING VILLAGE TRADITIONS

The nunneries in Sri Lanka are well-maintained, clean, and have a peaceful atmosphere. Like other Buddhist temples, they have a shrine room with a statue of the Buddha where the nuns make daily offerings and do daily sitting meditation. The nunneries always have a *bodhi* tree in their courtyard, enclosed by a traditional wall that surrounds the sacred tree (*prakaraya*), where they perform services (*pūjā*) daily. Devotees come especially to attend the *bodhi pūjā*, a very common sacred ritual in Sri Lanka. When they are sick, in distress, or going through a difficult period according to their astrological charts, they believe that the *bodhi pūjā* will impart blessings to overcome their problems. The devotees request the nuns to perform these *pūjā*s, which have become very popular in the villages. The nuns receive food and medicines and the devotees receive blessings, establishing a mutually beneficial symbiotic relationship between the ordained and lay communities.

In the past, only monks were allowed to chant *sutta*s in laypeople's homes. Now the nuns are being invited into the homes. The people have found that it is less expensive and more practical to have nuns come to perform the readings. The nuns recite the *sutta*s well and are willing to stay all night, from 7:30 p.m. until 5:30 a.m. Unlike the monks, who may be much more demanding of the families, the nuns are very humble and sincere in their devotions.

Nuns are also becoming recognized as leaders in their villages. When people have difficulties in their families, they often come to the nunneries to seek advice from a nun, instead of asking the monks for help. Because most of the nuns come from humble backgrounds, they understand the people's needs and problems. The nuns offer compassionate counseling in times of need and some have even been consulted by local provincial councils for their opinions regarding development work in their villages. When it comes time to construct a road, dig a well, or erect a new school, the villagers and government officials will seek the support and advice of the head nun of the *aramaya* in the village. The nuns are becoming highly respected and are gaining self-confidence and strength. They provide many other services to the people, too, such as visiting patients in the hospital and chanting *sutta*s in the homes of the sick and elderly.

The recent controversy surrounding the movement to revive the Bhikkhunī Saṅgha has brought nuns into the limelight. They have begun to glimpse what is possible, and are striving their utmost to become as well trained and educated as they can. After receiving higher ordination, the *bhikkhunī*s observe the required Vinaya procedures (*karma*) and a number of ordination platforms (*sima malaka*) have been erected at various nunneries in different districts for the observance of the *uposatha sila*. The *bhikkhunī*s usually receive instruction from their *bhikkhu* teachers. Sakyadhita Sri Lanka has organized training programs that not only provide traditional Buddhist learning for nuns, but also training in health care, leadership, preschool education, and economic and community development.

In 2000, with the help of the Heinrich Böll Foundation of Germany, Sakyadhita Sri Lanka established its own training institute for nuns, which currently has seven nuns in residence. During the weekends, other nuns who have already received *bhikkhunī* ordination come for further training. Prior to the establishment of this center, from 1996 to 1999, the nuns were supported by Mapalagama Vipulasara Thera, who provided food and facilities for their training. Now Sakyadhita provides the money for their tea, medicine, travel, and educational expenses. The training institute is a significant step toward gaining greater recognition for the nuns and their contributions from the wider community. The nunneries are gradually improving in quality and acceptance from society is coming faster and sooner than anyone expected.

Sakyadhita Sri Lanka is engaged in training these *bhikkhunī*s to serve the community. With the professional training they receive in mediation and counseling, nuns are able to serve the community in many ways, including helping with family disputes, child abuse, drug and alcohol abuse, and suicide. Increasingly, nunneries serve as emergency medical clinics in the villages and the villagers look up to nuns as community leaders.

THE NEW BHIKKHUNĪ SAṄGHA IN SRI LANKA

Since the third Sakyadhita Conference in Sri Lanka in 1993, Sakyadhita Sri Lanka has been working to benefit Buddhist women, with a special focus on nuns. Before 1993, Sri Lankan nuns did not receive much support and did not have the self-confidence they needed to become a strong force in society. Since the conference, Sakyadhita members, particularly laywomen, have been helping to motivate the nuns and increase their self-confidence. In recent years, many nuns have become strong members of their communities and have begun recognizing their rights not only to work for their own liberation, but also to regain their lost heritage as *bhikkhunī*s.

From the time of the International Ordination Ceremony in Bodhgaya in 1998 until the end of 2001, seven *bhikkhunī* ordination ceremonies were held in Sri Lanka and more than 350 *bhikkhunī*s were ordained. All seven ceremonies were held at Rangiri Dambulu Maha Vihara at Dambulla, due to the initiative of Inamaluwe Sumangala, the chief incumbent. Before becoming eligible for higher ordination, the *dasasilmātā*s were selected after an interview and trained for a period of six months by senior *bhikkhu*s and *bhikkhunī*s. In April 2000, three Indonesian nuns joined twenty-two Sri Lankan nuns to receive higher ordination at an international ordination ceremony at Foguangshan Monastery in Taiwan, becoming Indonesia's first Theravāda *bhikkhunī*s.

As more and more *dasasilmātā*s have become interested and qualified to receive the higher ordination, it has become necessary to organize more *bhikkhunī* ordination ceremonies in Sri Lanka. In March 2002, an international dual ordination ceremony was held under the guidance of Talalle Dhammaloka, Deputy Chief Saṅgha of Amarapura Nikaya at his temple, Tapodhanaramaya, in Mount Lavinia. Ten senior *bhikkhus* attended the ceremony to serve as the *upajjhāya* and *kammācariya* precept masters. In addition, in accordance with the Vinaya procedures, ten Sri Lankan *bhikkhunīs* served as *kammācariya*, while two senior *bhikkhunīs* from Korea and two from Taiwan attended the ceremony as *upajjhāya*. At this ceremony, seventeen nuns from Sri Lanka, four from Vietnam, and one from Malaysia received *bhikkhunī* ordination. A ten-precept nun from Burma and one from Taiwan received *sāmaṇerī* ordination the same day. In response to applications, additional *bhikkhunī* ordination ceremonies were held in July 2002 at Dambulla and March 2003 at Tapodhanaramaya, Mount Lavinia.

The ordinations being held in Sri Lanka are having an impact on other Theravāda countries, too. In February 2001, Dr. Chatsumarn Kabilsingh, a professor of philosophy, received *sāmaṇerī* ordination and the name Dhammananda in Sri Lanka. Her ordination set off a storm of controversy when she returned to her native Thailand, where conservatives correctly feared that she would attempt to introduce the *bhikkhunī* ordination to Thailand. In February 2002, another Thai woman received *sāmaṇerī* ordination in the first such ceremony ever to be held in Thailand. She was given the Theravāda robe and the name Dhammarakkita, creating history in Thailand. Saddha Sumana, a Sri Lankan *bhikkhunī*, conferred the *sāmaṇerī* precepts on both occasions. Western nuns have also traveled to Sri Lanka to receive ordination in the Theravāda tradition.

Dr. Chatsumarn Kabilsingh (now Bhikkhunī Dhammananda) received her higher ordination in Sri Lanka in February 2003 at Tatalle Dhammaloka's temple, Tapodanaramaya, at Mount Lavinia. Ten senior monks and ten senior *bhikkhunīs* attended the ceremony. On same day, Bhikkhunī Sudhamma, an American nun; Bhikkhunī Gunasari, a Burmese national living in the United States; and Bhikkhunī Saccavadi, a young Burmese nun, also received the higher ordination. The ceremony was organized by Sakyadhita and a colorful reception was held at the Sakyadhita center to welcome the newly ordained *bhikkhunīs*. As over thirty *bhikkhunīs* were led in procession by drummers and dancers, hundreds of people gathered to greet them, waving flags and expressing their approval, saying "Sādhu! Sādhu! Sādhu!"

The *bhikkhunī*s in Sri Lanka are steadily gaining solid support from the public and from the *bhikkhu*s. A major aim of the Sakyadhita Conference in 1993 was to gain acceptance for nuns in Sri Lankan society and empower them to become leaders so that they could bring Dhamma into the villagers' daily lives. These aims are being completely fulfilled. Now, with the restoration of the Bhikkhunī Saṅgha, the nuns are becoming accepted on an equal footing with monks and are being invited to perform almost all the rituals that were previously performed only by monks. The villagers supply the four requisites (food, shelter, medicine, and clothing) and the nuns serve the community in many ways. In most villages, the *bhikkhu*s have also begun to appreciate the services of the *bhikkhunī*s and often invite them to the temple on full moon days to give Dhamma talks and to lead meditations. Even though the government prohibited mention of the term "*bhikkhunī*" as recently as the Sakyadhita Conference in 1993, the word is now used freely and will soon be accepted by all sectors of the community.

NOTES

1. The Pāli term for a fully ordained nun, *bhikkhunī*, is used in the Theravādin Buddhist traditions. The Sanskrit term, *bhikṣuṇī*, is used in the Mahāyāna traditions.

2. "Sinhala" is the term used to designate the indigenous people and language of Sri Lanka.

3. The Vinaya section of the Buddhist scriptures describes the standards of discipline by which nuns and monks live their lives.

4. See Karma Lekshe Tsomo, *Sisters in Solitude: Two Traditions of Buddhist Monastic Ethics for Women, A Comparative Analysis of the Dharmagupta and Mūlāsarvāstivāda* Bhikṣuṇī Prātimokṣa Sūtras (Albany, NY: State University of New York Press, 1996).

5. Sakyadhita, "Daughters of the Buddha," the International Association of Buddhist Women, was established in 1987 and has been instrumental in supporting and encouraging women in the Dhamma.

6. Stone inscriptions discovered in recent excavations in Burma indicate that the *bhikkhunī* order may have reached Burma, but nothing is known

about where the *bhikkhunīs* came from, whether they established themselves in Burma, and, if they did, why they disappeared. Burmese nuns today observe eight, nine, or ten precepts.

7. *Anujanami bhikkhave bhikkhunī bhikkhunīyo upasampadetum.*

8. Her doctoral dissertation committee reportedly found her work too controversial and would not accept her dissertation. In it, she openly discussed the absence of the *bhikkhunī* order in Sri Lanka, and suggested that there was no textual evidence for not allowing the order to be restored. The committee found this problematic and did not pass her. She set about writing a second dissertation, and finally received her PhD in Buddhist Philosophy in 2000.

9. See Yuchen Li, "Ordination, Legitimacy, and Sisterhood: The International Full Ordination Ceremony in Bodhgaya," in *Innovative Women in Buddhism: Swimming Against the Stream*, Karma Lekshe Tsomo, ed. (Richmond, Surrey: Curzon Press, 2000).

10. The *pāṭimokkha* (Sanskrit: *prātimokṣa*) includes the rules of discipline that regulate the lives of Buddhist monastics.

Chapter 8

Dharma Education for Women in the Theravāda Buddhist Community of Nepal

SARAH LEVINE

Dharma education for women of all ages has been a central feature of the Theravāda Buddhist movement in Nepal from the 1930s to the present. After a review of the social and religious conditions that gave rise to the Theravāda mission to Nepal and the evolution of the nuns' order,[1] there is a discussion of the nuns' efforts to educate the laity. There follows an account of their own educational development and finally, some thoughts about the direction that Dharma education for women may take in the twenty-first century.[2] Included at many junctures are excerpts from interviews with nuns and their devotees.

THE MISSION PERIOD: 1930-1951

Theravāda Buddhism is a relative newcomer to Nepal. In the late 1920s and early 1930s, a handful of young Newar Buddhists, dissatisfied with the traditional form of Buddhism, began looking for an alternative. In their search, they encountered Mahabodhi Society missionary monks from Burma and Sri Lanka at the sacred Buddhist sites of North India. After receiving ordination *(pabbajjā)* from them, they returned to their homeland determined to "purify" their own long-laicized Vajrayāna tradition. Their objectives included, first, reintroducing monasticism and second, spreading their modernist message in a community whose baroque rituals and practices they viewed as elitist and largely irrelevant to the needs of ordinary laypeople. This early generation of Theravādin monastics faced almost overwhelming opposition from: 1. a government prohibition against religious conversion, which meant they were only allowed to approach people who already identified themselves as Buddhists, and 2. the implacable hostility of the ruling Rana regime and their orthodox *brahmin* counselors. For the first twenty years of their mission, both monks and nuns suffered intermittent harassment, persecution, and even exile for spreading "treasonable" egalitarian (anticaste) ideas.

While male converts to Theravāda Buddhism in the early years ordinarily chose monks as their teachers,[3] laywomen were more often drawn to a prominent nun named Dhammacari whose own life experience, sorrow, and courage held particular meaning for them. At a time when very few children—all of them male—attended school[4] and less than two percent of the adult population of Nepal was literate,[5] Dhammacari (born Laksminani Tuladhar) not only learned to read Newari, but Nepali and Hindi as well. Widowed in her twenties, she soon suffered the death of both her children and turned to her religion for solace. For several years, she was a devotee of Tibetan lamas she encountered among the pilgrim-teachers at the great stupas in the Kathmandu Valley. Later, she and several of her friends were converted to Theravāda Buddhism by Dharmaloka, one of the first Nepalese monks to return to Nepal following ordination in India.[6] After taking the ten precepts[7] in Arakan, Burma, in 1934, Dhammacari and five companions returned to Nepal and settled in Kimdo Baha, a seventeenth-century Newar Buddhist temple near Svayambhu Stupa which, at that time, was home to a half-dozen Theravāda monks and novices, as well as a handful of nuns. Although the nuns had been designated *anagārikā* (meaning "homeless ones" in Sanskrit) by their Burmese preceptors, when they returned to Nepal they were customarily addressed as "*guruma*" ("mother teacher"), the traditional form of address to the wife of a Newar Buddhist Vajracarya household priest.

Few of the women who gathered around Dhammacari at Kimdo in the 1930s and 1940s were able to read or write. Dhammacari taught new ordinands how to perform Buddha *pūjā* and had them commit *sūtras* to memory for the purpose of ritual recitation. But with very few vernacular Buddhist books in print and barely literate themselves, these *gurumas* had little to offer the laity in the way of instruction. In return for the *dāna* they received, they conducted devotional and protective rituals, recounted Jataka tales, and gave counsel regarding domestic problems.[8] Their position in the community was distressingly marginal. In addition to being the subject of salacious gossip, they experienced harassment both from the government and from the monks.[9] Meanwhile the meeker ones among them found themselves pressed into performing domestic tasks for the monks with whom they shared quarters.

Because the schools that existed at the time were for the Hindu elite, few if any recruits to the monks' order had received formal schooling. Nevertheless, virtually all were able to read Nepali and Hindi, as well as Newari, their native language. Those who had been ordained later in life did not always wish to travel abroad, but with the help of the Mahabodhi Society, all the younger novices (*samanera*) had the opportunity to study in Buddhist institutions in India, Burma, or Sri Lanka and to take higher ordination (*upasampadā*).[10] By contrast, female recruits left Nepal only to receive the precepts at the Mahabodhi Society's monastery in Kushinagar after which some took a quick tour of the sacred Buddhist sites of North India before returning to Nepal.[11]

In 1944, the Rana government prohibited the eight monks and novices who lived in Kimdo Baha from preaching and giving five precepts to the laity on lunar days. When they ignored the ban, the government sent them into exile in India, where they remained until 1946 when the eminent Sri Lankan monk Narada Mahathera negotiated their return. Their two years' enforced stay abroad proved to be a valuable opportunity to develop contacts that, in some instances, led to further opportunities for study.[12] Dhammacari and her group of nuns were also expelled from the Kathmandu Valley; however they spent their exile in Trisuli, a Nepalese town just a day's journey away, rather than abroad. Even so, their exile experience proved fruitful since for the first time they were free to do as they wished without interference from the *bhikkhus*. When they were permitted to return to Kathmandu, it was with the determination to live separately from the monks. In the late 1940s Dhammacari was able to purchase land near Kimdo Baha. She called the nunnery she built Kimdol Vihāra ("monastery"), to distinguish it from the traditional Newar Buddhist *baha*. Once they were established in it, she and her colleagues were much better able to conduct their affairs as they saw fit and soon laywomen were flocking to them for Buddhadharma instruction. With the ousting of the Rana regime and the "coming of democracy" (*pajratantra)* in 1951, the Theravādins, now free to proselytize, moved from the margins to a respected position within Nepalese society.

NEW LEADERSHIP

Long before her death in 1978 at age 80, Dhammacari had surrendered her position as the leading female Theravādin teacher to a much younger nun named Dhammavati. Returning to Kathmandu in 1963 after a thirteen-year stay in Burma, Dhammavati had applied her considerable intellectual talents and organizational skills to educating a new generation in the Dharma. To her Buddhist modernist way of thinking, everyone, regardless of age, sex, or status, should have access to the Dharma. In her view, the greatest obstacles in Nepal were lack of literacy on the one hand and lack of Buddhist vernacular materials on the other. She saw her life's work as the elimination of these obstacles.[13]

She herself had had no formal schooling but had learned to read from a private tutor and later studied Buddhadharma and Pāli with Bhikkhu Buddhaghosa at Sumangal Vihāra in Patan. Soon after her teacher left for Burma in 1950, fourteen-year-old Ganesh Kumari Shakya (Dhammavati is the name she received on taking the precepts) also set off for Burma where, having reached Kemarama Nunnery in Moulmein, she plunged into the four-level Burmese monastic curriculum. Although the Burmese nuns lived and studied separately from the monks, the curriculum they followed and the examinations they took were identical. Burmese nuns were technically ordained laywomen (*thilashin)* not *bhikkhunī*; nevertheless the scholarly nuns among them were highly regarded by the monks as well as by the laity.

For a decade, Dhammavati was the only Nepalese nun studying in Burma, but in 1960, when she returned for a brief visit to Nepal, she arranged for some other young Newar women to be trained at Moulmein. After she had passed the Dharmacarya exams, the first Nepalese to do so,[14] she was offered a teaching position at Moulmein; however, determined to teach Dharma in her own community, she decided to return to Nepal. Ratnamanjeri, a Nepalese nun who had also studied in Moulmein, and Daw Gunavati, a Burmese nun who, like Dhammavati, had passed the Dharmacarya, accompanied her to Kathmandu.[15] In 1965, Dhammavati realized her wish to be independent from the senior male and female monastics by establishing Dharmakirti Vihāra at Sri Gha in the center of Kathmandu. She and her companions were soon joined there by two other newly returned Burma-trained nuns, Kamala and Dhammadinna. The goal of these five women was straightforward and heroic: they would teach Buddhadharma to anyone willing to listen, to the benefit of all, particularly women, whom they saw as having been ignored by Newar Buddhist society and Nepalese society as a whole. Their main teaching tool was the sermon or textual exposition (*dharma deśanā)* delivered in the nunnery during the observance of Buddha *pūjā* on lunar days, or in a private home following a meal offered to them by the laity (*bhojanadāna).*

DHARMA FOR CHILDREN

From the outset, children, especially girls, were a second very important focus of their mission. As Dhammadinna observed decades later, "Children's minds are still clear, without prejudice, unlike their elders who always think in terms of caste and the superiority of men to women."[16] At the time of the 1951 revolution, there were only 321 primary schools in Nepal, attended by about 8,500 students.[17] When Dhammavati and her companions returned to Nepal twelve years later, the number of schools had considerably increased—at least in urban areas—but even so, the large majority of children, especially girls, still had no access. During their first year in Kathmandu the nuns taught at a school opened by Bhikkhu Sumangal in Gana Baha, a tumble-down Newar Buddhist monastery in the center of the city. When Sumangal left to study in Japan, he handed the school over to Dhammavati, and as soon as Dharmakirti Vihāra was habitable, she moved it there. Recalling the school's beginnings, she says,

> We took in children who were hanging around our courtyard. Since there were no schools for poor children in those days, and no work either, they just played most of the day. The first week we had 20 boys and girls, but word spread and soon we found ourselves with 150 children! We had no particular educational model in mind. We just thought that children first need to learn the alphabet and everything else followed from that.[18]

School began at 6:00 a.m. in the summer, 7:00 a.m. in the cold winter, and ran for two or three hours, depending on the season, until 9:00

a.m. The nuns taught reading, writing, and arithmetic, and Dhammavati began designing materials for teaching Buddhadharma to children. One woman who attended Dharmakirti School in the late 1960s recalls:

> My older sister would drop my little brother and me off at the *vihāra* every morning and we just stayed until she picked us up. I loved going there. The *guruma*s were like members of my own family.[19]

Dharmakirti was one of several Buddhist schools established by monks and nuns in the 1950s and 1960s. Gradually, however, as new government schools opened, the Newar Buddhist parents no longer looked to monks and nuns to teach their children basic literacy and mathematics. But, although other monastery schools were soon taken over by the Ministry of Education and lost any trace of their religious affiliation, Dharmakirti continued its program for fourteen years. When the school finally closed, the nuns replaced it with a Buddhadharma Saturday school. One former student reminisces:

> The younger children came in the morning and twenty-five of us older girls and boys—we were about twelve and thirteen at that time—came in the afternoon. The *guruma*s explained what the *sūtras* meant, and we memorized and chanted them. Now and then some *bhante*s [monks] would come to teach us, too. We had to take our studies seriously, because every year we took stiff examinations, and we had quiz competitions with teams of children from other Saturday schools that the *bhante*s ran. We also had a leadership program. We had to get up in front of the class and make speeches about social problems and how to solve them. Dhammavati Guruma used to tell us girls that we were just as talented as the boys. Most of us had read the book a Burmese monk wrote about her,[20] and she would tell us girls, "You must be brave, like I was." We weren't always serious, we had fun too. When we passed our exams we were given prizes, and sometimes we went on trips around the city.[21]

DHARMA FOR ADOLESCENTS: THE BUDDHIST STUDY CIRCLE

Believing that all Buddhists should be able to read the scriptures for themselves, from the earliest days of their mission, the Theravādins had been teaching laypeople—a few men, but mostly women—to read. Sometimes they did so on a one-on-one basis and sometimes they gathered several students together for informal classes. Starting with a labored deciphering of the *devanāgarī* alphabet, students progressed to reading stories of the past lives of the Buddha. The Dharmakirti nuns taught their share of laypeople to read, but they soon discovered that young people who were in or had recently graduated from secondary school were also interested in learning Buddhadharma. In 1970, with the help of Bhikkhu Buddhaghosa, some laymen founded the Nepal Young Men's Buddhist Association. However, members were all in their twenties if not older and almost all were male. The following year the nuns took an important step when, with the help of Aswaghosa Bhante, they started the Buddhist Study Circle (*Bauddha Adhyayan Gosthi*). The original group, numbering only a few dozen members, rapidly expanded to more than one hundred. Although the program was designed for adolescents, people tended to stay on so that, thirty-four years later, many of the original members still attend regularly. One woman, looking back on her teenage years, described her experience in this way:

> My father and his brothers were very interested in Tibetan Buddhism and they often invited Tibetan *lama*s to the house. But the *lama*s who came only performed rituals and did not to teach the Dharma. Meanwhile my grandmother was a devotee of Dhammacari Guruma, and sometimes I went to Kimdol Vihāra with her. In those days, Dhammacari had many lady devotees, but she didn't seem to want to teach girls like me. Her *celi*s [disciples] were all much older than I was. I thought, "I want to learn too, but where can I go?" Then the *guruma*s started the Buddhist Study Circle, and my cousins and I began going on Saturdays. We were all in secondary school at the time and it was like having our own club![22]

Young people came to the Buddhist Study Circle to hear a wide range of speakers, and to read and discuss texts that Dhammavati and others had translated into the vernacular from Pāli and Burmese. A professional woman recalls:

> Those *guruma*s were so determined! We all admired them. And the nice thing about them was that even if you got too busy with your studies and had to stop going to the meetings, the nuns were as friendly as ever when you ran into them in the street. They greeted you as if they had just been talking to you yesterday, even though you hadn't spoken for months or even years. They never made you feel guilty about dropping out.[23]

DHARMA PUBLICATIONS

In 1972, the Study Circle began to publish a magazine entitled *Dharmakirti*. The magazine's editor, Bhikkhu Aswaghosa, is one of the very few monks who, over many years, has given unqualified support to the nuns. At first published annually, in 1990 *Dharmakirti* became a monthly magazine with articles in Newari, Nepali, and English. The Study Circle became a prodigious publisher of books and pamphlets as well: a total of 195, as of 1999, many authored by Dhammavati as well as other nuns.[24] The monks have translated many texts, also, and written and published a great many books, including a multivolume ten-level *pariyatti* curriculum for the laity, edited by Buddhaghosa. However, hearing complaints that "the *bhikkhu*s' books" were too difficult, Dhammavati started to write a series especially for Dharmakirti devotees in language that ordinary people could understand. She had already written several books for children and now she began writing a series for adults, eventually producing a seven-level *pariyatti* syllabus for use in classes held at Dharmakirti Vihāra on Friday afternoons.

TEACHING IN THE COUNTRYSIDE

In 1950, the *Dhammodaya Sabha* (Buddhist Society of Nepal) announced that one of their objectives was to build a *vihāra* in every town or village that had a sizeable Buddhist population, and to have one or two monks in residence in each to provide religious instruction. In the final years of Rana rule and in the years immediately following their removal, monks and nuns did indeed establish dozens of outposts; but, given the shortage of human resources, few of these new *vihāra*s ever had a monastic in permanent residence. Most stood empty for long periods while others were abandoned altogether. What had once identified itself as a missionary movement was being rapidly transformed into a much more narrowly focused organization. Urban institution-building was now the first priority. Whether to continue missionary work or not was up to the individual abbot and abbess.

In 1972, although busy with daily devotions, teaching Buddhadharma to people of all ages, running a circulation library, a weekly clinic, and a hospital visitors' program (not to mention cooking, washing clothes, and cleaning the nunnery[25]), the Dharmakirti nuns started going out, along with some of their Study Circle students, to teach in villages in which no monastic had been seen in years. On arrival they would gather a group of children together in a house, a courtyard, often under a tree, and teach them the alphabet along with the fundamentals of Buddhism. After a few days, they would have to move on to another village. Ideally, they would return the following year and slowly the seeds they had sown would germinate, a community would begin to form, and the *vihāra* would be repaired or a new one built.

The village program received a new lease on life when, freed from teaching basic literacy by the expansion of schools into rural areas following the 1990 revolution, some of the younger nuns, led by an astonishingly energetic nun named Dhammasangha, started a Buddhadharma program in government schools. From initial forays in urban locations, they extended their program to a dozen villages within the Kathmandu Valley, and, in the spring of 1996, Dhammasangha started teaching in Khungai, a village a day's bus ride from Kathmandu and only three miles from Lumbini, the Buddha's birthplace.[26] Today the population of this particular village, like that of the entire district, is Hindu and Muslim. Dhammasangha explained her choice of location in this way:

> The Buddha was born there, he grew up not far away at Kapilavastu, and after enlightenment he continued to teach in the area. But Buddhism vanished many centuries ago and all we see now are the ruins of places where Buddhists once lived. It's very important to bring the Dharma back, and because children are more open-minded, it's easier to start with them than with adults.[27]

She made friends with the local headmaster, who was eager for any help he could get for his dilapidated school set in the midst of wheat fields. If the help consisted of having the children take refuge in Buddha, Dharma, and Saṅgha, so be it. Any attention from outsiders was better than none, he said. So everyday for six weeks in late winter and early spring, in her pink dress and straw sun hat, Dhammasangha bicycled the three miles from Lumbini to the school. Determined as she was, she admitted to being sometimes daunted by the task she had set herself. Many parents forbade their children to attend classes on Buddhism. The mother tongue of those who were permitted to come was a dialect of Hindi; there were no Buddhist books written in that dialect and many children did not speak or read Nepali, the national language. She was well aware that the main reason some of the one hundred children enrolled in her classes was to receive the free pens and notebooks that she handed out. Nevertheless, they did the homework assigned to them and took the test at the end of the course. Five years later, in 2001, enrollment had risen to 350. The school buildings were newly whitewashed, Dhammasangha had exchanged her sun hat and bicycle for a helmet and motorcycle (gifts of an admiring Taiwanese donor), and a shrine, housing a large Buddha image, had been erected in the school yard. Although, as Dhammasangha admitted, she may have made no converts, there was a new awareness of Buddhism in the villages surrounding Lumbini.

BUDDHADHARMA FOR THE *GURUMAS*: TRAINING YOUNG NUNS

Until the 1980s, the assumption of senior monks and nuns alike was that religious education was of primary—even sole—importance. But, because there was no Theravāda training center in Nepal, novice monks and young nuns would have to go abroad. During the U Nu years, Burma opened its doors to foreign students, including a few Nepalese nuns. Following the military takeover in 1962 however, foreign monastics were barred from studying in Burma, and although those who were already there were permitted to finish their courses, conditions deteriorated rapidly. As one nun who was in Moulmein at the time recalls:

> The economy collapsed and laypeople had almost no *dāna* to give us. Because we were always hungry, we couldn't concentrate on our studies and when we got sick there was no medicine. Our dresses fell into rags and we didn't have cloth with which to sew new ones.[28]

She and her companions stayed on for a few years but they felt that, from an educational point of view at least, their time was largely wasted.

After Burma was closed to foreigners, alternatives were hard to find. Nepalese novices were sometimes offered places in monastic training institutions in Sri Lanka and, in the mid-1970s, some started going to Thailand. But opportunities for young nuns to study abroad opened up much more slowly. Between 1966 and 1980, no Nepalese nuns studied abroad. Their only recourse was to learn what they could from the senior nuns or, failing that, on their own. A nun named Padmavati, who went to live in Dharmakirti in 1974, recalls:

> Dhammavati Guruma was going out all the time. She was too busy to teach me and so were the other nuns. Gunavati Guruma was always cooking and cleaning and helping laypeople. So I cooked and cleaned, too, and memorized *sūtras*, and I studied the *pariyatti* textbooks by myself and tried to understand what I read.[29]

When, in 1980, after a hiatus of fourteen years, Burma opened its doors a crack and Dhammavati arranged for two young nuns to go to Moulmein, it was their parents who bought their airplane tickets and provided money for their expenses, and they entered the country on visas that required renewed every three months. The following year they were joined by four other young women. Padmavati recalls:

> We spent the first three months in retreat in Mahasi Sayadaw's meditation center in Rangoon. That first month was terrible. . . . we were meditating fourteen hours a day! At the end of the retreat, we joined the other two Kathmandu nuns at Moulmein. We were assigned a teacher who was supposed to teach us Burmese, but I, for one, never managed to learn much of the language. For one thing, we six Nepalese shared a room and we spoke Newari all the time. We were supposed to be studying Abhidhamma, but again, speaking for myself, I didn't learn much because I didn't understand what the teacher was saying. And then, after one year we couldn't get any more extensions on our visas and we were forced to leave.[30]

It was not until the late 1980s that the Burmese military regime began issuing long-term visas to foreign monastics, at which point Nepalese nuns started going to study in institutions in Rangoon and Sagaing, as well as Moulmein. After stays of a dozen years or more, three received the Dharmacarya. But most did not set their sights so high; rather, having followed the government-approved Buddhadharma course for five or six years, they came home.

THE 1987 BODHGAYA CONFERENCE

The First International Conference of Buddhist Nuns, which took place at Bodhgaya in February 1987, had several important consequences for Nepalese nuns. The conference, which brought together seventy monks and nuns and eighty laypeople from twenty-six countries, focused on issues of central importance to Buddhist women in general, and Buddhist nuns in particular. Primary among them was education. For Dhammavati, who went to Bodhgaya accompanied by a male interpreter from the Dharmakirti community, the conference was a revelation. She, like the other senior nuns, recognized the need for formal *religious* training but had been slow in seeing the need for *secular* education. By the 1980s, however, the nuns' order was starting to attract a more diverse group of recruits than in the past. Though some, as before, were formerly married women, the majority were adolescent girls and single women. These recruits had different notions from their elders' about what the renunciant life required. Coming of age in a rapidly developing location, the Kathmandu Valley, they wanted as much secular education as their talents warranted, which in many cases meant continuing their education long after ordination, through to university.

Exposed at the Bodhgaya conference to Western feminist ideas of individualism, self-realization, and gender equality for the first time and frustrated by her inability to communicate directly with the other delegates, Dhammavati did an about-face with regard not only to full ordination for Theravāda nuns[31] but, just as important, education. In order to engage in the momentous changes that Buddhist women, both lay and monastic, were working to bring about, she conceded that Nepalese nuns needed secular education as well as religious training. From that point on, instead of discouraging recruits from continuing their studies as she sometimes had in the past, she began pressuring them to remain in school. Since Bodhgaya, young nuns have been expected to complete secondary school. Those who fail the school-leaving certificate examination are expected to take it again and again until they pass.[32] Only then should they focus fully on religious training.

DHARMA TRAINING ABROAD

At Bodhgaya, Dhammavati made several contacts that, in time, opened up opportunities for Nepalese nuns to study Buddhadharma abroad. In 1989 the first of several nuns went to Thailand, and in the 1990s others went to Sri Lanka and Taiwan. Arrangements had to be made on a case-by-case basis. Once a place in a foreign institution had been secured, each young woman required a local sponsor to assume financial responsibility for her during her stay in the country; her family contributed what they could to her travel expenses, and Dhammavati and other senior nuns raised the balance from the community.

The education a young nun receives abroad varies depending on the country and institution to which she is sent as well as on individual talent and motivation. The first task is to learn the local language. Whereas Nepalese novice monks who study in monasteries to which foreigners have been coming for decades report that language instruction is reasonably effective, this is not the case for the nuns, most of whom study in much smaller and more insular institutions. Study aids, including dictionaries and grammars, may be entirely lacking. One young nun who went to Burma described the tutor who was assigned to her as kind, but too busy:

> To begin with, we met every afternoon and she taught me the alphabet and words for many things, which I'd write down and memorize. But after a short while she left for Sagaing for a month's meditation, and when she came back to the *vihāra* she didn't have time for me.

Dhammaratna, a graduate degree holder in her thirties who spent nine months in Sala Santi Suk in Thailand in the 1990s, had similar complaints. She admits that she was lucky, because both she and the abbess who prepared her for taking the precepts knew some English, which enabled them to communicate reasonably well. But her main purpose was to learn Thai as quickly as possible so that she could get on with studying the Dharma, and with that she had little help.

Unlike Nepalese monks who study abroad, the large majority of whom are enrolled in Buddhist universities, few Nepalese nuns who are involved in Dharma studies in foreign countries pursue university-level courses. Theoretically, Thai Buddhist universities now admit nuns, but few if any Thai nuns have enrolled thus far. A lower-level *pariyatti* course, specifically designed for nuns, takes nine years, and to date, no Nepalese has completed it. This is in part because of an acute awareness that, back in Nepal, Thai training earns less respect than Burmese training. Chandravati, who arrived at Sual Santi Suk at the age of eighteen after finishing secondary school in Kathmandu, was surprised by many things she found there.

> First of all, there were very few *maechi* (nuns) my age. In Thailand, nuns shave their heads when they're older, so almost everyone was a lot older than I. Second, although a few studied Buddhadharma, most worked like servants for the monks in the monastery next-door, or else they meditated in little huts up in trees in the orchard. There were a good many nuns whom I hardly ever saw because they meditated every night and slept in the daytime. As for social work—I never saw nuns going out to work in the community like we do here in Kathmandu. Unless the Santi Suk nuns went to work for the monks in the monastery next-door, they stayed in the *vihāra*.

Chandravati was surprised—even shocked—by the fact that all Dharma talks were given by monks.

> Even the learned nuns didn't give them, and when we went to chant and eat our midday meal in the homes of laypeople, after *bhojanadāna*, we'd read aloud Dharma talks from books that monks had given somewhere else and then published![35]

An alternative to the *pariyatti* course is the program offered by Mahapajapati Theri College, which opened in Bangkok in 1999. But to study in Thailand is expensive and requires a high level of proficiency in written Thai. To date only one Nepalese nun—who had already spent four years in a Thai nunnery and is from a well-to-do family who can afford to pay her tuition costs—has been accepted. Sri Lankan nuns, previously excluded from Buddhist universities, are now being admitted and, as of this writing, two Nepalese nuns have enrolled in university courses. Several Nepalese have spent from two to four years in the Buddhist College at Foguangshan Monastery in Taiwan and one Nepalese nun recently received her bachelor's degree from the Buddhist International Mission University in Rangoon. In general, however, Nepalese nuns seem less excited about foreign education than their male counterparts. This reflects the fact that few nuns are admitted to university courses, and again that, other than in Burma, nunnery-based religious education is widely regarded as inferior to that which monks receive. Thus, for tertiary education—which today's young Nepalese nuns consider mandatory—college in Kathmandu remains their best option. Many do spend time abroad, but aside from being exposed to foreign ways in great Asian cities such as Bangkok and Colombo and acquiring a certain cosmopolitan "polish," for most, the main benefits are that they make foreign friends and learn another language that from time to time they have an opportunity to practice with foreign pilgrims in Nepal.

EDUCATION FOR NUNS IN A CHANGING WORLD

Although 70 years after Theravāda Buddhism made its first appearance in modern times in Nepal and 50 years after monks and nuns won the right to proselytize freely, the lay community flourishes, the nuns' order remains small. As of last count, there are 118 nuns, of whom 20 are abroad (5 in Sri Lanka, 4 in Thailand, 8 in Burma, and 3 in Taiwan).[36] Given that many nuns who live in Nepal are either school-age adolescents or advanced in years, the work of the order falls upon a rather small group. Like their missionary predecessors, teaching Buddha-dharma is their first priority. With the assistance of devoted laymen and women, they organize classes and courses for people of all ages in *vihāra*s and government schools in the cities, towns, and villages of the Kathmandu Valley and beyond, as far away as Pokhara, Daran, Jiri, and the Terai. They are also involved in teaching *vipassanā* meditation, introduced from Burma by Daw Panyacari, founder and abbess of Moulmein Nunnery, who in 1980 led a retreat for the nuns of Dharmakirti Vihāra and a few of their devotees. She was followed by the well-known Burmese meditation master Mahasi Sayadaw in 1981, and by the Indian U.S.N. Goenka in 1982. Nepalese people took to *vipassanā* almost immediately and, overnight, meditation teachers were in high demand.

In addition to their own nunneries to which local people come daily to meditate, nuns are involved in three large meditation centers, the International Buddhist Meditation Center at Sankumol in Kathmandu; Dharmasingha, north of the city above the village of Buddha Nilkantha; and Gautami Vihāra in Lumbini. In the not-so-distant past, recruits to the Nepalese nuns' order had little if any formal education and nuns with secondary education were exceedingly rare. But as the level of education has risen in the general population, so too has it risen among recruits. Today, it is not uncommon for women with university training to renounce lay life, and although they are eager to go abroad on pilgrimages, to conferences, and on meditation courses, few are interested in *studying* abroad. Their objective is to work in their home community. As one nun who holds a master's degree put it, "I'm already an educated person. I know how to learn what I need to know from books in my own country." A few years ago she took *bhikṣuṇī* ordination in China. She wants to work for others now. She does not want to delay fulfillment of her bodhisattva vow while she commits the Tripiṭaka (the Buddhist canon) to memory!

An important, and in many cases the *most* important, initial motivation for seeking ordination is to avoid the traditional gender roles of wife and mother. But renunciation is not an escape from the world. Rather, in the view of young recruits to the order in today's global community, becoming a nun is equivalent to entering a very demanding profession that requires lengthy and rigorous training and the acquisition of a wide range of skills. Advanced Dharma study is still only available abroad. But today's recruits are more likely to pursue a secular qualification at a local university than to study Buddhadharma in a foreign institution. Knowing they will need them in order to be effective in their calling, they seek the same qualifications as their lay-sisters and brothers—and monks. Although a few may enroll in the Buddhist studies postgraduate course that has been offered at Tribhuvan University since 1999, most will continue to study Buddhadharma "on their own time."

NOTES

1. See Sarah LeVine, "At the Cutting Edge: Theravāda Nuns in the Kathmandu Valley," in *Innovative Buddhist Women: Swimming Against the Stream,* Karma Lekshe Tsomo, ed. (Richmond, Surrey: Curzon, 2000).

2. All names of monastics have been changed except in the case of prominent monks and nuns whose identity could not be concealed.

3. Notable among them were Mahapragya and Pragyananda. Both these monks first received ordination in the Tibetan Nyingma tradition but, dissatisfied, in 1929 traveled to Kushinagar, India, where they took first ordination *(pabbajjā)* in the Theravada tradition from the celebrated monk Chandramani. Chandramani resided at Kushinagara, the place where the Buddha attained *parinirvāna,* from 1901 until his death, at age ninety-six, in 1972. He gave the precepts to most of the first generation of Nepalese monastics.

4. The first school for girls in Kathmandu opened at Hanuman Dhoka in 1942. Few parents were willing to let their daughters attend, however. A second school, Kanya Mandhir, opened in Kathmandu in 1947. The first girls' school in Patan opened in 1948.

5. At the "coming of democracy," the overthrow of the Rana regime in 1951, only 0.5 percent of school-age children were actually enrolled in school. See T. R. Khaniya and M. A. Kiernan, "Nepal: System of Education," in *International Encyclopedia of Education,* 2nd ed., Torsten Husen and T. Neville Postlethwaite, eds. (Tarrytown, N.Y.: Elsevier Science, 1994), p. 4062.

6. Dharmaloka, who, like Mahapragya and Pragyananda, was also a charismatic teacher, took first ordination in Kushinagar and higher ordination (*upasampadā*) in Sri Lanka.

7. After three days, they gave up the precept that prohibits touching money because it was impractical.

8. S. M. Tuladhar, "Kindo Baha: A Centre for the Resurgence of Buddhism in the Kathmandu Valley," *Lost Horizon* 3 (1996): 7–12.

9. M. B. Shakya, *Bhjkkhunī Dhammacari: A Short Biography,* unpublished paper.

10. Amritananda, Bhikkhu, *A Short History of Theravāda Buddhism in Nepal* (Kathmandu: Anandakuti Trust, 1986).

11. Khema, a nun from Tansen, who had taken the precepts from Chandramani in 1942, went to Burma where she died in 1946. Although she became rather well known in Burma because her original home was outside the Kathmandu Valley, she never returned to her native land after ordination. She is hardly remembered in Nepal.

12. Ria Kloppenborg, "Theravāda Buddhism in Nepal," *Kailash* 5 (1977): 301–22.

13. S. K. Tuladhar, "Dhammavati Guruma: The Yomha Mhyaaya of Nepal," in *Dhamma and Dhammavati,* S. R. Tuladhar and R. Tuladhar, eds. (Kathmandu: New Nepal Press, 1999).

14. In 1966, Gyanapurna Mahasthavira became the first, and so far the only, Nepalese monk to pass Dharmacarya.

15. Daw Gunavati lived in Kathmandu for almost thirty years, only returning to her homeland in 1996 to found Nepal-Burma Vihāra in Rangoon.

16. Interview with Dhammadinna, Kathmandu, June 18, 1998.

17. K. N. Shrestha, *On Primary Education in Nepal* (Kathmandu, 1988), p. 82.

18. Interview with Dhammavati, Kathmandu, June 10, 1997.

19. Interview with Anjali (a pseudonym), November 30, 1997.

20. M. K. Shakya, *Snehi Chori (Beloved Daughter): A Biography of Anagarika Dhammavati* translated into Nepali (Kathmandu, 1990) from Gyanapurnik Bhikkhu's Newari translation *Yomha Myaaya* (Kathmandu, 1967) of the Burmese original by We Thonm (Rangoon, 1963).

21. Interview with Anjali, Kathmandu, April 30, 1998.

22. Interview with Rita (a pseudonym), Kathmandu, March 11, 2001.

23. Interview with Anjali, Kathmandu, April 30, 1998.

24. As of 1999, Dhammavati had thirty-nine publications, Gunavati one, Sushila four, Madebhi one, and Ratnamanjari one. Although a majority of Dharmakirti Vihāra publications were produced by monastics, laypeople authored a sizeable number, too. The Study Circle included many young people eager to publish their ideas and they were encouraged to do so. Of the 195

works published by Dharmakirti through 1999, 134 were in Newari, 57 in Nepali, and 4 in English. In most cases, production costs of individual publications were underwritten by families in memory of a deceased relative.

25. They did not employ a servant until the 1990s.

26. The Lumbini Development Trust was established by U.N. Secretary General U Thant during the Fourth World Buddhist Conference, which was held in Kathmandu to mark the 2500th anniversary of the Buddha's birth. An area several miles square surrounding the spot where the Buddha is believed to have been born was designated "Lumbini Garden." Villages were destroyed and their inhabitants given land elsewhere in compensation, trees were planted, and a Nepalese temple was built close to the Aśoka pillar, after which development of the site came to a halt. Only after thirty years and several financial scandals was a fresh start made, lots parceled out to Buddhist countries interested in building temples, and construction begun. By 2000 more than a dozen temples, many of them extremely elaborate, had been completed or were nearing completion and several hotels were open to receive pilgrims. However, thus far, aside from members of the Newar Buddhist community who frequent Lumbini in the winter months, few visitors come to the place.

27. Interview with Dhammasangha (a pseudonym), Lumbini, April 7, 1997.

28. Interview with Dhammadinna, Kathmandu, April 8, 1998.

29. Interview with Padmavati (a pseudonym), Kathmandu, March 5, 2001.

30. Ibid.

31. Like her preceptors, until the Bodhgaya conference, Dhammavati had believed that the Theravāda *bhikkhunī* ordination lineage had died out centuries before and could never be revived. At the conference she was persuaded otherwise and, in 1988, took *bhikkhunī* ordination from Chinese monks and nuns at Hsi Lai Monastery in Hacienda Heights, California. To date, more than thirty Nepalese nuns who are old enough (twenty years) to take full ordination have done so.

32. In 2000 the Nepalese nuns' order received five years' funding from an American foundation to cover the cost of education through university. By 2003 more than forty young nuns were receiving support.

33. Interview with Ittara (a pseudonym), April 11, 1998.

34. Interview with Chandravati, Kathmandu, June 14, 1998.

35. Ibid.

36. In 2001 there were 166 Nepalese monks, including 89 novices. See Bhikkhu Kondanya, "*Bhiksu, sramanera, anagarika tatha viharharu,*" *Ananda Bhumi* 30:1 (2002): 49–55.

Chapter 9

Buddhism, Women, and Caste: The Case of the Newar Buddhists of the Kathmandu Valley

DAVID N. GELLNER

It is natural for modern observers and interested Western Buddhists to ask, "How did caste get into Buddhism?" It is perhaps equally natural for scholars of Buddhism, and especially for an anthropologist, to be tempted to deconstruct this question by asking more questions: What is caste? What is Buddhism? It would be easy to argue, and easier still to insinuate, that neither Buddhism nor caste has an unchanging essence across all the ages and in all the regions where it has appeared. It is tempting, in other words, for specialists to refuse to answer the question, to reject it as anachronistic, and to bury their heads in the texts and their notes. I shall resist this temptation and attempt to answer the question in the spirit in which it was put.

CASTE IN BUDDHISM

We can take "caste" to refer to hereditary, ranked, and endogamous groups. Castes resemble the ethnic groups of the modern world, except that they are hierarchically ranked. They normally share a language, both in the literal and the extended senses, and form a single social system. Before the twentieth century, all the societies in which

Buddhism spread were hierarchical to a greater or lesser extent. They may not have had as many subdivisions as South Asia, but they all had hereditary, ranked "estates" of some sort. It is well known that the monastic orders of Sri Lanka are divided on the basis of caste and that, traditionally, the lowest castes were excluded from Buddhist temples.[1] The marginalization of the *burakumin* in Japan, an outcaste group that is considered polluted and polluting, may have had something to do with Buddhist influence. In Tibetan societies, there are hereditary caste-like groups. Some Hindu polemical texts responded to Buddhist attacks on Brahmanical claims to spiritual preeminence by saying, in effect, "You, too, accept caste; you do not accept low caste people or slaves into your monasteries."

Hierarchy existed in all Buddhist countries. Did Buddhism change the way the caste system operated? Richard Gombrich describes how a very large number of the Buddha's teachings, as recorded in the Pāli canon, represent a reworking—a sometimes satirical, but always fundamental and revolutionary reworking—of the *brahmins*' religious ideas.[2] This applied as much to caste as to anything else. Caste status was no guarantee of spiritual worth. It is correct that Brahmanical texts stress that true brahmin status required good character,[3] but the *sociological* significance of this doctrine was very different from the seemingly similar Buddhist teaching. The Hindu stress on good character reflected intra-Brahmanical debate about different ways of seeking status, but it did not undermine, in their eyes, the superior entitlements of all *brahmins* over all non-*brahmins*. Thus Buddhist parts of South Asia were caste societies because all South Asian societies were caste societies; but it is possible to argue that where Buddhism was prominent this made a small but significant difference to the severity with which caste principles applied in everyday life.

Despite this difference between Hinduism and Buddhism, and contrary to the picture of the Buddha that is dear to many modernist Buddhists, it is not really plausible to assert that the Buddha was interested in social reform. Perhaps he would have been interested in social reform had he been alive today, but it remains true that social work by monks or nuns, worthy though it is, is a modernist adaptation of traditional Buddhist practice.

At the time of the Buddha, caste was a fact of life. There were many grades of social status, including despised outcastes. Some of these people found their way into the Saṅgha. Most of the Buddha's followers were *brahmin*s or *kshatriya*s. In theory, no distinctions were to be made inside the Saṅgha. But the fact that caste consciousness carried over during the Buddha's time is evident in the responses given (in the *Tittira Jataka*) to the Buddha's question, "Who should have the best quarters, the best water, the best food?" Some replied, "Monks of the *brahmin* caste" and others, "monks of the *kshatriya* caste."[4] From this, Yuvaraj Krishnan concludes that the Buddha "accepted the caste system among laypeople as a fact of life." Furthermore, he taught that their status in the next life, as well as their degree of happiness and suffering in that life, were determined by their actions in the previous life. He thus "established a link between caste (*varna*, *jati*) and karma. The origin of the caste system based on the mythology contained in the *Puruṣa-sukta* of the *Ṛg-veda* is now replaced by the causal cosmic law of karma."[5]

There are no exhortations to laypeople to treat everyone as a social equal in early Buddhist texts,[6] but monks and nuns *are* expected to do so. The *Ambattha Sutta* states that anyone who makes snobbish distinctions of rank is far from wisdom.[7] Thus monks and nuns are supposed to accept food from everyone, irrespective of caste. In short, caste was accepted in society, but it was rejected in the Saṅgha. So the first answer to the question, "How did caste get into Buddhism?" is clear—from society.

THE NEWARS

The Newars are the "indigenous" inhabitants of the Kathmandu Valley.[8] They are divided into approximately twenty castes; some of these are found throughout the valley and beyond, others are localized in one city or several villages and not found elsewhere. In terms of the range of castes and specializations, they are fairly typical of North Indian regional systems. But in other ways they are atypical: they speak a Tibeto-Burman language, practice Mahāyāna Buddhism and Hinduism equally (though in differing proportions, according to caste), and their relatively small population (around a million) means that the smaller castes can sometimes have considerable difficulty finding brides who are not related within the proscribed limits of kinship.[9]

There has been a continuous history of contact and exchange between the Newar Buddhist tradition and the Tibetan tradition.[10] The holiest Buddhist *stupa*s and temples in the Kathmandu Valley (including Swayambhu and Bauddha) are important pilgrimage sites for Tibetans.[11] Many Newar Buddhists, whose forebears traded in Tibet, have adopted Tibetan Buddhism as the idiom for their own personal religious practice, and some Newars have become monks and nuns in the Tibetan traditions. Many Newars are lay followers of Tibetan Buddhist teachers, and some Newar Buddhist sites have had chapels redesigned in Tibetan style (e.g., Kwa Bahah and Uku Bahah, Lalitpur) or have been taken over by Tibetans (e.g., Kindol Bahah).[12] Tibetan-style prayer wheels were added to most prominent Newar Buddhist sites between the 1860s and the first half of the twentieth century.

Despite these links, the organization of Newar Buddhism is quite different from Tibetan Buddhism. Its scriptures, liturgies, and practices are preserved in and carried out in Sanskrit by members of the composite Vajracharya-Sakya caste. At the age of five, seven, or nine, the boys of this caste are initiated as monks in the monastery-temple complex of their fathers (providing their father has had a correct marriage, that is, their mother is from the same caste).[13] The boys remain as monks for four days, during which time they observe a monastic regimen: sleeping on the floor, eating only one full meal a day, and receiving alms from their relatives. On the fourth day, the boys go through a ritual in which they return to lay life. Throughout their life, they take on this monastic identity at various times and in various contexts: once a year they traditionally participate in the festival of Panchadan, during which time they receive alms from private households and from *guthi*s (special socioreligious associations endowed for the purpose). When it is their turn to carry out the daily monastic rituals in the temple complex to which they belong, Sakya and Vajracharya men likewise revert to their monastic identity. The rest of the time they are householders, eventually marrying and having children themselves. But they combine their householder identity with their monastic identity, as is reflected in the name "Sakya," short either for Sakyabhiksu (meaning "Buddhist monk") or Sakyavamsa (meaning "of the Buddha's lineage"). The latter interpretation is more prevalent in the city of Lalitpur than in Kathmandu and reflects the tradition that the Sakyas are descended from the last surviving members of the Buddha's tribe, who migrated from the Tarai region of Nepal to the Kathmandu Valley.[14]

CASTE AND GENDER IDENTITY

Vajracharya men have an additional religious identity. This identity is reflected in their surname, which means "master of the adamantine scepter," that is, a preceptor of the Vajrayana form of Buddhism. After receiving monastic initiation, Vajracharya boys go through an additional ritual that entitles them to serve as domestic priests for others, making them the equivalent of *brahmin*s in Hinduism, as some have noted.[15] Like *brahmin* priests, they have hereditary links to various households who must summon "their" Vajracharya to carry out any obligatory life cycle rituals in their house. The Vajracharya, in turn, is obliged to officiate at such rites or to send a substitute in his place if he is unable to go. Vajracharyas refer to those they serve as *jajman* or *jayma*. This may be translated as "patron" or "parishioner" (many scholars have preferred "clients").

The wife of a Vajracharya priest has an important role to play, always accompanying her husband to rituals. She is addressed as "*guruma*" and is entitled to half the ritual stipend (*daksina*) that is given to her husband. In exoteric rituals her role is that of ritual assistant. Rituals are highly complex affairs, requiring the mobilization and efficient marshalling of numerous ingredients. The priest's wife or other accompanying female must have considerable expertise and experience, and it is for this reason that Vajracharyas prefer to marry their sons to girls from Vajracharya families, even though there is no caste bar on them marrying Sakyas. In esoteric rituals the Vajracharya's wife becomes even more central. She often has to adopt the role of the goddess Vajradevi, the incarnation of Buddhist wisdom, becoming possessed by her.[16]

Thus it is Vajracharya priests, assisted by their wives, who preserve and transmit traditional Newar Buddhism. It is they who learn how to perform the rituals and who read the scriptures. Attempts to revive Newar Buddhism from what is widely seen as a terminal decline have focused on educating the younger generation of Vajracharyas who are responsible for carrying on the tradition. Other strongly Buddhist castes—the Sakyas, Manandhars, and, increasingly, the Maharjans—have tended to support the newly imported Theravāda movement, both becoming monks and nuns, and acting as crucial lay support for building monasteries and other activities. With the exception of one or two prominent Vajracharya families, Vajracharyas have generally been conspicuous by their absence in Theravāda circles.[17]

The traditional role of women in Newar society was to preserve religious traditions at the household level, whereas the Vajracharyas were responsible for spreading Buddhism more widely. Certainly, a very large part of daily and calendrical practices were in female hands. Senior women were relied upon to remember what rituals needed to be performed and when. Each caste had, and, to a considerable extent, still has, a slightly different subculture with different traditions for different occasions. One justification often heard for arranged marriages is that the traditions of the two families involved must be in harmony with one another. Marriage partners from families following similar religious traditions are thought to encounter far less of the interactional awkwardness that inevitably results from a union between members of different castes.

The position of women as preservers of tradition is clearly reflected in an informative book on the customs of Kathmandu Newars written by the late Ratna Kaji Vajracharya.[18] He recorded in detail what had to be done in seventeen different castes for each life cycle ritual. I would suggest that it was no coincidence that a majority of his informants were women.

Among the Buddhist castes, the relatively high status of senior women, and of the priest's wife in particular, may have had something to do with the symbolic importance of the female within Vajrayana Buddhism. The highest practices within the Vajrayana tradition are ideally performed as a couple. Far from women being excluded from these practices, their presence is essential. Such practices are, however, restricted to practitioners of high caste. There is, then, a subtle interplay between social and gender hierarchies. Furthermore, it is certainly the case that caste, as an institution, is dependent on arranged marriage. Arranged marriage, in turn, is itself dependent on, and crucially helps to reproduce, the joint household. The joint household system, in turn, is built upon the labor (in both senses) of the subservient daughter-in-law. Modernization, with its expectations of equality and daughters-in-law who work outside the home, is beginning to undermine the whole edifice.

In different ways, then, all forms of hierarchy are being questioned and transformed in modern life. Castes may still be separate and are ideally endogamous, yet they are separate and equal, rather than separated and hierarchically ordered. Newar women are beginning to take greatly expanded roles in all spheres, including, and perhaps especially, the sphere of religion.[19]

CONCLUSION

For the Buddha, so far as we know from the Pāli canon, caste was irrelevant to salvation and to moral worth, but it was, nonetheless, a fact of life in the social world. As Buddhism adapted to the world in which it existed, it was hardly surprising that influences from the social world should affect its organization, and in particular the Saṅgha. This has led over time to what may be called the "householderization" of the Saṅgha. Clearly Newar Buddhism—with its hereditary households of domestic priests acting out their monastic status occasionally and living in privately owned residential courtyards ritually defined as monasteries—has taken this process a long way.

In the past century or more the process has been put into reverse as the monastic ideals of meditation, book learning, and an overriding soteriological orientation have spread from monastic practitioners to laypeople, including, significantly, laywomen. Caste, which came into Buddhism from the social world, is on its way out again, in line with the egalitarian ideals of the modern world.

NOTES

1. Richard F. Gombrich, *Buddhist Precept and Practice: Traditional Buddhism in the Rural Highlands of Ceylon* (Delhi: Motilal Banarsidass, 1991).

2. Richard F. Gombrich, *Theravāda Buddhism: A Social History from Ancient Benares to Modern Colombo* (London and New York: Routledge, 1988).

3. N. K. Dutt, *Origin and Growth of Caste in India* (Calcutta: F. K. L. Mukhopadhyay, 1968), p. 216.

4. Ibid.

5. Y. Krishnan, *The Doctrine of Karman: Its Origin and Development in Brahmanical, Buddhist and Jaina Traditions* (Delhi: Motilal Banarsidass, 1997), p. 87.

6. Gombrich, *Buddhist Precept and Practice*, p. 356.

7. *Ambattha Sutta* 2.1.

8. Gérard Toffin, *Religion et Société chez les Néwar du Népal* (Paris: CNRS, 1984); and David N. Gellner and D. Quigley eds., *Contested Hierarchies: A Collaborative Ethnography of Caste among the Newars of the Kathmandu Valley, Nepal* (Oxford: Clarendon, 1995). On Newar Buddhism, see John K. Locke, *Karunamaya: The Cult of Avalokitesvara-Matsyendranath in the Valley of Nepal* (Kathmandu: Sahayogi, 1980); David N. Gellner, *Monk, Householder, and Tantric Priest: Newar Buddhism and Its Hierarchy of Ritual* (Cambridge: Cambridge University Press, 1992); and Todd T. Lewis, *Popular Buddhist Texts from Nepal: Narratives and Rituals of Newar Buddhism* (Albany, N.Y.: State University of New York Press, 2000).

9. Gellner and Quigley, *Contested Hierarchies*, pp. 30, 193, 246.

10. See T. T. Lewis and L. Jamspal, "Newars and Tibetans in the Kathmandu Valley: Three New Translations from Tibetan Sources," *Journal of Asian and African Studies* 36 (1988): 187–221; and T. T. Lewis, "Newars and Tibetans in the Kathmandu Valley: Ethnic Boundaries and Religious History," *Journal of Asian and African Studies* 38 (1989): 31–57.

11. Keith Dowman, "A Buddhist Guide to the Power Places of the Kathmandu Valley," *Kailash* 8:3–4 (1981): 183–291.

12. On Newar Buddhist monasteries, see John K. Locke, *The Buddhist Monasteries of Nepal: A Survey of the Bahas and Bahis of the Kathmandu Valley* (Kathmandu, Sahayogi, 1985); and David N. Gellner, "The Newar Buddhist Monastery: An Anthropological and Historical Typology," in *Heritage of the Kathmandu Valley*, Niels Gutschow and Axel Michaels, eds. (Sankt Augustin: VGH Wissenschaftsverlag, 1987), abridged version in David N. Gellner, *The Anthropology of Buddhism and Hinduism: Weberian Themes* (Delhi: OUP, 2001).

13. John K. Locke, "Newar Buddhist Initiation Rites," *Contributions to Nepalese Studies* 2:2 (1975): 1–23; and David N. Gellner, "Monastic Initiation in Newar Buddhism," in *Indian Ritual and its Exegesis*, Richard F. Gombrich, ed. (Delhi: Cambridge University Press, 1988).

14. For more on Sakya identity, see Gellner, *Monk, Householder, and Tantric Priest*; and David N. Gellner "Buddhist Monks or Kinsmen of the Buddha? Reflections on the Titles Traditionally used by Sakyas in the Kathmandu Valley," *Kailash* 15:1–2 (1989): 5–25.

15. Locke, "Newar Buddhist Initiation Rites;" and David N. Gellner, "The Consecration of a Vajra Master in Newar Buddhism," in *Les Habitants du Toît du Monde*, S. Karmay and P. Sagant, eds. (Nanterre: Société d'Ethnologie, 1997).

16. See Gellner, *Monk, Householder, and Tantric Priest*, p. 285.

17. On the newly imported Theravāda movement, see R. Kloppenberg, "Theravāda Buddhism in Nepal" *Kailash* 5:4 (1977): 301–21, H. Bechert and J. U. Hartmann "Observations on the Reform of Buddhism in Nepal," *Journal of the Nepal Reseach Centre* 8 (1987): 1–30 and note 19.

18. Ratna Kaji Vajracharya, *Newah Samskara Samskritiya Tahca* (Cultural Heritage of the Newars) (Kathmandu: Vajracharya Prakashan, 1989).

19. See Sarah LeVine, this volume, and also, "At the Cutting Edge: Theravāda Nuns in the Kathmandu Valley," in *Innovative Buddhist Women: Swimming Against the Stream,* Karma Lekshe Tsomo, ed. (Richmond, Surrey: Curzon Press, 2000).

Chapter 10

Trafficking in Buddhist Girls: Empowerment through Prevention

KHANDU LAMA

Trafficking in human beings is so incomprehensible to many people that it is almost beyond their power to conceptualize.[1] Yet if we cannot conceive of the extent of the problem, it will be difficult to conceive of solutions. Therefore, at the Hyolmo Women's Development Association where I work, we use visualization and small group discussions to evoke empathy toward the victims and an understanding of the depth and horror of the problem.

We begin with a visualization. We ask participants to sit in a comfortable position and close their eyes, inhaling and exhaling slowly. Next, we ask them to listen deeply to the true story of a young girl and imagine what it feels like to be her:

> You are a girl born in an extremely poor Buddhist village in the mountains of Nepal. Only three months after your birth, your mother dies. Your relatives take you in because your father believes it is not his role to raise children and because he doesn't have enough food to provide for you. Like most girls in rural Nepal, you wake up early to collect firewood and water, and to cook, wash clothes, tend the buffalo, work in the field, polish the floors, and take care of your other siblings.
>
> At age fifteen your relatives take you on a trip to India. In Bombay, your relatives introduce you to a man that you will work for. They explain that it is your duty to raise money for the family.

> Your relatives return to Nepal. You quickly learn that the work your relatives have found for you is to have sex repeatedly with men of all ages while living in a brothel with twenty-five other young girls. To make you submissive and willing to lie on dirt floors and have sex with men day and night, you are continually raped, beaten, and starved by the man your relatives sold you to, until you are sufficiently "broken in." Your life continues like this for twenty years.
>
> Back in the village your relatives have spent the money they earned from selling you to build two homes and to buy jewelry and many large copper pots to display their earnings. One day you escape from the brothel in Bombay and try to return home, but when you go to cross the border, the police recognize the markings of a prostitute that have been branded onto the backs of your heels, and put you in jail. You call your relatives and ask them to send one of the necklaces they had bought. You promise to pay the money back when you get out of jail, but they refuse to help. When you are finally released, you return to India to continue working. Years later, your family finds out that you have died, but the details of your death are unknown.

After guiding people through this visualization exercise, we ask participants to pay attention to the feelings that arise as they listen to this young girl's story. Afterward, we then give them a chance to articulate the feelings and thoughts that come to mind. The thoughts and emotions people experience are varied: rage, danger, terror, horror, violation, despair, tragedy, sadness, powerlessness, helplessness, sympathy, hatred, exploitation, grief, and betrayal, among others.

The next thing we do is share definitions and information gathered from organizations in Nepal that are working to prevent trafficking and to facilitate the rehabilitation of girls and women who are trafficked. The definition of trafficking that these organizations have developed refers not only to trafficking in girls, but to trafficking in general: "Trafficking is an act of selling someone anywhere, whether within a country or across international borders, to exploit that individual for financial gain." Using this as a working definition, we then focus specifically on trafficking in girls, investigating who the girls are, what their lives are like, and why they are being exploited and sold for sex.

UNDERSTANDING AND ADDRESSING THE PROBLEM OF TRAFFICKING

The Hyolmo Women's Development Association, which I founded and still chair, is one of a number of grassroots organizations that have been founded to address the problem of trafficking in Nepal. Based in the village of Shermatang in the Helambhu region of northern Nepal, about a hundred kilometers north of Kathmandu, the association works with indigenous women from the Himalayan region. In Shermatang, I work with a staff of between fifteen to twenty people to help improve the vocational skills of the women in Helambhu. Our goal is to help the women make a living, so that they can stay in the region. In the past, women have had to leave the Helambhu region to seek wage-earning employment. Learning skills such as sewing and knitting has enabled many women to earn an income and stay in Helambhu. We also conduct literacy courses so that the women will be able to communicate with the tourists that visit the area. With their improved English skills, the women are able to run lodges, sell their products, and gain independence. In the literacy classes, we also teach the women basic health and environmental awareness.

Unfortunately, in our work with the Hyolmo Women's Development Association, our awareness of girl trafficking has increased. Learning about the history of girl trafficking in Nepal is one step toward addressing the problem. By learning more about what has happened so far, we can learn how to stop this disastrous practice in the future. Girl trafficking is a problem in all of Nepal, but here we describe the history of the problem in my home district of Sindhupalchowk.

Many years ago the queen of Nepal had some problems with her husband. She needed to get away from him, so she traveled to the region of Helambhu, in the mountains to the north of Kathmandu. While in Helambhu, she hired many women to work as her maids and caretakers, and she became very fond of the women who worked for her. When it was time for her to return to Kathmandu, because her husband died, she brought some of the women with her. The men of Kathmandu, especially the men from the palace, noticed how beautiful the Helambhu women were and decided to keep some of them as *bhitinees*. This Nepali term denotes a woman who is not married to the man she stays with, but who is not considered a prostitute.

Once the Rana family took over the country (1846–1951), they started to send men up to Helambhu to get more women. The women were used as *bhitinees* (concubines) and maids in the palaces of the Ranas. The women came under false pretenses, thinking they would be working for the queen. During those days, working in the palaces of the Ranas was a matter of prestige. Later, members of the Rana family began to give the women to the kings of India as impressive gifts. This practice of providing girls to the royal palace was the beginning of the trafficking in girls in Helambhu, which has continually increased up through today.[2]

Once the women came to the city, it was very difficult for them to return to their villages, because they lacked an education. This led to poverty and unemployment. The Rana government policy did not allow mountain people to be educated, perpetuating the problem. Today 90 percent of the girls and young women who are trafficked in Nepal are Tamang indigenous people or members of other disadvantaged tribes and castes. The districts most severely affected by girl trafficking are Sindhupalchowk, Nuwakot, Dhading, and Makwanpur. Furthermore, 75 percent of the girls are Buddhist. It is difficult to statistically document the numbers of women from the area who have worked or are working in brothels in India because people in the area try to be discreet. When examining trafficking patterns, it is also important to differentiate between safe migration to India and unsafe migration.[3]

For the past ten years, a law has been in effect that sentences anyone found guilty of girl trafficking to twenty years of imprisonment. Since this law was passed, agencies and government organizations have been established to eliminate girl trafficking, but so far, for unknown reasons, these organizations have been ineffective in controlling the problem. Hundreds of people have been arrested for girl trafficking, brought to court with evidence of their guilt, but have been found not guilty and set free. Those people who have been found guilty have been imprisoned for no more than twenty days to twenty months, rather than the stated twenty-year sentence. It is unclear why people who have been convicted have not been properly punished. Either the agents are accusing innocent people or the police and the courts are corrupt. If the agents are accusing innocent people, they need to be more careful about whom they arrest. If the police and the courts are corrupt, then the organizations established to stop trafficking need to raise strong objections to this corruption, but so far this has not happened.

We, the people, also need to let our voices be heard concerning girl trafficking. Up until now, concerned organizations have been doing the job of the police. They have been going to the border areas and arresting the girl traffickers. But these activities are not sufficient to prevent this disaster. If we really want to prevent girl trafficking, we need to address the urgency of this issue at a grassroots level. We need to visit the affected areas and discover the real reasons why women are leaving their homes, whether willingly or unwillingly, and we must create alternatives for them. For example, we must teach women skills so that they may earn a living and become more independent, as the Hyolmo Women's Development Association project has been doing for women in Shermatang.

One reason for this project's success is the research we did in the area. The data we collected on demographics, education, local trades, and the problems of the village allowed us to address the specific needs of the people of Shermatang. This is a small, grassroots project that is run by just thirty local women. To effectively put an end to girl trafficking, however, the government needs to get involved as well. Until now, the government has not gone to the affected areas, nor has it punished those who have committed the crimes. It has not created educational programs about the issues surrounding girl trafficking either. Most of the agencies have not even begun to do research at a grassroots level. Even assuming that the girl traffickers are sent to jail, this will not solve all the problems associated with girl trafficking.

Some people are working to help remedy some of these problems already. Agents have developed rehabilitation centers for women who have been brought back from the brothels and for those who have contracted the AIDS virus. We appreciate their efforts. Most agencies are centered in Kathmandu, however, with more than 50 percent of their budgets being spent on administrative costs. This is not helping. It is only perpetuating the idea of helplessness, the "beggar's bowl" (*mangi khane bhando*). The agencies need to work at the grassroots level and give practical support, so that people in the affected areas can become more economically independent. Social workers need to take a clear look at the problem, stop talking, and take action. This is our main responsibility. Although the majority of the victims of girl trafficking in Nepal are Buddhist, it will take the efforts of both Buddhists and non-Buddhists to overcome this problem. Although we, as Buddhists, are especially concerned, the whole society has been hit hard by this disaster, which is a huge responsibility and challenge for all of us.

Another aspect of the issue that needs to be addressed concerns the women who have contracted HIV/AIDS in the brothels. It is estimated that 60 percent of prostitutes from the brothels have contracted HIV/AIDS. This raises grave concerns about the safety and well-being of future generations. This concern is not limited to those with AIDS; all of us with daughters are concerned about their future, too. The main issue confronting social workers in Nepal is how we can protect future generations from this epidemic, but the problem is not isolated to Nepal. It is a problem in both developed and developing countries around the world. Yet, whereas the developed countries have many resources to address the issue, Nepal is a small country with limited resources. Although the problem affects the whole society and the whole nation, the responsibility for tackling the problem falls on the shoulders of just a few social workers.

Trafficking in girls and women is both a national and an international problem, and the problem is multifaceted. Many people are astounded when they hear that parents sell their children. They comment that even dogs take care of their puppies, so how can human beings not take care of their children? But the problem is greater than the parent/child relationship, since parents living in poverty must make tough decisions about the survival of their whole family. Peer pressure and consumer patterns are factors that affect their decisions, too. When young women return to their villages with money to buy homes for their parents, they create expectations among other poverty-stricken families in the villages.

To prevent girls and their families from succumbing to material desires, there is a need for good role models for girls, better opportunities for education, and meetings to strengthen community awareness and prevent other girls from falling victims to trafficking. Economic development schemes are vital. If girls and young women are financially independent and able to live successful, happy, healthy lives, they will naturally resist situations that lead to trafficking.

Because of the incredible poverty in the villages, girls and young women need alternatives, particularly education and ways to earn their own living. Training women as social workers for the villages is vital, too; these women can keep an eye on the girl children, sense problems, and take the responsibility for problem solving. Education, empowerment, and economic alternatives work together; families who realize the value of girl children will not sell them, but educate them, realizing that women are an economical asset to the community.

If 75 percent of the victims of trafficking are Buddhists in a country that is predominantly Hindu, there is also a religious element to the issue of girl trafficking. The international Buddhist community must put pressure on the government on Nepal to combat this injustice. Buddhists must frankly consider those aspects of Buddhism that may be disempowering for women.[4]

Techniques developed in child abuse programs can educate young children, both boys and girls, to recognize situations of danger, to resist them, and to recognize resources in their communities—parents, teachers, religious figures, and trusted people in their neighborhoods—in whom they can confide their anxieties.

OVERCOMING SOCIAL INJUSTICES

In closing our seminars, we ask participants to recall the strengths we associate with women. Typically, the qualities they list include: virtuous, intuitive, cooperative, sensitive, loving, resourceful, courageous, spiritual, self-sacrificing, kind, powerful, and diligent. We then ask them to place the list of strengths alongside the list of responses they gave to the story of the young woman sold in Bombay. The contrast between these two lists helps illustrate the contradictions between women's exploitation and women's human potential. To eradicate social injustices against women and instead visualize women's positive potential is a way to call that potential into being.

The visualization that I did at the beginning of this chapter is a true story about a real family that I personally know. It is difficult to imagine that parents would sell their own children, but the grinding poverty of their lives is also difficult to imagine. The best way to prevent trafficking is to provide economic alternatives for families so that they will not need to sell their children. We need to educate the villagers and convince them that educating their daughters, rather than selling them off, will be more economically advantageous in the future. We need to teach the villagers about human rights and Buddhist ethics in order to increase their social awareness and renew their own spiritual roots. And, perhaps most importantly, we need to awaken the women to the enlightened qualities within themselves.

NOTES

1. The extent of global trafficking in women and children was the topic of a four-day conference in Manila in April 2000. Since then, this 17-billion-dollar industry has increasingly become the focus of international attention. See Nancie Caraway, "Traffic Pattern," in *Honolulu Weekly* 10:29 (2000): 6–8.

2. Having been born and raised in Helambhu, I am personally acquainted with people who have worked in the palaces of the Ranas. For example, one of my grandmothers, who passed away in 2000, worked in the palace.

3. I am grateful to John Frederick for pointing out the importance of this distinction. His six-year project to investigate trafficking as a social problem rather than as a criminal problem is documented in *Fallen Angels: The Sex Workers of South Asia*, edited by John Frederick and Thomas L. Kelly (New Delhi: Roli Books, 2000).

4. For a brief discussion of Buddhism and gender identity formation, see Lucinda Joy Peach, "Buddhist and Human Rights in the Thai Sex Trade," in *Religious Fundamentalisms and the Human Rights of Women*, Courtney W. Howland, ed. (New York: St. Martin's Press, 1999), pp. 215–26.

Chapter 11

Khunying Kanitha: Thailand's Advocate for Women

KARMA LEKSHE TSOMO

The first time I met Khunying Kanitha was during the Second Sakyadhita International Conference on Buddhist Women, which was held in 1991 at Thammasat University in Bangkok. I wanted to send five nuns from Jamyang Choling, our monastery in India, to attend a meditation course at Suan Moke Monastery in southern Thailand, and was looking for someone with a car to help purchase the train tickets. Someone pointed out a tall, stately figure standing by a jeep across the way, and said, "Ask Khunying. She will help you." As soon as I explained the situation to this distinguished woman, she happily agreed to go to the train station and get tickets for the nuns. Later, when I realized how highly esteemed she was in Thai society and how many responsibilities she shouldered, I felt deeply embarrassed to have imposed on her time. But I soon learned that Khunying is well known as a model of humility, generosity, and loving-kindness.

Over the next ten years, I was fortunate to meet and correspond with Khunying frequently and was continually impressed by her many talents and personal qualities. Even before her death in early 2002, I had begun to interview her and the people who knew her, with the intention of documenting her achievements for future generations. Now that she has passed away, I hope this chapter will serve in some small way as a tribute to her memory and her contributions to social justice in Thailand.

First, I trace Khunying's early life and education, to understand the roots of her concern for social service.[1] Second, I document her achievements in working for social justice in Thailand, especially her efforts to benefit women. Third, I attempt to place her life and her work within the context of women's social history in Thailand and in the broader context of the Buddhist women's movement as a whole.

FAMILY LIFE AND EDUCATION

Khunying was born Kanitha Samsen in Bangkok on November 4, 1922. She was one of four sisters—Boonkua, Kingkaew, Kanok, and herself. Her family also took in several boys, whom she addressed as brothers. As a child, she loved animals and was fond of visiting the sick, even tuberculosis patients who might have been contagious. She attended St. Joseph's Convent High School in Bangkok, a school that was also attended by the children of prominent families. Her father was a lawyer and she also decided to pursue law. Today women comprise almost half the students in law schools in Thailand, but at the time she studied law at Thammasat University in Bangkok, she was one of only ten women in a class of three hundred men. After graduation, she went abroad for further studies. First, she spent a year studying French at Couvent des Oiseaux in Dalat, Vietnam. Next, after World War II ended, she studied international law at American University in Washington, D.C., and law at Columbia University in New York. Later, she studied international relations at L'Institut des Hautes Etudes Internationale in Geneva

After returning to Thailand, Khunying worked at the Ministry of Foreign Affairs in Bangkok. There she met Adul Wichiencharoen, who impressed her with his refined manners and erudition. A year later, in 1950, they were married, and within two weeks, he set off for the United States on a U.S. State Department fellowship. While studying for his master's degree during the McCarthy era, conservatives at Georgetown University labeled him a communist for advocating a one-China policy. He even came under suspicion from the Thai Embassy in Washington for his left-of-center social sentiments. Eventually, he became the Vice-Rector of Thammasat University and the Rector of

Silpakorn University. He and Khunying had three children—two sons, Aim and Art, and one daughter, Anik—and eight grandchildren, including two grandsons now studying in Boston and Honolulu.

Khunying graduated from a convent high school in 1940 that was also attended by children of the nobility and the royal family. After the queen married the king of Thailand, Khunying helped her with several projects, including a drama performance and an art exhibit that she organized to support the Red Cross Foundation, which helps women. After the first showing, she was invited to produce the musical again at Thammasat University, where many people were able to watch it. Because she helped organize this event, the king granted her the title of "Khunying" as a tribute to her distinguished social service, perhaps at the urging of the queen.[2] When Khunying later met the queen in Paris, they were already acquainted from school, and because of their long-standing acquaintance, Khunying was able to make a request of the queen—that she encourage the nuns of Thailand to gain legal status.[3]

A BUDDHIST ADVOCATE FOR GENDER JUSTICE

From 1962 to 1965, Khunying served as president of the Women Lawyers' Association of Thailand. While traveling abroad, she was impressed by the women's shelters she saw and decided to create such a shelter when she returned to Thailand. In 1979, she established the Emergency Home and Relief Fund for Women and Children in Distress to counsel and care for battered and deserted women. Remodeling a small house in the center of Bangkok that belonged to her family, she started a center where abandoned and abused women, often from rural areas, could seek shelter from the streets. This was the first women's shelter to be built in Thailand and it is still flourishing today. When I asked Khunying, "How do the women find their way to the Home?" she replied, "The police bring them to us."

As the number of women needing assistance increased, the home was no longer adequate in size. At that point, a former high school classmate donated a sizable plot of land in Donmuang, near Bangkok International Airport, for the purpose of building a larger women's shelter and a vocational training center. Eventually, the women who took refuge at the first shelter complained that they had no place to rest, so Khunying and her associates joined their efforts, found a donor, and built the first building on the new property. They then organized their first art exhibition and used the proceeds to construct the building that later became a nursery.

It was at this site that Khunying founded the Association for the Promotion of the Status of Women (APSW), which she officially registered with the Thai government in 1982.[4] By that time, there were already many organizations and women working for the advancement of women, so the project proposal received widespread support.[5] Khunying served as the president of APSW from its founding in 1982 until she resigned in 2000 to devote her energies to founding Mahapajapati Theri College. In 1995, she represented the APSW at the Fourth International Women's Conference in Beijing. One of APSW's supporters, the same classmate who had donated the Donmuang site to her, sponsored the construction of a building to be used for administrative purposes. In addition, Khunying gradually built not only a women's shelter, but also an AIDS hospice, an orphanage and child care center, and a clinic for homeless pregnant women and their infants. She was able to do this with the help of the Sasakawa Foundation, the Jimmy and Rosalyn Carter Foundation, and other donors.

In 1979, Khunying founded Friendship Force International, an exchange program to promote trust and friendship between Thai and American host families. Because of her international experience, when President Jimmy Carter came to Bangkok with his wife Rosalyn in 1981 to attend a Habitat for Humanity conference, Khunying was selected as the coordinator of the conference. After the conference, she had an opportunity to speak with the First Lady of the United States as she escorted her on a shopping expedition. Khunying later recalled that, "The car went very fast through the Bangkok traffic, because police cars drove in front of us to clear the way."

During this outing, Khunying had an opportunity to share information with Rosalyn Carter about life in Thailand. In the process, she happened to mention the social development projects that she was involved in. Later, when Jimmy and Rosalyn Carter came through Bangkok on another trip, Khunying invited them to visit the Women's Education and Training Center. As a result of this visit, the Carters contributed one million baht (approximately $40,000) to build a medical clinic and a home for pregnant women and children at the Donmuang site. The clinic and home have continued to grow and to serve the needs of women and children, including many people infected with HIV, up to the present day.

Later, when Khunying attended the Friendship Force International conference in the United States in 1983, she had an occasion to meet the Carters again. President Carter introduced her to Ryoichi Sasakawa, a Japanese shipping magnate and director of the Atlanta-based Sasakawa Foundation that supported Friendship Force International. The Sasakawa Foundation has also supported Khunying's projects over the years by donating a total of fifty-two million baht (over $2,000,000) to the emergency home for the construction of buildings, vocational training programs for women, and other programs to benefit deserted and battered women, unwed pregnant women, children, and AIDS patients.

To address social problems on a structural level, Khunying also established the Women's Education and Training Center, serving as its director from 1988–93, and the Gender and Development Research Institute. Waskorn Pinyosinwat, who worked with Khunying on a voluntary basis for more than twenty years, said, "She felt that if women of different backgrounds and professions could work together, we could fight for women's rights and build a better world." Gradually, well-wishers donated money to build a small house where the donor of the land could stay. Eventually, Khunying lived in that house and created a small residence for nuns with a pond beside it, where I have stayed many times.

Recently, the Sasakawa Foundation contributed 6.6 million baht for the construction of an administration building at the newly constructed Mahapajapati Theri College in Pakthongchai, Nakhornratchasima Province. Mahapajapati Theri College (in Thai, Mahapachabodi Theri Wittayalai) was established by Khunying because she realized the crucial importance of higher education for women and had long dreamed of establishing a Buddhist college for women. Funding for the construction of the college was raised primarily due to Khunying's personal charisma and connections. Once, after Khunying fell seriously ill with cancer in 1999, Yohei Sasakawa, the son of Ryoichi Sasakawa, left three thousand dollars in Khunying's retreat hut (*kuti*) for her personal healthcare. In a letter of thanks, Khunying said that she would not use the money for herself, because, as she said, "I'm O.K. now." Instead, she proposed building a Sasakawa Centenary Bell in honor of Yohei's father, Ryoichi. Yohei replied by sending twenty thousand dollars to build the bell tower, which was soon completed on the grounds of the new college. The college was consecrated in 2001 and is the first such institution ever established for women in Thailand.

Over the years, Khunying has initiated numerous social welfare projects. All of these projects are still flourishing, including Donmuang Youth Center, which was inaugurated in 1995 to facilitate educational, spiritual, and recreational activities for the benefit of over thirty thousand young people in the area. This facility provides a place where young people can go to swim, play basketball, and participate in training programs and symposia designed especially to meet the needs of young people. It provides alternatives to drugs, gangs, and prostitution in a time of rapid social change in Thai society. Donmuang Youth Center has been the site of many gatherings of young people from around the country, with an emphasis on promoting interreligious dialogue, character development, and social justice.

In addition to funds from the Sasakawa Foundation, Khunying has gained support for her many community development projects through art exhibitions and other fundraising events. Waskorn recalls:

> At the beginning, I contributed some of my paintings to the first international art exhibition that Khunying organized. Her classmate had given her land in Donmuang. This was just like a dream to us, but she had no money at all for constructing buildings or operating expenses. She didn't even have enough money to pay the fee at the district office for registering the land. She dug soil from the *klong* herself to build the first road. A European man donated about one hundred mango trees and the members of the organizing committee and their family members dug holes to plant the trees ourselves, because we didn't have money to hire laborers. This was a very happy time, with everyone working harmoniously together.[6]

In 1997, Khunying and her staff held a Women's Art Exhibition for Youth at the Bangkok Hilton that displayed and sold the paintings, ceramics, sculptures, textiles, jewelry, and photographs of twenty-five women artists, including Her Royal Highness Princess Bajrakitiyabha. In 1999, an exhibit featuring three young artists—Waskorn Pinyosinwat, Brancha, and Thani—raised three million baht to construct the Princess Mother Centenary Library at Mahapajapati Theri College in Pakthongchai.

In Thailand, organizations are required to register with the government. Khunying's sister, a supporter of the Girl Guides Association, and many other people supported APSW's application, especially because of its concern with social equality. Toward this goal, in 1990 APSW established the Gender and Development Research Institute (GDRI) in cooperation with Dr. Suteera Thomson Vichitranonda. Its objectives are to advance the status of women, promote democratization, support women's equal participation in public life and decision making, and eradicate gender bias in law and public policy.

ENCOURAGING HUMAN POTENTIAL

Khunying's work for social justice has inspired many people in Thailand. Not only have her many accomplishments become a model for others, especially women, but she was also widely admired for the way in which she worked with other people, modeling the Buddhist principles that are highly valued in Thai society. Waskorn recalls,

> Khunying's social service activities to benefit women and children have been the inspiration for almost all similar projects. She is a respected role model for Thai women in the field of social action. Khunying was like a mother to me. I lived and worked with her as a volunteer for many years and I understand that she is someone who gives people a chance to try out any project that is beneficial to others. The way she manages the staff here is like a family. She always encouraged us to forgive each other for any misunderstandings and to think of the good qualities of our adversaries. Especially, she encouraged us to be kind to those who are weaker or disabled. She also encouraged us to get further education and she gave us the opportunity to go overseas to get more experience. Whenever she got a grant from overseas, she took us along. She is very humble and, most importantly, whenever she knows she has made a mistake, she always apologizes to everyone, even the drivers or laborers. Whenever we have activities and work hard, she supports us in every way, takes care of us, and feeds us. Almost every night, from 1:00 to 2:00 a.m., she walks around the center to make sure that the water and sewage and other facilities are in order and encourages us to save electric energy. Many social workers think more about material welfare, but she tries to convince us to appreciate anyone who contributes volunteer energy or money, no matter what they look like.[7]

Khunying's practice of Buddhist principles was not limited to formal meditation practice, but permeated every daily encounter. Her ideals of empowering women were continually translated into direct action, however challenging the circumstances:

> [Khunying] told me, "When we think ill of others, we are the ones at fault. One who is more concerned about others than oneself will find happiness. One's own unhappiness is one's own responsibility and no one else's." She gave opportunities for women in the Emergency Home to become staff members. She always cares more about others than herself. She always gets along with everyone and is friendly even to problematic people.[8]

Khunying's life was her practice, yet her goals reached far beyond her personal sphere. Although she enjoyed many privileges in her life, she used her educational advantages in the service of others and her legal skills to achieve legal recognition for nuns in Thailand.

WOMEN'S RIGHTS IN THAI SOCIETY

Khunying's achievements are even more impressive, given the present-day societal context of Thailand, where tensions between traditional and modern values are palpable. The lack of options for women in Thai society has driven an estimated half a million women into prostitution. This number is especially staggering, considering that it is double the number of monks in Thailand. The combination of poverty in rural areas, the new consumer culture, tourism, and a decline in traditional Buddhist values are blamed for the flourishing sex trade. Without access to higher ordination, women have few alternatives other than marriage, prostitution, or a life of tedious, unhealthy factory work. Inequalities in education also contribute to these economic and social injustices; girls have fewer educational opportunities than boys who, as monks, may study for free at village temple schools and a nation-wide system of Buddhist universities.

Buddhism plays a central role in Thai society, but women do not have equal access to their religious heritage. Women are prohibited from touching a monk or sitting alone in a room with him. These monastic regulations limit women's access to Buddhist teachings. Although becoming a *mae chii*—a female renunciant with eight, nine, or ten precepts—is a meritorious avenue of spiritual practice, Thailand's estimated ten thousand *mae chii*s lack legal recognition. This lack of legal status and the absence of higher ordination for nuns in Thailand mean that women are consigned indefinitely to a lesser, marginal status in Thai society. Although the status of *mae chii*s has improved in recent years, and *mae chii*s in some communities have begun going on the traditional almsround, becoming a *mae chii* is not an attractive career goal for most Thai women today. The Buddha granted women the right to full ordination, but subsequent generations in Buddhist societies have not always honored this right.[9] The establishment of a *bhikkhunī* lineage in Thailand would not only be a means for women to create merit and learn more about Buddhism, but it would also be a great service to society, especially to women, by providing an enormous resource of religious specialists, teachers, spiritual counselors, and mentors.

The establishment of a *bhikkhunī* lineage in Thailand is especially necessary given the problems of poverty and social dislocation in the country. In Thailand, as in other developing countries, such problems are linked to global economic structures that exploit human and material resources. A vivid case in point is Thailand's sex industry, where women are "doubly exploited by the combination of global economic and traditional gender structures."[10] Multinationals exploit women for cheap labor and wealthy men exploit women for sex through prostitution, which Tavivat Puntarigvivat aptly calls "gender oppression in its crudest form."[11] Race, class, neocolonialism, and the military have also contributed to the sexual economics of prostitution in Asia. Some families exploit their own daughters for economic gain by encouraging them to seek employment with better pay, even when doing so may lead to prostitution. Although prostitution is illegal in Thailand, the sex trade has become a mainstay of the Thai economy, and the brothels and massage parlors are conveniently overlooked. Moreover, these institutions have no problem finding women to work for them, as many young women are enticed into the sex industry to repay a debt of kindness to their parents, despite the risks of abuse, exploitation, and HIV/AIDS.[12] Many women find themselves faced by a clash between traditional Buddhist values, Confucian filial piety, and consumer culture in which social conventions and economic necessity often win over moral principles.

Suwanna Satha-Anand argues that "when truth of convention comes into conflict with Buddhist truth, the latter is to overrule the former."[13] By this, she means that Buddhist principles supercede social conventions; specifically, "As the Buddha finally decided to allow female ordination, he was, in fact, respecting the rights of women to religious practice. Convention was thus overruled in favor of women's rights. This principle of truth over convention, in and of itself, can serve as a philosophical basis for women's rights in Buddhism."[14] She further hypothesizes that, "If the Buddha had denied female ordination, then such a denial would imply that his truth was not universal, for his truth would have been irrelevant to half of humanity."[15] Given the diversity of Buddhist traditions, the existence of a "universal Buddhist truth" other than simple human kindness is debatable, but it is nevertheless legitimate to question the universality of the Buddhist teachings if access to the highest ordination is available only to men. By admitting women to the Saṅgha, the Buddha affirmed that his teachings are applicable to all human beings, not only to men. To deny women access to the choicest avenue of Buddhist practice is to limit their abilities to achieve the highest religious goal of enlightenment.

Satha-Anand concludes that the obstacles that hinder women's enlightenment are not intrinsic to human nature, but relate to human conventions. She ascribes the Buddha's initial hesitation to admit women to the Saṅgha to his "deference to the force of convention."[16] Today, 2500 years later, the same dynamic tension exists in many societies, including Thailand, where traditional patriarchal religious structures clash with contemporary attitudes toward women's equality. For centuries, Thai women have been the primary supporters of the Bhikkhu Saṅgha and a religious hierarchy in which they have no official voice.

In Thailand, religious structures have not been reformed to reflect values of gender equity; on the contrary, the Bhikkhu Saṅgha is more closely linked to government power than ever. As Satha-Anand notes, "The influence of Buddhism is also manifested through a close alliance between the Buddhist establishment and the Thai state. For example, the National Sangha Act of 1962 promulgated a highly centralized Saṅgha (the monks' order) as an arm of the state."[17] Royal government patronage of the Bhikkhu Saṅgha guarantees protection and many privileges for the order of monks. The close relationship between the Sangha and the Thai state is a double-edged sword, however, since it also entails government control of the order. Thus far, unlike the monks, the majority of Thai nuns have not pressed for government recognition and support, preferring instead to maintain their independence from government control. In fact, when the Institute of Thai Nuns conducted a national survey of *mae chii*s in 1985, many nuns, suspicious of the authorities, did not return the questionnaires. The independence of the order of nuns from government control is therefore also a double-edged sword, and there is no way to predict how receiving royal government patronage might affect their autonomy.

THE STATUS OF NUNS IN THAILAND

One of the most significant social justice projects that Khunying Kanitha undertook was advocating justice for Thailand's nuns. Unfortunately, historically the Bhikkhunī Saṅgha was never established in Thailand. There are an estimated ten thousand nuns, called *mae chii*s, but they are regarded merely as laywomen (*upāsikā*s) with shaved heads. They wear white, the color worn by laypeople at religious ceremonies, which symbolically blurs their identify with the mundane world. The vast majority of *mae chii*s are elderly women who have lost their husbands or fulfilled their worldly obligations. Because they are celibate, they are trusted to work in the temples and are often found cooking and cleaning for the monks. Rather than seeing this as oppression, most *mae chii*s view this as a privilege; not only do they have a safe, spiritually enriching environment in which to live and practice, but they have many opportunities to gain merit by serving the temple and the monks. Whereas *bhikkhu*s are highly regarded, even revered, and therefore a "field of merit," or objects worthy of the laypeople's generosity (*dāna*), the ambiguous status of the *mae chii*, as neither lay nor ordained, signals to the laity that they are less worthy of support.

The *mae chii*s' lack of status in the Saṅgha is mirrored by their lack of status in the society as a whole. Neither *bhikkhunī*, nor *samaṇerī*, nor fully lay, the *mae chii*s are on a precarious footing in society. Because they are not full-fledged members of the Saṅgha, they do not reap the benefits of monastic membership, such as tuition waivers for education and discounts on public transport. They do not enjoy the exalted legal status of the Saṅgha, nor the legal status of a layperson. Thus, they are legally and religiously disenfranchised, deprived of both civil and religious rights. According to Waskorn, Khunying was deeply concerned about the *mae chii*s' lack of legal recognition and was well aware of its ramifications for the educational advancement of nuns:

> Presently, nuns in Thailand have no legal status. They are not allowed to vote during elections. Monks do not vote either, but they have many privileges that nuns do not have. Before Khunying began

> her work, nuns did not have opportunities for higher education either, unless they found some private means of support. In contrast, monks are more highly respected than nuns and receive many privileges. If they pursue higher studies, they are eligible for a nominal tuition fee and receive free room and board in the temples. In Thailand, only a few nuns have bachelor's degrees; most have very little education. Khunying wanted nuns to have access to education. She wanted them to become self-sufficient teachers and administrators who could staff Mahapajapati Theri College.[18]

The ramifications of legal disenfranchisement extend to the economic sphere as well. Because *mae chii*s are not fully ordained and have no legal status in society, the laypeople feel no obligation to support them. Most *mae chii*s are therefore dependent on the charity of their families or the temple where they live. Because the *bhikkhu*s are revered as worthy objects of lay generosity, in prosperous towns and cities they receive far more than they require. A novice monk or temple boy often accompanies a *bhikkhu* on his almsround and carries the surplus donations back to the temple. This surplus supplies meals for the temple staff, including the nuns who serve the monks.

For many years, Khunying wished to receive ordination as a nun. As her sister Khunying Kanok Samsen Vil put it:

> She was a completely engaged Buddhist, social activist, and legal scholar throughout her life. After many years of service to women in need—women and children who escaped forced prostitution, women and children without homes as a result of domestic violence, women and young girls pregnant from rape and incest with nowhere to turn—her life deepened into the spiritual realm.[19]

In Buddhist societies, it is not uncommon for a woman who has finished raising a family or lost her husband and children to become a nun. Rarely, however, does a woman give up professional success to become a nun in Thailand, since the status of nuns in Thai society is ambiguous. For example, when nuns use public transportation, they do not get free or discounted transportation like the monks because they are considered laywomen with shaved heads; and, when elections come, they are not allowed to vote because they are nuns. The ambivalent status of nuns is reflected in their living conditions and roles in Thai society. The *mae chii*s follow a worthy spiritual path, but are far from being treated as equals to monks. Monks are regarded as superior "fields of merit" and hence garner greater material support. Nuns are free to pursue a religious education and some have developed as exemplary meditation teachers, but opportunities and encouragement are often lacking. Unless their families support them in their spiritual pursuit, nuns generally work in the temples for room and board.

In 1993, following the Third Sakyadhita International Conference on Buddhist Women in Sri Lanka, Khunying was encouraged to become a nun by Dr. Chatsumarn Kabilsingh, a Thai professor of philosophy and Buddhist women's rights activist. It was my good fortune to be present at this historic event, watching as Khunying's head was shaved and as she received the ten precepts of a novice nun at Sri Dhamma Buddhist Center in Dehiwala. Five *bhikkhus* and five *bhikkhunīs* presided at the ordination ceremony. The five *bhikkhunīs* included Ayya Khema and Jampa Tsedroen from Germany, Wun Weol from Korea, and Karuna Dharma and myself from the United States. Khunying made a conscious decision to dress in the white robes of a Thai *mae chii*. To wear orange or brown robes like a Sri Lankan nun would have sparked serious controversy in Thailand, technically making her subject to arrest for "impersonating a monk." On one hand, if she had worn orange or brown robes, her high social standing might have helped gain greater acceptance and support for nuns; on the other hand, a clamor of protest from the monks might have undermined her work to gain legal status for the nuns.

In 1994, Khunying submitted a petition to the Royal Government of Thailand requesting the legal recognition of *mae chiis* in Thailand. The following year, she laid plans to create Mahapajapati Theri College, the first Buddhist college for women in Thailand. Serving as president of the project, she forwarded a proposal to Mahamakut Rajawittayalai Vidhayalai University in 1998 and the following year, received approval to begin the project. In 2002, her request to place the college under the patronage of the Sangharaja, the supreme religious authority in Thailand, was approved. As an expression of support, the Sangharaja made a substantial donation toward the construction of a meditation hall at the college.

As an attorney and a champion of human rights, Khunying aspired to achieve gender equity for nuns and all Buddhist women. Associates believe that she ultimately hoped to see the Bhikkhunī Saṅgha established in Thailand. However, the issue of full ordination for nuns is an extremely sensitive one, due to Thailand's unique history and the opposition of some monks.[20] Therefore, throughout her life, Khunying adopted a very careful approach to accomplish her aims. The first phase of her work was the effort to gain legal recognition for nuns in Thailand. The second phase was the establishment of Mahapajapati Theri College, officially registered as Mahapachabodi Theri Wittayalai. In 1999, the college was officially accepted as part of the Mahamakut Rajawittayalai, a leading monks' university in Bangkok, under the patronage of the Sangharaja, Supreme Patriarch of Thailand.

In her careful handling of the effort to gain legal recognition for nuns in Thailand, Khunying refrained from advocating full ordination for nuns, so as to not jeopardize her work for the nuns. According to the people who worked with her, she believed that, once the nuns gained wide social acceptance and their status became stable, the institution of the Bhikkhunī Saṅgha would naturally follow. Gaining official acceptance for the college as part of the Mahamakut Rajawittayalai under the patronage of the Supreme Patriarch was viewed as a tremendous achievement, but some feared that this move effectively placed the nuns under the domination of the monks. Dissenters feared that achieving legal status for the *mae chii*s would also put them under the control of the Saṅgha Council. Khunying did not see this as a problem; that is, the risks were negligible compared to the benefits that legal status would confer.

SISTERS IN SOCIAL ACTIVISM

Insight into Khunying's approach to social activism can be better understood by discussing her work in relation to three other pioneer nuns of Thailand: Maechee Sansanee, Dr. Chatsumarn Kabilsingh (now Bhikkhunī Dhammananda), and Khunmae Prathin. All these nuns have gained international attention as spokeswomen for Thai Buddhism and are actively engaged in social welfare programs. Although Khunying is the eldest and was the forerunner in advocating women's rights in Thailand, it is fair to say that these four nuns have taken inspiration from each other. Their individual styles and objectives, however, are quite distinct.

The work of these nuns, in turn, needs to be considered in relation to the socialization of women and the position of nuns in Thai society. As yet, there have been few attempts to analyze notions of gender identity and the self-perceptions, ideas, and activities of women who hold positions of leadership in Thai Buddhist society.[21] Beginning in the family environment, the social conditioning of children in Thailand is very different for girls and boys. Gender equality therefore begins with basic identity formation, which is culture specific. In Asian cultures, children are trained to submerge their individual identity in a larger nexus of family relationships and are conditioned to value the harmony and well-being of the group above their own personal needs and desires. The qualities of gentleness and humility are greatly admired in Thai culture, especially for women. In the Thai social context, women are expected to embody the values of nurturance, virtue, and stability in the domestic sphere, whereas men are assigned power, prestige, and risk in the public sphere.

Khunmae Prathin is a leading example of grassroots social action for women in Thailand. After completing the sixth level of Pāli education at Mahamakut University, she went to India, where she completed a master's degree at Magadha University in Bodhgaya. After returning to Thailand, through great perseverance, she established Dhammacharini School. Located in Rajburi Province, about two hours outside of Bangkok, Dhammacharini provides both secondary and high school education for girls, as well as vocational training, Buddhist studies, and meditation training. Two special features of the school are its Buddhist orientation and its focus on providing training and education for girls from poor families, especially from poverty-stricken areas in northeast Thailand, providing them with alternatives to prostitution and other risky livelihoods. Khunmae Prathin was a founding member of the Institute of Thai Maechees, served as its secretary for many years, and is currently serving as president. In this capacity, she has worked steadily on an institutional level to gain higher education for nuns and has contributed substantially to the improved public perception of nuns in Thailand.

Mae chii Sansanee Sthirasuta is the founder of Sathira Dhamma Community, a six-acre Dhamma community founded in 1987 in Bangkok. Her special gift is creating an aesthetically pleasing natural environment where the public can listen to the Buddhist teachings and learn to meditate. She transformed deserted rice fields into a landscape of peaceful gardens, simple cottages, lotus ponds, and tented pavilions where nuns and laypeople of all backgrounds can escape the chaos of urban life, practice meditation, and learn about the Dhamma. The community's primary aim is to improve the quality of life of women, children, and nuns, guided by Buddhist principles. The community runs a shelter for unwed mothers and their children, called Ban Sai Sampan; a nursery school for the children of underemployed laborers; and weekend retreats where people of all ages can practice mindfulness of breathing (*anapanasati*). Maechee Sansanee also started Siripongse Temple Kindergarten, a place where children can learn in a lovely natural setting and where the basic curriculum is infused with spiritual values. In 2002, Maechee Sansanee attended the Global Peace Initiative of Women Religious and Spiritual Leaders held at the United Nations headquarters in Geneva; gradually she is becoming more active in the women's international peace and justice movement.

The most pointed critiques of the religious status quo in Thailand have come from Dr. Chatsumarn Kabilsingh, a professor of philosophy at Thammasat University, who charted a different course in her campaign for Buddhist women's rights in Thailand. Although she voices her opinions more freely abroad than in Thailand, her support for the full ordination of women is well known. She points out that the stereotypes of women as unclean and a threat to the purity of monks reinforce negative images that impede women in actualizing their full potential. Translating her principles into action, she writes, lectures, organizes seminars for the empowerment of Buddhist women, and has established a shelter for victims of forced prostitution and rape called the Home of Peace and Love. Chatsumarn's mother, Voramai Kabilsingh, received full ordination in Taiwan in 1972 and headed a successful temple outside of Bangkok, but her ordination as a *bhikkhunī* was never been recognized by the Thai Bhikkhu Saṅgha. In February 2001, Chatsumarn received the *samanerī* (novice nun) precepts in Sri Lanka and the name Dhammananda. This set off a storm of protest among the monks, who, with justification, fear that she will attempt to establish the Bhikkhunī Saṅgha in Thailand.[22] The storm intensified when she receive *bhikkhunī* ordination in Sri Lanka in February 2003.

These four nuns have all stepped outside the mold and moved into leadership roles by establishing women's shelters and working for women's rights. Whether subtly or overtly, all four drew attention to the gender inequalities that exist in Thai society and to the subordination and abuse of women by men. They have not been the only women to do so; many other women have also been working steadily and diligently to improve conditions for Buddhist women in Thailand. For example, many nuns have worked with the Institute of Thai Maechee.

Founded in 1969 by the Sangharaja, the Supreme Patriarch of Thailand, the Institute has been instrumental in creating solidarity among Thai nuns and a serves as a vehicle for their empowerment and education. Because the institute operates under the auspices of Mahamakut University and is housed on its premises, however, it is dependent upon monks for its very existence. Like most of the estimated ten thousand nuns in Thailand,[23] the institute's members have not directly challenged the monks' domination, preferring instead to work quietly and steadily for the advancement of nuns through specific projects, particularly education and networking. Even though the majority of the *mae chii*s do not receive as much media attention as the four nuns discussed here, their contributions are gaining recognition as Thai nuns gradually move into positions of teaching and leadership.

PASSING THE TORCH

When Khunying passed away in 2002, Thailand lost its leading advocate of legal equality for nuns and a luminary figure in the struggle for gender equity.[24] She was not only a guiding light for nuns in Thailand, but for all Buddhist women. Sakyadhita: International Association for Buddhist Women expressed its condolences by saying, "To express our boundless respect, we can only hope to emulate her example of wisdom, humility, and compassion. May the love she expressed in selfless service throughout her life continue to inspire us all and may we help bring about her vision for a peaceful society."[25] Through her work for both laywomen and nuns, Khunying Kanitha left an historically significant legacy. It is still unclear who will carry her work through to completion.

The new Thai constitution, promulgated in 1999, declares that women and men are equal in status. This declaration contradicts the actual status of women in Thai society. The existence of nearly half a million prostitutes in Thailand, despite the technical illegality of prostitution, is a stark example of women's disenfranchised position. The existence of thousands of *mae chii*s without legal recognition and without access to full ordination and membership in the Saṅgha is another. In an international climate of human rights and gender justice, the de facto disenfranchisement of Thailand's women has yet to be adequately addressed. It can only be hoped that the efforts of Khunying Kanitha and her work for the social, legal, and religious equality of women will soon bear fruit.

NOTES

1. For information on Khunying's early life, I draw on personal communications with her and her longtime associate Waskorn Pinyosinwat that took place in January 2002, and on Chan Khai Nghiem's *White Lotus, Reflections of Venerable Maechee Khunying Kanith Wichiencharoen* (Bangkok: Association for the Promotion of the Status of Women, 2000).

2. Eventually two of her sisters were also awarded the title Khunying for distinguished social service.

3. Queen Mom Rajawongse Sirikit's support for Buddhist nuns is widely recognized: "A special group that has received the Queen's attention is the Buddhist Nuns Association. Hoping to encourage the nuns to participate in social service for the community, Her Majesty has for several years accepted an invitation from the nuns to preside at their annual meeting and has given patronage to their organization. Her gracious support has succeeded in inspiring the nuns to promote self development and to actively participate in social service." *Thai Women* (Bangkok: The National Commission of Women's Affairs, Office of the Prime Minister, 1993), p. 20.

4. Khunying credits the queen with the founding of the Association for the Promotion of the Status of Women and says that she only procured the land. The public generally recognizes Khunying as the founder.

5. Among those supporters were Khunying Kanitha's sister, Khunying Kanok, who founded the Girl Guides Association in Thailand, and Dr. Suteera Thomson Vichitranonda, who served as director of APSW's Institute of Equality and Development and became director of APSW after Khunying Kanitha decided to establish Mahapajapati Theri College.

6. Personal communication with Waskorn Pinyosinwat, January 13, 2002.

7. Personal communication with Waskorn Pinyosinwat, January 14, 2002.

8. Ibid.

9. Tavivat Puntarigvivat, "A Thai Buddhist Perspective," in *What Men Owe to Women: Men's Voices ftom World Religions,* John C. Raines and Daniel C. Maguire, eds. (Albany, N.Y.: State University of New York Press, 2000), p. 227.

10. Ibid., p. 225.

11. Ibid., p. 227.

12. Chatsumarn Kabilsingh, *Thai Women in Buddhism* (Berkeley: Parallax Press, 1991), p. 78.

13. Suwanna Satha-Anand, "Truth over Convention: Feminist Interpretations of Buddhism," in *Religious Fundamentalisms and the Human Rights of Women,* Courtney W. Howland, ed. (New York: St. Martin's Press, 1999), p. 282.

14. Ibid.

15. Ibid., p. 284.

16. Ibid., p. 288.

17. Ibid., p. 289.

18. Personal communication with Waskorn Pinyosinwat, January 14, 2002.

19. Khunyin Kanok Samsen Vil in the preface to Nghiem, *White Lotus*, p. 8.

20. One historically significant episode is documented in Chatsumarn Kabilsingh, *Thai Women in Buddhism* (Berkeley: Parallax Press, 1991), pp. 45–48.

21. Noteworthy exceptions include Charles F. Keyes, "Mother or Mistress but Never a Monk: Buddhist Notions of Female Gender in Rural Thailand," *American Ethnologist* 11(2): (1984) 223–35; and various articles in *Women of Southeast Asia,* Penny Van Esterik, ed. (DeKalb, Ill.: Northern Illinois University, Center for Southeast Asian Studies, 1982), pp. 13–32.

22. "Thai Monk Blazes Path for Equality for Women," *New York Times,* October 14, 2001.

23. Due to the lack of a complete census and because nuns are free to disrobe and reordain, the precise number of nuns in Thailand can only be estimated.

24. Tributes to Khunying appeared regularly in the Thai press with such titles as "Thailand's fighting lady who won't take 'no' for an answer" *(Bangkok* Post, March 22, 1982) and "With the strength to follow her heart" *(Bangkok Post,* March 17, 1990). An article also appeared in *Reader's Digest* in August 1987, titled "Thailand's Protector of Prostitutes" and subtitled "For four decades, Kanith Wichiencharoen has championed the rights of her country's oppressed women and children."

25. Letter sent from Sakyadhita to the Wichiencharoen family, May 20, 2002.

Chapter 12

Crisis as Opportunity: Nuns and Cultural Change in the Spiti Valley

MARGARET COBERLY

In this chapter, I describe several of the innovative religious education programs for women that have been introduced into the north Indian Himalayan region of Spiti. In particular, I analyze their potential impact on constructs of gender identity among Spiti women and on the reconfiguration of traditional religious institutions there. Cultural change is a multidimensional, multidynamic process in which external influences on indigenous cultures may work to strengthen traditions as well as to erode them. In the case of Spiti, amidst a crisis in which multiple forces have threatened cultural and religious values and institutions, there are also instances where these outside influences, particularly those related to the feminist values of inclusion and empowerment, are working to strengthen traditional principles by creating new institutions that contribute to equitable gender relations. The inclusion and empowerment of women in Spiti is revitalizing its ancient religious heritage.

SPITI VALLEY

Spiti is a remote region in the Indian Himalayas that shares a border with Tibet and was once a major trade route between India and China. The altitude in Spiti ranges from 11,000–14,000 feet, with peaks as high as 21,000 feet. For nine months of the year, the two mountain passes into the isolated area are closed by snow. Travel to the isolated villages of Spiti is restricted, not only because of its geographical extremes but also because of its proximity to Chinese occupied Tibet. For centuries, Spiti looked to Tibet as the source and center of its culture. In recent years, however, the Chinese government has effectively broken the historical ties between India and Tibet by sealing the border between them. The small but self-sufficient population of Spiti is ethnically Tibetan and speaks a dialect that retains grammatical forms of classical Tibetan that have effectively disappeared from modern Tibetan. Many other aspects of Spiti's ancient Buddhist culture also have remained intact until today. For example, the custom of the village temple, wherein families collectively support a monk to maintain the temple and perform rituals on their behalf, is still found. The village temple not only provides protection and blessings, but also serves as a cultural center where the villagers gather for Buddhist ceremonies, teachings, and celebrations.[1]

Spiti came under British rule in 1904 when the British drew the border of India along the top of the Himalayas (the MacMahon line). Later, in 1949, when the Indian subcontinent was partitioned, the people of Spiti became Indian citizens and eligible to apply for Indian passports. Thus, inadvertently, one hundred thousand Himalayan Buddhist people were spared the direct and brutal consequences of the Chinese takeover of Tibet. In fact, the crisis of Chinese rule in Tibet has had the unintended impact of renewing and strengthening Spiti's cultural and religious traditions as a result of an influx of Tibetan religious teachers who fled to India.

BEGINNING TRANSFORMATIONS

Although it was not until 1991 that foreign visitors were permitted to visit Spiti, the Indian government laid dirt tracks along the sides of the mountains that allowed access to the isolated region in 1980. This road opened the area to more frequent contact with outside ideas and influences. As Indian and Western commodities began to trickle in, Spiti's subsistent agricultural economy started to develop into a more lucrative cash economy. Predictably, these changes have had a significant impact on Spiti's social structure and cultural values. The most remarkable of these has been the change in women's roles and women's leadership.

Women have always shouldered a major share of the labor in Spiti, both in the home and field, but today their roles are expanding. Many Spiti men have begun to leave the area to work during the winter in Shimla, Manali, or as far away as Delhi, in order to earn the cash necessary to buy Indian and Western commodities such as thermoses, tools, kitchen utensils, yarn, cloth, or even, on occasion, a jeep. Prior to this exodus, winters in Spiti were traditionally a time for prayer, meditation, and visiting with friends while staying warm around the household fire. Now, as priorities shift, so do the traditional roles of men and women in the community.

As men migrate down to the Indian cities in search of work, the formerly male-dominated community leadership positions in Spiti's villages are increasingly being assumed by women. This change allows women to fulfill a larger role in the politics of the region, but since it adds to the sum of their many other proscribed duties, political freedoms have not necessarily given women greater power or social freedom. Surprisingly, the greatest changes for Spiti women in recent years have occurred in the field of religion, a field traditionally dominated by men.[2] The catalyst for change has been the introduction of Buddhist studies programs that have not only opened up new vistas for young women, but have also created a shift in the religious structures that portend wider social changes to come.

A MONASTERY OF THEIR OWN

In 1987, Dorje Tsering, a young Spiti monk in his thirties, was serving as the attendant of Lochen Rinpoche, the highest ranking lama of Spiti (then only about twenty-five). At that time, he met Karma Lekshe Tsomo and explained to her that there were some nuns in his homeland who were very eager to study. Dorje told the story of how the nuns had previously attempted and failed to establish a nunnery for lack of support. Moved by his story, Tsomo sent copies of Tibetan grammar books, Buddhist scriptural texts, and English textbooks for each of the eighteen young nuns who wished to study. When Dorje returned to Spiti, he invited Kachen Drubgye, a senior monk-scholar who had studied for thirty years in Tibet, to teach the nuns religious texts.

One year later, after receiving reports of the nuns' diligence and success with their studies, Tsomo raised enough money to build a monastery and named it Yangchen Chöling Monastery for Women.

The name *Yangchen*, the female bodhisattva patron of learning, was selected to encourage studies; *Chöling* means a "realm of spiritual practice." The description "monastery for women" was given in hopes that laywomen as well as nuns would feel encouraged to join. For a nun to name the monastery, rather than a highly placed male monastic, was considered an auspicious indication (*tendrel*) that this monastery would encourage leadership among laywomen and nuns.

Yangchen Chöling Monastery for Women was built in Pangmo, a village in northern Spiti with 35 households and a total population of 207. The first few nuns in Pangmo lived in a cave cut into the cliffs above the village.[3] These nuns cleared out the scorpions as best they could and constructed two rooms in the cave, complete with a wood-burning stove. The cave dwelling was close enough to town for them to fetch supplies and far enough away to remain undisturbed by village events. As simple as it was, the nuns were delighted to have a space of their own—a space dedicated to spiritual practice—instead of living and working in their family homes.

The nuns, with the community's help, built the monastery themselves, with the help of an "architect," a mason, and the villagers of Pangmo. The first stage of construction included a main building to house an assembly hall, living quarters arranged around a central rectangular courtyard, a kitchen, and several small rooms for an office, storeroom, and dispensary. The villagers of Pangmo came for several successive days to clear the ground, set the wooden beams, pound the rammed-earth bricks, and whitewash the walls. In accordance with tradition, when the community mobilized to work on this project, the nuns provided them with tea and meals throughout the day. The construction of Yangchen Chöling Monastery for Women was an especially joyous occasion for the villagers, who were delighted to have the opportunity to accumulate large quantities of good karma. Only the architect and two masons were paid for their work. The villagers worked as volunteers to accrue the maximum karmic benefit.

THE STUDENTS OF YANGCHEN CHÖLING MONASTERY FOR WOMEN

All the nuns at Yangchen Chöling have been nuns since they were young.[4] Even as children, most of them expressed such strong interest in religious practice that their parents allowed them to shave their heads and wear robes, and encouraged their interest in religious devotions when they had finished their chores. All of the nuns' parents are farmers and most of them are quite poor. Although parents who lose a daughter to study sacrifice harvest labor, it is considered very meritorious to have a child in the monastery.[5] Many of the parents say they feel fortunate to have daughters who chose to become nuns. With their relatively increased exposure to Indian culture, many have also come to admire secular education and the importance of learning Hindi as well as English. With rising educational expectations and a greater acceptance of education for women, the study program at Yangchen Chöling soon became a lively learning center for eighteen students.

Most of the students at Yangchen Chöling are humble and shy at the first meeting. In interactions with their siblings, they occasionally relax, laugh, and tell stories, but generally they are fully occupied with their studies and the work of maintaining the monastery. Visitors to the monastery are invariably impressed with the nuns' industriousness and warmth. The nuns are extremely hospitable to visitors and offer them the best of everything they have, from food to prayers. Visitors' cultural ineptitudes are treated with kindness and, once friendships are established, guests experience the good humor that prevails throughout Spiti's population.

The nuns' motivation in joining the monastery is simply to receive as many teachings as possible and devote themselves to religious practice. Every nun in the monastery has her own altar where she arranges butter lamps, water bowls, silk or natural flowers, and various religious images. Many of these images are photographs and postcards of paintings. Although altars in Spiti, whether at home or at the monastery, have no formal structure, there is not one without an image of the XIVth Dalai Lama.

Support for the nuns costs an average of twenty U.S. dollars per nun each month. This amount has remained constant due to the devaluation of the Indian rupee. The money goes to provide food, fuel, ongoing and emergency medical care, and educational expenses such as the teacher's salary, books, and supplies. Although financial support is difficult to maintain, and comes mostly from visitors to the area, the nuns are encouraged to be content with their resources and not seek outside employment. Early in the monastery's history, the nuns were helping in the yearly harvest and occasionally worked at road repair for the Indian government, but these activities disrupted their study and were eventually discontinued. Various revenue generating projects have been proposed but rejected as incompatible with the nuns primarily spiritual objectives.

THE TEACHERS OF YANGCHEN CHÖLING MONASTERY FOR WOMEN

When Kachen Drubgye, the greatest living scholar of Spiti, retired from his position as abbot of Kyi Monastery, he lived in a small retreat house where he engaged in intensive meditation. As a young monk, Kachen had been sent from Spiti to study in Tibet. For thirty years he studied at Tashi Lungpo Monastery, where he achieved the highly regarded scholastic degree of Kachen ("Great Teacher") before returning to Spiti in 1951. By the time Yangchen Chöling was established in 1989, he was already eighty-four years old, hard of hearing, and nearly blind. Yet when Tsomo requested his services, Kachen recognized the nuns' sincere interest in Buddhist studies and agreed to teach them Buddhist texts, such as the *Bodhicarya-avatara*, *The 37 Practices of the Bodhisattvas*, and a Vinaya text on the novice precepts. In 1995 after teaching at Yangchen Chöling intermittently for five years, Kachen asked to retire because he could no longer see or hear. The nuns said that they really enjoyed his teachings but, toward the end of his stay at Yangchen Chöling, it was difficult for them to understand him because he had no teeth left. Even after he retired to his retreat house near Kyi Monastery, until his death in 2000 at the age of 92, Kachen maintained a strong interest in the nuns' learning progress and was instrumental in obtaining their present teacher, Tsering Tashi.

Tsering Tashi is a well-respected meditator and scholar who left his retreat cave in 1993 to teach the nuns of Yangchen Chöling Monastery. The nuns were making progress in their studies with him, when in 1994 Tsering Tashi was compelled to leave. A party of monks from Kyi Monastery arrived in a jeep and told him that he had to leave Yangchen Chöling. Although Tsering Tashi was forced to leave with the monks, he returned to Yangchen Chöling in August of 1996 and resumed teaching the nuns on the advice of Kachen Drubgye, who appreciated the nuns' dedication to Buddhist studies. This incident demonstrates that women continue to face gender discrimination when it comes to educational opportunities.

Obtaining instructors for women's study programs in Spiti has proven extremely difficult. The few qualified lamas that live in the region are in constant demand as administrators and ritual specialists, and naturally tend to teach at the better supported monks' monasteries. In Spiti, the ideal philosophy teacher would be both a monk and a geshe, that is, a person with moral integrity and compassion who is also a highly trained scholar of Buddhist philosophical texts. Some argue that the higher philosophical studies a fully qualified teacher provides are not necessary for nuns. Others argue that a fully qualified teacher who is a nun with advanced knowledge of Buddhist philosophy would be the ideal teacher for the nuns. A number of highly successful study programs in Dharamsala, South India, and Nepal have demonstrated that, when given the opportunity, nuns take a keen interest in the philosophical texts and do extremely well at their studies and at dialectical debate.

In Spiti, Yangchen Choling received so many applications for admission that a second women's monastery was established on a hillside above Morang, a tiny village with only eight households and a total population of fifty-four. A remote location such as this is regarded as an ideal site for nuns.

SHERAB CHÖLING INSTITUTE

Sherab Chöling arose out of a need for an additional Buddhist studies program to accommodate twenty-five nuns who were waiting for admissions to Yangchen Chöling. In 1992, three nuns from Morang were living in their families' homes, helping with the household chores and reciting prayers whenever they got time, hoping and praying for a monastery. Earlier, these nuns had joined with several others to construct two rooms in Dankhar where they began to receive instruction in Buddhism from a lama from the area. Unfortunately, the lama soon died, and the rooms collapsed under the weight of the heavy snows. The nuns from Morang salvaged a few of the costly wooden beams and stored them in the village, hoping that some day in the future a monastery could be constructed.

In 1993, the villagers of Morang generously donated a piece of land with an abundant supply of water, to be used as a construction site for a new monastery. Dorje Tsering, who was to be the first instructor at Sherab Choling, was traveling through Kinnaur that summer, and he requested that the local people donate lumber for beams to build the monastery school. The school was named Sherab Chöling, *sherab* meaning "wisdom" in Tibetan—a reference to the female bodhisattva of wisdom, Prajñāpāramitā. The older nuns who had cherished the dream of establishing a monastery and education program at Morang for so many years, ever since their earlier failed attempt, were completely uneducated and illiterate. Nevertheless, these middle-aged nuns were determined to make monastic education available to the young women of Spiti. To that end, they have dedicated their lives to building and maintaining Sherab Chöling Institute. They reason that even if they are too old to study, they can work to provide educational facilities for others.

All of the nuns who joined Sherab Chöling Institute are from Spiti, mostly from the villages of Morang, Hull, Rangrik, and Sumling. The young nuns put their names on a waiting list when the idea of Sherab Chöling arose in 1994, were admitted in 1996, and attended Hindi-medium schools in their villages until the institute was built. All of these young nuns have completed grade seven and some have completed grades eight, nine, or ten. A few girls who wish to become nuns and join the program at Sherab Chöling are still attending government schools and plan to complete grade ten before beginning Buddhist studies at the institute. The students at Sherab Chöling are typical young women of Spiti, shy and self-effacing upon first meeting, but competent and very friendly once they feel comfortable with people.

Dorje Tsering, a self-educated former monk, became the first teacher at Sherab Chöling. The next teacher was Karma Tsering, a lay Tibetan who completed grade ten at the Tibetan Children's Village in Dharamsala and was recruited in Delhi in August 1996. He taught Tibetan, English, and math at Sherab Chöling until 2000. The present teacher is Tsering Dhondrup, a monk graduate of the Institute of Buddhist Dialectics in Dharamsala who taught at Namgyal High School in Kathmandu from 1986 to 1994. He teaches a Buddhist studies curriculum, including logic, philosophy, and debate, as well as English, Hindi, and math.

The villagers, who are all related to the nuns in some way, not only donate *tsampa* (roasted barley flour, the staple diet in the Tibetan cultural region), but also contribute their time and moral support to encourage the nuns in their practice and studies. Although the students must begin by acquiring basic reading and writing skills, it is hoped that the institute will develop into a Buddhist studies program with high academic standards and be a model for further Buddhist education projects in the future. It may also serve as an impetus to the monks to study more!

XIVth DALAI LAMA VISITS YANGCHEN CHÖLING AND SHERAB CHÖLING

Monasteries in Spiti support themselves primarily by conducting prayers and rituals on behalf of individuals, families, or the community as a whole. In return for services, the patron, an individual or a family, donates food, tea, and a monetary contribution to the monks. In the Tibetan tradition, monasteries follow the custom of performing prayers and rituals for laypeople on a commission basis. Monasteries also receive private donations made by the family and friends of resident monks and nuns.

In contrast, the nuns' communities are funded almost solely through private donations. When His Holiness the Dalai Lama visited Yangchen Chöling and Sherab Chöling after giving the Kalachakra empowerment in Spiti in 1996, he donated ten thousand rupees to each monastery for the performance of specific prayers. Without support from the lay community in some form, nuns would not be able to maintain their practice.

In mountain areas, the ancient Buddhist custom of going for alms is still followed. Typically, after the harvest of barley and peas has been reaped, monastics may supplement their income by going from door to door to collect alms. Families are happy to supply donations, usually in the form of barley and occasionally in the form of cash. As devout Buddhists, the people believe that they accumulate merit or good karma by making offerings to monastics. Although nuns in Spiti, doubting their own worthiness, are often reluctant to seek alms, they are certainly allowed and encouraged to do so. As the nuns' educational standard has improved, contributions from the laity have noticeably increased.

NEW IDEAS, NEW LEADERSHIP

To address the problem of cultural erosion and to preserve traditional learning, students at Yangchen Chöling and Sherab Chöling study Tibetan language, Buddhist philosophy, and meditation. In addition, they study general subjects such as math, English, Hindi, and health and hygiene in order to become better equipped at negotiating the contemporary world. After completing their studies, these women will serve as teachers, health-care workers, community workers, and mentors to others. Not only will they become qualified as teachers for future generations of both women and men, but they will also gain the administrative skills needed to create other study programs in their homeland and elsewhere. Nuns who master their own Buddhist traditions will be able to serve their communities and also revitalize their special Buddhist cultural heritage. They can help to bridge the gap between the mostly illiterate, but devoutly religious, older generation and the better educated, but secularly oriented, younger generation.

The central dilemma for nuns in Spiti is getting well-qualified teachers to travel to such a remote and barren region. Their hopes for female teachers lie with the dozen or so Spiti nuns who are now studying at Jamyang Chöling in Dharamsala. If these nuns successfully complete their studies and return to teach at Yangchen Chöling and Sherab Chöling, there is every reason to believe that the monasteries will prosper and give rise to women teachers fully capable of transmitting the Dharma for the benefit of future generations. Of the Spiti nuns currently studying at Jamyang Chöling in Dharamsala, several will soon be eligible to take the *geshe* degree in Buddhist philosophy—an unprecedented breakthrough for nuns in the Tibetan Buddhist tradition and a first in religious history.

One of these nuns, Lobsang Chödron, arrived in Dharamsala from her home village of Hansa when she was just eleven years old. She has excelled at her studies and is eager to learn whatever she can, from electrical repair to e-mail. She relates:

> Since we came here we have been able to learn so many things, take so many teachings with His Holiness. It is like the difference between night and day. Now we can understand His Holiness's teachings, speak English, and don't feel embarrassed when people ask us questions about Buddhism. Before we were like lumps, just sitting around wasting our time. We wore the robes of a Saṅgha member, but we

> had none of the qualifications or qualities a Saṅgha member should have. Now we have a chance to study the teachings and we really plan to return to our homeland and devote our lives to teaching the Dharma there. Before we had no way to help our people, but now, because we had a chance to study, when we return home, we will be able to help by explaining the teachings to people.[5]

In 1995, during the winter break, Lobsang Chödron and Tenzin Chödron, another nun studying in Dharamsala, returned to visit their families and stayed for two months teaching the nuns at Yangchen Chöling. This was the first time that Lobsang Chödron had formally taught and it was also the first time that the Yangchen Chöling nuns had been taught by a nun. The rapport between the young nuns and the respect they accorded a learned member of their ranks was a powerful shift in awareness in a culture where religious teachers are invariably male. These developments bode well for the future, not only for nuns, but for laywomen of all generations and social classes in Spiti.

The sphere of Tibetan culture looks to a glorious past in which religious practice was valued above any worldly pursuit. The Buddhist traditions that constitute the core of Tibetan culture are worthy of admiration for their rich contributions to philosophy, art, music, drama, and meditation. These Tibetan traditions have endured for over a thousand years, spreading to areas as remote as Spiti and Siberia. In the past, male-dominated religious institutions set a pattern for male-dominated social structures. Today, however, these structures are being questioned and challenged by the actions and dedication of the two small but fiercely determined groups of nuns at Yangchen Chöling and Sherab Chöling

The Spiti nuns are well-trained and competent to represent the Tibetan Buddhist tradition. They offer encouragement to laywomen who are becoming emboldened to acquire marketing skills for their traditional handicrafts, such as weaving and knitting. Some women have served in leadership positions as *panchāyat* (village government) heads in the villages. Many are gaining confidence to seek information about reproductive health care and methods of contraception. The response of the villagers to the improvements in the lives of the nuns has been overwhelmingly positive. With nuns emerging as leaders of social transformation, they are establishing new paradigms of what is possible for women. Once an innovation such as religious education for women catches on in areas such as Spiti, it gains its own momentum, particularly when the advances are in line with cultural priorities, such as the Buddhist teachings. Since Buddhism promotes universally cherished religious values such as honesty, simplicity, and contentment, it provides valuable resources to help people to cope with the social changes inherent in an increasingly complex world. By actualizing and modeling these values, women in Spiti are transforming this critical moment into an opportunity for awakening.

NOTES

1. Much of the information and research about Spiti that is reported in this chapter is based on original fieldwork and documentation by Emily Mariko Sanders in her unpublished master's thesis, *Culture Change and Tibetan Buddhism*, San Francisco State University, 2000.

2. For a more in-depth discussion of this topic see Karma Lekshe Tsomo, "Change in Consciousness: Women's Religious Identity in Himalayan Buddhist Cultures," in *Buddhist Women Across Cultures: Realizations*, Karma Lekshe Tsomo, ed. (Albany, N.Y.: State University of New York Press, 1999), pp. 169–89.

3. The story of a journey to Tibet by Himalayan women is told in Kim Gutschow, "Yeshe's Tibetan Pilgrimage and the Founding of a Himalayan Nunnery," in *Innovative Women in Buddhism: Swimming Against the Stream*, Karma Lekshe Tsomo, ed. (Richmond, Surrey: Curzon Press, 2000).

4. Interestingly, case histories of the nuns reveal that 99 percent of the nuns were middle children and 82 percent were second daughters. Traditionally in Spiti, first sons were responsible for the fields, home, and parents; middle sons were sent to monasteries; and younger sons were encouraged to engage in trade. It is likely that families are more willing to allow a second daughter to join the monastery, keeping the elder daughter at home to help with the housework until she is of marriageable age.

5. Personal communication between Lobsang Chodron and Emily Mariko Sanders, July 24, 1996.

Chapter 13

Spiritual Piety, Social Activism, and Economic Realities: The Nuns of Mantokuji

DIANA E. WRIGHT

While much is known about the daily lives of Buddhist monks in premodern Japan, relatively little is known about the lives of nuns, particularly Jishū (Time Sect) nuns. The degree to which these women (and female clerics in general) interacted with the secular world around them has been underestimated and under-appreciated. This lacuna is addressed here by analyzing records concerning life in Mantokuji, a Jishū temple-shrine complex known as a "divorce temple" (*enkiridera*, literally, "temple for the severing of [karmic] ties"). This convent, which operated as both an ancestral temple of the Tokugawa shogunal line and as one of Edo Japan's two official divorce temples, was neither "purely" religious nor "purely" secular. Accordingly, Mantokuji's nuns played a vital, multi-dimensional role in the society around them.

OF PIETY AND ACTIVISM

Located in what today is Ojimamachi in Gunma Prefecture, Mantokuji (Temple Overflowing with Virtue) was the nucleus of the community. Inhabitants included members of both the Saṅgha and the laity throughout the Edo period (1603–1868). On the religious side, the convent's clerics served in three basic capacities: "ordinary" nuns, incumbent abbess, and retired abbess (*goshōninsama*). This simple organizational structure belies the complex nature of each of these divisions.

Little is known about Mantokuji's ordinary nuns; their names do not appear in Mantokuji's official death register (*kakochō*)[1] and only rarely in temple documents. Even their exact numbers are unclear, a problem complicated by the fact that this component included both ordained and lay nuns. What is apparent, however, is that these nuns occasionally were divided in their loyalties to Mantokuji's head clerics. Each abbess had her own disciples and becoming a retired abbess in no way invalidated their ties to her. If the successor was not a personal disciple of the former abbess, or only nominally so, the new abbess would develop her own group of disciples. Under such conditions, factionalism could develop. Thus, it is not surprising then to find that one of Mantokuji's precepts (rules of behavior) stresses that harmony within the group must be maintained.

Contrary to popular belief, the temple's community was not limited to women. While the abbesses dealt with high priority matters, it was Mantokuji's secular male employees who were responsible for the temple's nonecclesiastical daily routine. These men resided within their own, fenced-off section of the temple compound. The highest ranked of such individuals were the convent's "secular temple officers" (*terayakunin*). Besides specific duties connected with the temple's divorce procedures, *terayakunin* acted as judges in local dispute cases, oversaw the temple's land holdings, and attended to temple interests in Edo. In addition to these officials, Mantokuji's divorce process required that the temple employ some well-to-do villagers (*gōnō*) as part-time "Temple Inn" managers. These males had three major functions in the temple. They—and often their wives—ensured that the families of the parties involved in temple-officiated divorce proceedings were separately housed. They were to act as mediators for informal discussions between the two factions and to arrange a reconciliation, if at all possible, and serve as legal advisors. Finally, the convent employed nonelite male villagers as manual laborers and couriers. These men, who also served as temple gate guards, or temple "muscle," lived within the *terayakunin*'s section of the temple complex.

Mantokuji housed a mixed-gender community whose members were involved in both secular and religio-political activities. There is not enough data to estimate accurately the size of Mantokuji's community prior to the nineteenth century. During the 1800s, however, records attest that between thirteen and twenty-one individuals lived there at any given time. The population of the temple complex fluctuated depending on the temple's political fortunes and the number of women seeking divorce. Based on the records of public ceremonies, abbesses' funerals, and divorce cases, a limited number of residents could be accommodated at Mantokuji's precincts.

Though officially an independent convent, that is, one with neither an overseeing nor a branch temple, Mantokuji and its clerics did have ties to other temple complexes. The Ji sect's Shōrenji in nearby Iwamatsu Village had been interconnected with Mantokuji since at least the early Edo period. A 1702 Jishū document stated that the monks of Shōrenji were to instruct the nuns about sectarian laws and other ecclesiastical matters.[2] Eitokuji, a monastery immediately across from Mantokuji, was also connected with the convent vis-à-vis Tokugawa memorial services. The fact that Eitokuji belonged to the esoteric Tendai sect was irrelevant to both government officials and Mantokuji's clerics.

The convent also maintained close religio-political ties to many distant temples, judging from the institutions that sent high-ranking representatives to the funerals of Mantokuji abbesses. Significantly, the vast majority of these were not Jishū temple complexes; indeed, only two of the convent's allies—the aforementioned Shōrenji and its adjacent Saikōan hermitage—belonged to the Ji sect. The rest of the convent's allies belonged to a variety of sects: Jōdo, Tendai, Shingon, and even the eclectic Shingon-affiliated "Eastern Mountain" (Tōzan) branch of Shugendō. The latter fact is evident from the presence of a "mountain ascetic" (*yamabushi*) from Kōyasan's Kongozōin at the funeral of one of Mantokuji's most powerful head clerics, Retired Abbess Honsen (1778?–1860?).[3]

Duties expected of the convent's clerics varied according to the individual's rank. In general, however, Mantokuji's nuns were responsible for performing daily *nembutsu* chants (reciting the name of Amitabha Buddha) for the temple's deceased clerics, for individuals whose memorial tablets (*ihai*) were installed at Mantokuji, and for individuals whose names were recorded in the convent's death registry. Standard Jishū practices, such as praying six times each day, and extraordinary practices like the performance of the one million *nembutsu* recitations and special death anniversary rituals were also part of the job. Scheduled shogunal memorial ceremonies were performed as well.

Though important, these activities were eclipsed by ceremonies performed for the sake of the Tokugawa regime. From the time of the Tokugawa restoration in 1615, Mantokuji's clerics recited the *Lotus Sūtra* on the seventeenth day of every month to ensure the permanence of Tokugawa rule, an observance that began after a shogun's daughter recovered from a severe illness. Special rites were also performed on the seventeenth day of both the first and fourth lunar months in front of the temple's shrine to the Shintō god Tōshōgū-sama, the deified founder of the shogunal line, Tokugawa Ieyasu (1542–1616). In addition to such "private" services, the performance of public religio-political rituals for the *bakufu* (shogunate, the ruling military regime) were a central element of Mantokuji's activities. For example, Mantokuji's abbesses (and retired abbesses) and their retinues paraded to Edo to participate in New Year's celebrations, shogunal successions, and shogunal funerary rites. Participation in these processions demonstrated the convent's prominence in both the religious and political spheres, and at the same time bolstered the status of the Tokugawa shogunal line.

Less public, but equally political, were special fertility and postpartum rites for women of the shogunal women's quarters (*ōoku*) that were performed by or involved Mantokuji's clerics. In addition, Mantokuji's abbesses were often summoned to Edo to participate in ceremonies performed during the birth of shogunal offspring. It was services—and connections—such as these that enabled the nuns to increase their sphere(s) of influence during the latter part of Tokugawa rule.

The most assertive activity undertaken by either abbesses or retired abbesses was direct intervention with *bakufu* officials whenever the temple's rights, including those pertaining to its divorce system, were threatened. Because of Mantokuji's status as the Tokugawa ancestral temple, its personnel were able to bypass the *bakufu*'s lower bureaucratic strata when applying for funding, repairs, verification of authority, and other benefits. It must be emphasized that the vigorous, even aggressive, protection and extension of temple prerogatives by its head clerics were simultaneously a defense and an expansion of the temple leaders' own powers.

Despite all of this involvement with and membership in the ruling class, Mantokuji's clerics also were actively concerned with the welfare of commoners, particularly women. This is most evident in the convent's interdiction for nonelite women caught in unhappy marriages. At a time when women were theoretically prohibited from divorcing their husbands, Mantokuji provided a forum for them to do just that. A woman initiated the process by taking refuge (*kakekomi*) at Mantokuji, usually, though not necessarily, arriving at the temple unaccompanied. All that was required for her to claim sanctuary was for her to safely make it through the temple's main gate; after that, Mantokuji's male servants would protect her from any pursuers. According to tradition, these servants would also come to her aid if she were caught just before entering the temple's precincts, but to gain sanctuary in this way, the woman had to toss a personal item, such as a sandal, through the main gate.

The number of runaway wives sheltered by Mantokuji fluctuated and there was no cap on the number accepted at any one time. Once permitted to initiate divorce proceedings, such women began twenty-five (or, prior to the 1800s, thirty-six) months of in-temple service as lay nuns. During this period, they lived the life of ordained nuns, observing the temple's precepts and generating spiritual merit through daily *sūtra* chanting and meditation. More prosaically, sheltered women were expected to pay a minimal maintenance fee, which could be made in installments, and also to do light housekeeping and basic gardening within the nuns' quarters.

Having granted a woman sanctuary, Mantokuji's secular officials began engaging both her natal and marital families in formal talks and legal proceedings designed to secure a voluntary divorce. If this was not achieved by the time the woman successfully completed her time of service, temple officials placed the case before the *bakufu* authorities. These officials then issued a decreed (*okoegakari*) divorce and ordered the woman's husband to provide a writ of divorce to his former wife upon pain of imprisonment. Upon receiving this document, the woman was released from her marriage contract and returned to her family with the option to remarry, if she so chose.[4]

Mantokuji's divorce processes served the general community and the families involved by controlling the societal tensions that resulted from such potentially explosive interpersonal conflicts. The convent provided other social services to the surrounding communities also, including medical care, matchmaking services, and personal counseling to members of both genders. In addition, the nuns ran a temple school (*terakoya*) where neighborhood children were instructed in reading and writing.[5] Finally, Mantokuji aided villagers by being one of the area's most benevolent landlords and moneylenders, a situation that articulates the symbiotic nature of the nuns' relationship with the lay communities around them.

ECONOMIC REALITIES

Certainly, Mantokuji required a sizable and steady source of income to function effectively, and Tokugawa Ieyasu provided the base for this when he co-opted the temple for his family in the sixteenth century. According to a document issued in 1591 by Ieyasu (known then as the "Minamoto Ason"), the complex was granted holdings that provided an annual income of 100 *koku* (approximately 512 bushels) of rice. In addition, Mantokuji received extraterritoriality status and was exempted from unspecified corvee duties.[6] Although Mantokuji's allowance was not overwhelming, it was significantly greater than those granted by Ieyasu to the area's other Nitta-connected temples. Chōrakuji in Serada received only a sixty-three *koku* bequest, while Mantokuji's next-door neighbor, Eitokuji, received just fifty *koku*.[7] Exactly why Mantokuji was so important to Ieyasu can be explained by its role in legitimizing his claims to a proper shogunal genealogy. Ieyasu's grant was important not merely to Mantokuji, but also to the status of the Ji sect. A 1702 Jishū record emphasized that it was Tōshōgū (Tokugawa Ieyasu) himself who awarded Mantokuji its one hundred *koku* stipend.[8]

Due to the temple's connections with Ieyasu, Mantokuji's abbesses participated in the installation ceremonies of each shogun, and performed merit-generating rituals and prayers to ensure his rule. The abbesses were also granted a formal audience with each new shogun at the time of his accession to power, at which time the temple's endowment was reconfirmed. Not only did each shogun acknowledge the endowment, but also Mantokuji's extraterritorial status was recognized "in perpetuity." Such grants were validated by citing Ieyasu's 1591 document, and then those of each subsequent shogun.[9] It should be noted that the land that presumably produced this one hundred *koku* was actually producing seven hundred *koku* by the Kan'ei period (1624–1629).[10]

Although relatively few of Mantokuji's records have survived, a fair amount is known about the temple's holdings. This is primarily due to official reports sent to the *bakufu*. One constant lament in these documents concerned the temple's diminishing acreage. Some land was lost due to erosion and some was no longer arable due to the Tonegawa River's frequent flooding, which sharply reduced the rice available to support shogunal memorial rites and other ceremonies.

In truth, however, the lands allocated by the shogunate were only part of the temple's holdings. A 1716 document that was generated in response to local confusion over which lands belonged to Mantokuji and which belonged to Tokugawa citizens provides the most detailed extant assessment of the temple's holdings. The survey revealed that the temple complex itself covered 2.14 acres and owned a total of 104 units of land. Of these, 93 units were plots of farmland in 39 separate locations. Of the total 20.66 acres of farmland the temple possessed, the smallest plot was .03 acres of infertile (gravel) land and the largest was .49 acres of superior quality. Mantokuji also owned four plots of clover, three units of reeds (one plot of which was the smallest of all Mantokuji's holdings at 35.6 square yards), and three wooded areas (one of which was the largest of the temple's overall holdings at .55 acres). The document specifically noted that plots donated for shogunal memorial services (Ieyasu's one hundred *koku*) were excluded from the survey.[11]

Throughout the temple's history, Mantokuji's clerics continued to remind the *bakufu* of its duty to provide for them. Inevitably, the official one hundred *koku* grant was their trump card. A sign of this bequest's importance to the temple was that Mantokuji's clerics insisted on the grant even after the 1868 Meiji Restoration. When Meiji officials began reviewing the land holdings of religious institutions, Mantokuji's response was to submit a document stating that "from ancient times" the temple had been granted one hundred *koku*, and its clerics had the official duty of performing rites to ensure the peace and prosperity of the country. Given this history, convent officials pressed the new government to reconfirm both Mantokuji's one hundred *koku* and its formal, nation-protecting role.[12]

As for its nongovernmental income, the temple was a major landlord in the area. Lessees signed standard contracts, guaranteed by a senior family member and/or village elder, in which they vowed not to cut down any trees and to faithfully pay their annual rent (*nengu*).[13] Mantokuji treated its tenant farmers with compassion. In 1783 Mount

Asama in Shinano Province erupted, resulting in extensive lava flows that choked the Tonegawa, decreased the area's water supply, and caused flooding due to changes in the river's course. As Mantokuji's arable land and hence renters' harvests became significantly reduced, convent authorities sought to collect only a fraction of the usual annual rent—rent that was reasonable even during productive years.[14]

A convent-issued request for government aid in 1819 noted that, out of the approximately thirty-nine *koku* of barley and twenty *koku* of soybeans its tenant farmers produced, the temple received only 25 percent of each (plus cash payments totaling some five ryō), whereas it was common for other landlords to charge 50 percent or more of a tenant's crops. Even this limited revenue was sharply curtailed shortly thereafter by repeated years of harsh climatic conditions during the Tempō period (1830–1844). The resulting poor harvests during these years led to one of Edo Japan's most devastating famines.

In 1833 temple officials estimated that, on average, their tenants only managed to raise half of what they previously paid, even during good years. Given the temple's habit of reducing rents during difficult times, the convent found itself strapped for funds. As suggested in one petition for aid submitted by the temple to government officials, just paying the annual wages owed to its (many) male and female employees was a hardship.[15]

These events attest to the fact that, ultimately, Mantokuji required cash for its day-to-day operations. Shogunal and *ōoku* (women's quarters) donations, though usually generous, were sporadic at best, and the rent payments, which normally would have provided a steadier income, were dependent upon weather conditions. A more secure form of revenue was needed to help finance nongovernmental social service activities. Mantokuji's clerics therefore set up interest-bearing savings accounts with the *bakufu*'s Zōjōji Temple in Edo. Significantly, however, they also became involved in money lending at the local level. By so doing, the nuns not only guaranteed a steady income for their temple, but were also able to provide a badly needed community service—comparatively low-interest loans.

Certainly, the area's inhabitants were often in need of loans. Their harvests, like those of the temple itself, were frequently ruined by natural disasters. It is difficult to ascertain precisely when individuals began availing themselves of convent loans. Like many other temple documents, the majority of the convent's early fiscal records were destroyed in the Great Fire of 1809. The fire, which broke out on the twenty-fifth day of the first lunar month, nearly consumed the entire complex, including the records of nineteenth-century transactions. This dearth of documents hampers a full understanding of the source of seed money used for these loans. Still, surviving documents indicate the source of the capital. An 1868 statement to the new Meiji government noted that Jōkan'in (1795–1840), who was a member of the Imperial family and official wife to the twelfth shogun Ieyoshi (1793–1853), donated one hundred *ryō* to Mantokuji in 1820, twenty *ryō* in 1822, and fifty *ryō* in 1839. This cash was loaned to villagers and the interest was used to support monthly memorial services.[16] Jōkan'in's contributions were supplemented in 1821 by a collective gift from members of the Shogunal Women's Quarters, an amount of some two hundred *ryō* to be used for lending purposes. In this case, the donors specified that the interest generated was to be used as needed for building repairs.[17]

A bad harvest followed the Tonegawa flood in late 1829. By 1831 independent farmers were turning to Mantokuji for loans. In one case, with the help of his guarantor (Shōda Ainosuke), Ikuta Kuranosuke arranged to borrow eight *ryō* from the temple. As collateral, Ikuta put up some 712 square yards of superior-quality land (producing 3 bushels barley and 1.6 bushels soybeans) and almost .4 acres of medium-quality land (6.1 bushels barley, 3.9 bushels soybeans). The eight *ryō*, borrowed from the temple's memorial funds, was loaned at a monthly interest rate of 2 percent. Mantokuji's officials promised to return the borrower's land when the loan was paid off in full.[18]

The depth of the area's economic distress was amply demonstrated in 1846 when Mantokuji's *terayakunin* authorized a 248.5 *ryō* communal loan to twenty-four (male) Nitta District Odachi villagers. The loan was to be repaid over a period of fifteen years, with the annual interest (10 percent of the land's yearly taxes) to be paid on the twenty-fifth day of the sixth month. In a separate contract, the group's headmen, Yaichiemon and Gihee, anticipating difficulty in repaying the loan, arranged a forbearance for a portion of the yearly payment (approximately twenty-four *ryō*) and the temple officials agreed to reduce the annual payment to sixteen *ryō*[19] Whether this led to an extended repayment period or the nuns' writing off the loss is not known.

In all, Mantokuji is known to have executed 107 loan contracts between 1827 and 1867, involving a total principle of 958 *ryō*. Individual repayment periods ranged from five to twenty years. Both the amounts involved and the fact that loans were made not merely to neighborhood farmers, but to residents of the province's capital and villagers from outside the province, attest to Mantokuji's regional involvement.[20]

The nuns' outreach programs earned them not only the loyalty but also the affection of the villagers around them, judging from the records of local donations. An analysis of a report concerning donations received by the temple after the 1809 fire reveals that the nuns were well-cared for, despite belonging to a private temple, that is, one "without parishioners." The fact that this report was written by one of the nuns can be deduced from the greater use of *hiragana*, the so-called women's script. The report shows that the majority of emergency donations—food, clothing, utensils, and ritual paraphernalia—were received from villages throughout the district. Significantly, there were many donations made by women in their own names.[21]

Donated food stuffs ranged from staples like rice, flour, and tea to treats like multiple tubs of *ohagi* (red bean dumplings) and *mochi* candy. To help replace the nuns' robes that had been destroyed in the fire, contributions of muslin, cotton, and wool cloth were supplied by local supporters.[22] It is significant that food and clothing were not the only donations the convent received. The very day of the fire, donors saw to it that the nuns received tobacco pipes, tobacco, a lacquered traveling case (*hasami-bako*), and bags of straw to form enclosures. Local wealthy peasants (*gonō*) contributed workers for daily labor, a wicket gate, pillows, and paper, while less well-to-do villagers sent a *misō* filter, a crossbeam, round boxes, and *udo* (a medicinal plant of the ginseng family). Before the end of the first month, two second hand ink stones and covers, one set of bedding, pine firewood, and five small dining tables, among other things, had been received from the temple's neighbors. The communities' immediate response to the nuns' plight confound expectations of an aloof or possibly adversarial relationship between Mantokuji, a private temple and money lending institution, and the surrounding secular society.

Local support for and devotion to the nuns continued even after the fall of the Tokugawa regime in 1868. Documents attesting to this were revealed during the convent's negotiations with the new Meiji government, which moved quickly to defrock Mantokuji's clerics and confiscate the temple's properties en masse. Records reveal that the nuns did not passively submit to the State's plans. In 1868 the convent's last abbess, Chihon, pointed out to prefectural authorities that all of the temple's clerics were elderly and would be unable to support themselves if they were "separated from the temple" or if the temple's holdings were taken away. She also mentioned the temple's tenant farmers, perhaps implying that the nuns would not be the only ones to suffer if the temple's lands were to be confiscated.[23] Indicative of the villagers' ties with Mantokuji, a representative from the Department of (Tokugawa) Village Officials conveyed the general community's hopes that the temple would retain its holdings.

Chihon continued to fight even after the Meiji government had seized Mantokuji's "nonvermilion seal" property. In 1871, at the age of seventy, she sent a pointed letter to the Meiji government officials pressing for reparations. She began her argument by reminding those concerned that all of the temple's remaining inhabitants were daughters of Tokugawa retainers (hence, from upper-class families). These forcibly laicized nuns were elderly, unable to return to their natal families, and managed to survive only because the villagers provided them with rice, salt, miso, and so on. Due to the high cost of commodities, the temple had large debts, and because the women had no livelihood to speak of, life was difficult. In her letter, Chihon thanked the government (sarcastically, one suspects) for providing the ex-clerics with one-quarter of the temple's former stipend, though only after ordering them to leave the complex. She concluded her letter by trying to ensure that her recently adopted son Tetsugorō would inherit the convent's remaining land. Although the Meiji government turned a deaf ear to most of her petition, it did recognize Tetsugorō's right to the land. Chihon did not admit defeat. Documents reveal that she was still defending her own and the convent's interests in 1874, two years after Mantokuji had been officially decommissioned.

Though its nuns were gone, the complex itself continued to serve the surrounding community. In 1893 Tetsugorō successfully petitioned an influential government figure, Baron Nitta Manjirō (who was originally from the area) for help in reactivating the temple, albeit without resident clerics. After portions of the main hall had been demolished, the remaining structure was moved to the northeastern part of the temple's former precincts and resanctified by the incumbent head priest of Shōrenji. Although greatly reduced in size, this hall continued to serve as a public meeting place for Tokugawa citizens until its demolition in 1992. Symbolic of the long-standing ties between Mantokuji and the community, it was destroyed only so that a replica of the main hall at the height of its glory might be erected. This was done in order to establish the Enkiridera Mantokuji Shiryōkan (Divorce Temple Mantokuji Archives), a way for Ojimamachi citizens to memorialize both the convent and its clerics.

MANTOKUJI'S NUNS: PIOUS NEXUS OF THE SACRED AND THE MUNDANE

Because of their extensive connections to the world outside their sanctuary, Mantokuji's nuns inevitably concerned themselves with matters both sacred and mundane. Initially directed to ritually protect and legitimize Tokugawa rule, Mantokuji's nuns expanded this mandate to include assistance to nonelite members of society. Their most distinctive service was to provide women with a means of initiating divorce at a time when the severing of marital ties was generally a male prerogative. This was not, however, the convent's sole outreach program. It also offered financial assistance and other social services to the communities around it. In order to support such programs, the temple's clerics (and their secular aides) pursued numerous means of acquiring funds. Out of necessity, they were economic realists, as well as pious activists. Because of this, like their counterparts in convents throughout Edo Japan, Mantokuji's nuns were able to provide crucial services to the society and remain part of, yet apart from, this worldly realm.

NOTES

1. There is one quasi-exception: An unidentified Jōkyōin (d. 1807) listed in the *kakochō* had a special scroll donated to the temple in her honor by her mother Myōkai. Myōkai may have been a Mantokuji disciple.

2. Jishū Shūten Henshū Iinkaihen, ed., "Shibazaki bunko," *Teihon Jishū shūten* 2 (Shōjōkōji, Fujisawashi, Kanagawa: Jushū Shūmusho, 1979), p. 181.

3. Documents 14 (1860.9) and 15 (1860.11). Ojimamachi-shi Henshū Iinkai, ed., *Tokugawa Mantokuji shi: Ojimamachi shi shiryōshū* 3 (Ojimamachi, Gunma: Ojimamachi shi Senshū Iinkai, 1984), pp. 190–92 and pp. 192–95, respectively. Document 27, 1853.7 (Ibid., pp. 227–37) was copied for Mantokuji by "Kōyasan Shukubō."

4. For a more detailed examination of Mantokuji's divorce procedures, see Diana E. Wright, "Severing the Karmic 'Ties that Bind': The Divorce Temple Mantokuji," *Monumenta Nipponica* 52/3 (Autumn): 357–80.

5. Ojimamachi-shi Senmon Iinkai, ed., *Ojima chōshi: tsushihen I* (Ojimamachi, Gunma, Ojimamachi, 1993), p. 1091. During the early Meiji period, presumably prior to the convent's decommissioning in 1872, Mantokuji's *terakoya* was run by "Ikkaku Sensei." Among the materials then used for instruction were *Jigokyō (Teachings of the True Words), Imagawa, Shisho (The Four Books),* and *Teikun (Garden Readings).*

6. Document 18, 159 1.11. *Tokugawa Mantokuji shi: Ojimamachi shi shiryōshū* 3, p. 197. One *koku,* or 5.12 U.S. bushels of rice was considered to be the amount needed to feed one *man* for one year. Although its value varied over time depending on the going price of rice, one *koku* roughly equaled one gold *ryō* cash.

7. Document 2, 1803. 1. Ibid., pp. 168-75. This is from a record written by Shōda Yoshinobu and copied by (Shōda-) Hayato Yoshifusa (head of the thirtieth generation of Shōda-Hayato) in 1854.11.

8. Jishū Shūten Henshū Iinkaihen, ed., "Shibazaki bunko," p. 181.

9. Documents 19 (1636.11.9) and 20 (1665.7.11). *Tokugawa Mantokuji shi*, p. 197.

10. Document 40, 1847.2. Ibid., p. 289.

11. Document 23, 1716.1. Ibid., 211–17.

12. Document 25, 1868.[4?-] 9–11. Ibid., p. 219. Although the document purportedly spanned the ninth to eleventh months of 1868, it may have begun as early as the fourth month.

13. Document 42, 1812.8. Ibid., pp. 293–94.

14. Document 39, 1833.11. Ibid., p. 285.

15. Document 34, 1833.6. Ibid., p. 255.

16. Document 25, 1868.[4?-] 9–11. Ibid., p. 223. The nuns requested that this revenue be recognized.

17. Document 34, 1833.6. Ibid., p. 263.

18. Document 43, 1831.12. Ibid., p. 294.

19. Documents 46 (1846.5) and 47 (1846.5). Ibid., pp. 295–96 and 296, respectively.

20. Ibid., p. 78.

21. Document 35, 1809.1.26 (-4.?). Ibid., pp. 268–72.

22. Document 35, 1809.1.26 (-4.?). Ibid., pp. 268–72.

23. Document 25, 1868. [4?-] 9–11. Ibid., p. 221.

Chapter 14

The Infinite Worlds of Taiwan's Buddhist Nuns

ELISE ANNE DEVIDO

Since the mid-1980s, Taiwan has experienced a large-scale religious revival, not only within the traditional popular religious sphere, but also within institutionalized Buddhism and Daoism. This profound cultural phenomenon, heretofore overshadowed by worldwide scholarly and media attention to Taiwan's economic and political developments, deserves attention in its own right. One striking aspect of Taiwan's religious efflorescence is the rapid increase in the number of Buddhist nuns, unprecedented in world history. The present number of fully ordained nuns and monks number about thirty thousand, with nuns constituting about 75 percent of this clerical population. This statistic is the one commonly cited by scholars of monastic Buddhism in Taiwan, based on fieldwork observations and by estimating annual ordination records. It is an extremely difficult task to gather and verify statistics about Taiwan's Buddhist monastics and their communities and activities, especially for the period after the end of martial law in 1986.[1]

I submit that Taiwan has become the heartland of the Mahāyāna monastic world, not only because of its open environment conducive to the development of Buddhist doctrine, practice, and autonomous monastic communities, but in particular, Taiwan has become a center for female Buddhist novices, Asian and non-Asian, from all Buddhist traditions (Theravādin, Tibetan, Zen) to receive training and full ordination. This does not exist elsewhere, not even in India, due to male monastic opposition over the centuries. For example, female monastics (both Asian and non-Asian) of the Tibetan Buddhist tradition are widely known as Buddhist nuns, though most are "novices" (*śrāmaṇerikā*), not fully ordained nuns. Unless their lamas grant them permission to become ordained in the Chinese (or Korean or Vietnamese) monastic tradition, they may practice as novices their entire lives. For over fifteen years, the Dalai Lama has advocated the establishment of a fully ordained nuns' order within Tibetan Buddhism, and sent a special envoy to Taiwan in November 1997 to investigate the Taiwanese system. Whether any concrete progress has been made still remains to be seen.

The implications of the Buddhist renaissance in Taiwan, and in particular the contributions made by female monastics, are thus profound. Not only will Taiwanese institutionalized Buddhism continue to transform and invigorate world Buddhism, but this Buddhist renaissance, inspired by the mission to create a "Pure Land on Earth," through its notable contributions to charitable and philanthropic causes, secular and spiritual education, publishing, mass media, the arts, environmentalism, opposition to nuclear power, animal rights, and disaster relief, also plays a crucial role in the construction of a civil society in postauthoritarian Taiwan. Finally, the preponderance of women, both monastic and lay, in these developments is at once a product of the liberalization of traditional gender roles in Taiwan since the 1970s, and a force that is creating more diverse life opportunities and choices for women in Taiwan. However, whether and how the phenomenon of Taiwan's Buddhist nuns can be explained via the categories and theories of "feminism" is a complex enterprise, which will be discussed further.

Oddly, thus far there are no full-length monographs on Taiwanese Buddhist nuns in Chinese, English, or any other language, though nuns are the subject of ongoing and completed doctoral dissertations in Taiwan and abroad. Recently, scholars of religion in Taiwan, such as Jiang Canteng, Ding Min, Lu Hwei-syin, Chen Meihua, Li Yuzhen, and Zhang Wei-an, and scholar-nuns such as Shi Zhaohui and Shi Jianye, have published articles and participated in conferences organized by Buddhist seminaries on this subject. Charles B. Jones' pathbreaking book, *Buddhism in Taiwan: Religion and the State, 1660–1990*, gives an excellent overview of Buddhism in Taiwan in which he discusses "the vitality of the nun's order [in Taiwan] after 1952," though he does not concentrate on Buddhist nuns in particular.[2] The discussion here is part of a forthcoming book on Buddhism, women, and civil society in Taiwan that highlights six different nuns and their monasteries in Taiwan, and also includes an analysis of Buddhist laywomen.[3]

THE "INFINITE WORLDS" OF TAIWANESE NUNS (*TAIWAN BIQIUNI DE TIANKONG*)

Both in written accounts and in interviews, nuns often speak about how Taiwan is the *tiankong* (literally, heavenly firmament) for Buddhism and, in particular, for nuns. I translate this term as "infinite worlds" for two reasons: first, to indicate that Taiwan is a free and open space for Buddhist nuns' development, and second, because there is not simply one ideal type of Buddhist nun in Taiwan. Significant differences exist within each monastic community (according to monastic generation, family and educational background, talents, and temperament), not to mention the differences among monasteries. In Taiwan there are monastic communities composed of only nuns, only monks, and both monks and nuns.[4]

Here it is appropriate to mention the most visible and charismatic nun in Taiwan, Master Zhengyan. She is head of the large international nongovernmental organization, Ciji (Buddhist Compassion Relief Foundation), which is primarily a lay organization. Although over the past decades Zhengyan has cultivated a small core of nun disciples, Ciji Foundation's focus is the philanthropic activities undertaken by its numerous lay followers, not the education and training of female monastics. I do not, therefore, include this organization in my focus.[5]

In this chapter, I have drawn upon the following sources: interviews with a number of female monastics and scholars of Taiwan Buddhism, a phone survey of all officially registered Buddhist monasteries in Taipei, Chinese primary and secondary sources, the few English sources on Buddhism in Taiwan, and resources on women in Buddhism as a global movement.[6]

A SERIES OF QUESTIONS

Many factors have contributed to Taiwan's standing as having the greatest number of fully ordained Buddhist nuns in the world. During my interviews with Buddhist nuns and scholars of Taiwanese Buddhism, I suggested a number of possible factors that may have combined to explain this phenomenon, including historical, economic, educational, political, and social factors, including changes in gender roles. The first contributing factor relates to Taiwan's unique cultural heritage, in addition to Japanese Buddhist developments in Taiwan. Both during the Qing dynasty and during the Japanese colonial period (1895–1945), we find the existence of Buddhist-inspired popular religious sects called "vegetarian women." The majority of these women were laypersons, not fully ordained nuns. Those who were ordained necessarily received ordination in the Japanese tradition, because in Taiwan under the Qing there were no nuns ordained in the traditional Chinese manner. At any rate, Taiwan had a large pool of women who identified with Buddhism, even if they had not formally gone for refuge in the Three Jewels. Many of these women became fully ordained in the Chinese tradition after 1952.

A second factor is the overall high level of coeducation in Taiwan compared with other nations with a Buddhist heritage. Ever since the promulgation of public schools during the Japanese period, and especially after the post-1949 modernization of the education system, a compulsory, universal, nine-year education system was instituted in Taiwan. This education system provided Taiwanese women with a relatively high standard of general education.

Third, the Buddhist monks who fled mainland China and settled in Taiwan established links with local nuns and laywomen. Being relatively few in number, and without contacts in Taiwan, these monks had no means of support and therefore had to rely on Taiwanese nuns and the extensive networks of Buddhist organizations (*Lianshe*, or Lotus Societies) that were composed primarily of laywomen. Unless they had political ties with the Nationalists and the Buddhist Association of the Republic of China (BAROC), these monks depended upon female lay devotees for building temples and attracting disciples, thus initiating ongoing patterns of cooperation between monks and laywomen.

Under the harrowing conditions of martial law and the anticommunist "White Terror" years, these monks often proselytized in secret. Unless they enjoyed Nationalist government (KMT) political protection, they were often arrested and silenced. Among the movements to popularize Buddhist teachings, the widespread influence of Yinshun's Humanistic Buddhism was notable in its efforts to modernize and rejuvenate Mahāyāna Pure Land Buddhism. Following the practice of Catholic and Protestant proselytizing methods among Taiwan's young people, from the 1960s the Buddhists began to establish study groups and scholarships in vocational schools, high schools, and universities, and issued popular publications and tapes of instructional lectures, Buddhist *sūtras*, prayers, songs, and so forth. Many potential nuns and monks were and are recruited in this way.

In the post-1949 situation, the monks who arrived in Taiwan to spread the Chinese Mahāyāna tradition brought with them the formal monastic rules for monks and nuns. Thus, they began the process of institutionalizing Taiwanese Buddhism. In the 1960s and 1970s, leading monks in Taiwan encouraged the development of the nuns' order, emphasizing their education and training. Three leading masters—Yinshun, Xingyun, and Shengyan—did not especially stress obedience to the eight special rules (*gurudharma*s) that historically kept nuns in an inferior and subservient position to monks. On the contrary, these masters argued for equal status for monks and nuns.

The 1970s and 1980s brought dramatic societal transformations in Taiwan. These developments were a direct by-product of Taiwan's remarkable and rapid economic takeoff. During this time, Taiwan's citizens gained more freedom to leave the country to tour and study abroad. The ending of martial law allowed for the development of a civil society, and curtailed the Ministry of the Interior and BAROC's ability to strictly monitor Taiwan's Buddhist world.

An additional contributing factor was the influence of feminist ideas on society in Taiwan and upon nuns who studied abroad. The influence of these ideas is difficult to track. Certain male academics cite feminist influences as an "obvious main factor," but the responses of the nuns I interviewed were ambivalent and contradictory, as will be explained later.

Due to the strenuous efforts over the years of nuns and leading monks sympathetic to their development, beginning from the first formal ordination of nuns in 1952, nuns have achieved positions of high social status in Taiwan. Unlike the situation of nuns historically in China, they play active roles in society at large—in education, charity, publishing, and the mass media—and hold leadership roles in monastic affairs. In addition, through sponsorship by their monasteries, nuns may gain opportunities to pursue graduate studies both in Taiwan and abroad.[7]

The nuns attribute their improved status to improved educational opportunities for women, the influx of Buddhist monastic institutions from China, movements to popularize Buddhist monastic training programs for nuns, and hard work. Their thinking seems to reflect the nuns' desire to affirm their rightful place in the orthodox Buddhist heritage, which was established in Taiwan only after 1949. They credit their long years of training, hard work, and the sacrifices they made to help advance the centuries-old Mahāyāna Pure Land heritage over Taiwan's so-called unorthodox and superstitious popular religions. Whereas the analyses of historians and social scientists commonly cite an imported Western feminism or political developments, such as the repeal of martial law, the nuns generally attribute their successes to their own efforts.

WHY BECOME A NUN?

Though some potential nuns may have grown up in what they term "Buddhist" families, the form of worship prevalent in Taiwan until recently is more properly characterized as "popular religion,"often centered on the worship of Guanyin, the bodhisattva of compassion. The actual point of entry into the orthodox Buddhist world for many nuns was participation in formal Buddhist study groups in vocational schools, high schools, and universities. The first attraction for most is both religious and idealistic. Young women engaged in the study of arts and sciences, business, computer science, or vocational training hope to pursue more intensive study of Buddhism as a means of self-cultivation, toward the goal of enlightenment (*yi xiuxing wei zhu*).

As these young women move from the secure and highly protected moorings of the Taiwanese family and educational system into the world, they often grapple with personal crises involving identity, family, and relationships. At this juncture, some may consider entering monastic life, but few women in this category succeed in negotiating the intensive, multistep process of observation, examination, and evaluation necessary to reach even the novitiate stage. Other young women who are drawn to the possibility of the monastic life already possess skills in the areas of counseling, medicine, and children's education. Others are teachers who feel that they have reached a limit in the significance and effectiveness of their pedagogy, and conclude that only religion, specifically Buddhism, will allow them to explore beyond the limits of secular knowledge. Still others consider careers in academia, publishing, communications, the arts, social work, adult or community education, or active social service, all of which are possible by joining one or another monastic community, each defined by an emphasis on its own particular mission(s) (*zhiye*).

Another factor that may attract a young woman to monastic life is that monasteries often sponsor the graduate studies of their nuns, whether in Taiwan or abroad. For young women who lack economic means or family encouragement, this may represent their only chance to obtain advanced degrees. For example, Venerable Mingjia, a leading nun at Luminary Buddhist Temple, obtained her master's degree in business administration in the United States. It is not necessary to become a nun to develop one's individual career path, however, one can also remain a lay practitioner of Buddhism. Therefore, the purpose of the extended prenovitiate and novitiate screening process is to identify those who are suited to living and working in a disciplined, communal setting sworn to a lifetime of celibacy. Equally important is to identify those who are dedicated to furthering the interests and missions of that particular monastery. Above all, no matter what form their secular mission may take, the central purpose of every monastery is to propagate the Dharma, or Buddhist teachings (*hong fa wei zhu*).[8]

Many observers draw hasty conclusions about Taiwanese nuns based on their observations of the high-profile, resource-rich, and socially engaged monasteries, which are styled the "mountain tops" (*shantou*) of Humanistic Buddhism. Besides these scions, however, a young woman may join one of numerous smaller monasteries situated in central and southern Taiwan, outside of major cities. These monasteries, often inhabited by nuns over fifty years of age, stress the contemplative life. Their nuns rarely venture out into society, unless invited to perform traditional Buddhist rituals, such as funerals and memorials during the mourning period. More extensive research into the differences among Taiwan's all-nun monasteries is crucial for assessing the extent to which the body of doctrines and practices known as Humanistic Buddhism has become the mainstream (*zhuliu*) in the Taiwanese Buddhist world, or will become mainstream in the next generation.

THE QUESTIONS OF FEMINISM

An important question to consider is whether nuns in Taiwan identify with, or are linked with, the worldwide Buddhist nuns' movement. This movement can be defined as working to strengthen the monastic order of nuns (and as working to achieve equity with monks). Also, do Taiwanese nuns identify with the feminist movement in Taiwan? This movement can be defined as working to gain equal opportunities for women, as well as improve their legal status, quality of life, and the like. Recent years have seen a growing movement among nuns within all Buddhist traditions toward a greater equality in Buddhist institutions. For some, the debate centers around contradictions regarding the status and nature of women and nuns that seems inherent in Buddhist scriptures and historical commentaries. Others focus on establishing and strengthening education and training for nuns, and on achieving opportunities for full ordination in those traditions where they do not exist.

On the one hand, the Buddhist scriptures claim that "all can reach enlightenment" and "in Buddhahood, there is no gender." In Chinese Buddhist monastic practice, both monks and nuns wear similar clothing, are tonsured, and receive burn marks upon ordination. The Buddhist names and titles they receive are not gender specific. Following historical precedent, one can use the sobriquet "a virtuous man" (*da zhangfu*) to describe both monks and nuns. And, unlike in the Catholic Church, monks and nuns have equal rights to participate in and officiate at Buddhist ceremonies, take disciples, hold the position of master, vote on Buddhist affairs, continue their education, and proselytize.

On the other hand, it is not difficult to cite examples of misogyny and discrimination against nuns. In addition to negative stereotypes about women's "bad karma," various weaknesses, and inclinations to nonvirtue that prevent them from reaching enlightenment, there are also many strictures in monastic life. Monks are required to abide by 250 precepts, whereas nuns must observe 348. Male masters can take both male and female disciples, whereas female masters can only take female disciples. And, least subtle of all, the eight special rules (*gurudharmas*) place nuns in an inferior position to monks.

In Taiwan, however, due to the factors discussed earlier, the nuns' order has flourished. Nuns not only outnumber monks, but also are leading figures in Taiwanese civil society. Do these nuns identify with, and are their views congruent with, those of the Taiwanese feminist movement? One might first draw this conclusion after observing the many self-reliant, self-administered communities of highly talented and hardworking Taiwanese Buddhist women. It is not unusual to see slight

Taiwanese nuns, under the blazing sun, slicing lumber with power tools for fuel to be burnt in their kitchen ovens. When one observes this and also the significant strength and stamina needed to play the drums and bells throughout long morning and evening religious services, the Chinese phrase for a "untraditional" woman, *nu qiangren*, immediately comes to mind.

As I was conducting interviews, female Buddhist masters repeatedly stressed that modernization and liberalization have opened up more opportunities and choices within Taiwan society. In addition to the traditional path of marriage and family, women today enjoy the freedom to pursue higher education and a career. As Venerable Ming put it, young women can now "come out of the kitchen to get an education and become self-reliant; there is no need to rely on one's family and husband anymore."[9] When I asked newly ordained nuns why they chose the monastic life, a standard answer was, "In this way, I can contribute my time, energy, and talents to far more people and to society at large, rather than devote myself to a husband, children, and in-laws."[10]

Yet when I probed further, I found that many female masters over forty years old still retain essentialist notions of "Chinese" femininity.[11] When I asked why are there so many nuns in Taiwan, Venerable Shanhui told me, "Women possess a compassionate and warm heart." Venerable Mingjia said, "Women are especially suited to undertake the rigorous path of Buddhist studies and training, due to their patience, endurance, and attention to detail," and added, "Due to familial and social expectations thanks to the Confucian legacy, men in Taiwan are under far more pressure to succeed in career and family life, so fewer men than women can choose the monastic life." Venerable Wuyin contended that, "By their nature women are particularly suited as caregivers, and excel in healing and counseling roles." Further, she stated, "Women are more suited than men to live in communal groups due to their self-effacing, self-sacrificing nature," and "Nuns manifest the steadfast, persevering, hardworking character of Taiwanese women." Venerable Hengqing asserted that, "Women by nature are inclined to excel in the fields of culture, [secular] higher education and scholarship, Buddhist education, and adult/community education." In "Buddhism and Women: Deconstructing Male Chauvinism in Buddhism," Venerable Zhaohui maintains that, "Nuns have succeeded in Taiwan in propagating Buddhism due to their gentle feminine nature, which makes people feel like they have been bathed by spring winds."[12]

Far from asserting an androgynous egalitarian ideal, according to these female masters, nuns' strength lies precisely in their difference. What are termed "feminine traits," for example, warmth, compassion, desire for harmony and peace, patience, endurance, and sacrifice correspond closely to Buddhist ideals. Because women possess these traits, they have natural advantages over men in the monastic calling. Nuns often distinguish between the Taiwanese experience and western feminist notions of "self-awareness" and "fighting" for gender equality.

The nuns whom I have interviewed hold attitudes about gender that differ from those held by Taiwanese femininsts. Most nuns see themselves as working for the good of Taiwanese society as a whole and do not particularly emphasize women's issues. Although they do emphasize higher education for women and the importance of helping women realize their individual potentials, they seem to view these as a necessary concomitant of society's overall welfare.

It is likely that in the future, as the older generation of nuns who were ordained from the 1950s to the 1970s age and become less socially active, the younger generation might very well align themselves more closely with the Taiwanese feminist movement. Some younger nuns and novices have backgrounds in women's studies and many have had the experience of studying abroad. However, another scenario may present itself: As Taiwan's society undergoes further liberalization, it may become socially acceptable to remain as unmarried career women, with or without children. In this case, there would be no need to make the sacrifices required by monastic life.

The sudden increase in numbers of young women who became nuns in the 1980s may simply have been a passing phase. Many young women were attracted to charismatic Buddhist masters and nuns who were pioneers in Buddhist social activism in Taiwan. Venerable Mingjia of the Luminary Buddhist Temple responds that, "In the future, young people drawn to the monastic life will not do so due to the compelling presence of any master, but due to the appeal of living and working in a Buddhist community, as a member of a collective team. She/he will have to be drawn first for religious reasons, because in the modern 'information society,' the enticements and pressures of the secular world are only increasing." Although Venerable Mingjia stated that the number of newly ordained nuns is steadily increasing, she feels that, more important than numbers, is continuing to improve the quality of nuns by providing ever more thorough, comprehensive, and professional education and training. As Buddhist communities continue to expand abroad and become socially engaged nongovernmental organizations, their achievements will also continue to attract young people.

How will Taiwanese Buddhist society respond to the criticisms and grievances of the global Buddhist women's movement? Already, Taiwanese Buddhism plays a central role in the development of the nuns' orders worldwide, by having preserved and developed the lineage of ordination, the monastic rules, and full ordination ceremonies for female monastics, and by having created outstanding nuns' communities. Venerable Zhaohui, who identifies herself as a feminist Buddhist (*yige fojiao de nuxing zhuyizhe*), is an influential voice in Taiwan who has achieved celebrity status. Her indefatigable work for animal rights and environmental protection has also brought Buddhist women's issues to the public's attention. At the seventh Sakyadhita International Conference on Buddhist Women, held at Huafan University in Taipei in June 2002, it was clear that many Buddhist nuns and laywomen in Taiwan are similarly interested in links with the global Buddhist women's movement and the Engaged Buddhist movement.

Taiwan has the potential to make an impact on Buddhism globally for several reasons: Taiwan holds full ordination ceremonies for nuns from other countries and traditions; Taiwan's nuns are well educated and have high social status, so hopefully they can serve as role models to other nations and traditions; and Taiwan's monasteries are resource rich, so hopefully they can do more to promote Buddhism and gender equality in Buddhism worldwide. Venerable Jingxin, a monk and director of the Chinese Buddhist Studies Association in Taiwan, has declared that, "The future of Taiwan's Buddhism belongs to the nuns." Given their dynamism and dedication, Taiwanese nuns are especially likely to make major contributions to the future of world Buddhism.

NOTES

1. Before 1986 all religious groups had to register as lawful organizations with the Ministry of the Interior (MOI) while each year the number of newly ordained nuns and monks were registered with the Buddhist Association of the Republic of China (BAROC), an official arm of the Nationalist party-state. After 1986, however, monasteries holding annual ordination ceremonies were no longer required to register with BAROC, and the MOI's statistics are vague and do not distinguish institutional Buddhism from the popular religions, let alone relate reliable numbers of ordained clergy. In addition, the monasteries

themselves are reluctant to reveal their own statistics. As for mainland China, the Pure Land monastic tradition has been revived in recent years but remains ideologically and institutionally fettered, while the opportunities for monastic education are limited. I have not yet found a number for fully ordained nuns, only eighty thousand for the total number of monks and nuns (Pure Land tradition). But I suspect that this number includes students, novitiates, and self-styled "monastics" who are in fact laypersons. I have also been told the following estimates, by a scholar who wishes to remain anonymous until the figures can be proven: 1500 fully ordained nuns in mainland China and approximately 18,000 fully ordained nuns in the world, excluding Taiwan.

2. Charles B. Jones, *Buddhism in Taiwan: Religion and the State, 1660–1990* (Honolulu: University of Hawaii Press, 1999). The American scholar of Buddhism, Yu Junfang, is currently conducting research on the Luminary Buddhist Temple, an all-nun monastic community and seminary in southern Taiwan noted for its high scholastic standards and rigorous monastic training process.

3. An earlier form of this essay appeared in the *Taipei Ricci Bulletin* 3 (1999–2000): 79–89.

4. As stipulated by the Vinaya, the monastic rules, a male master can take both monks and nuns as disciples, but a female master can only take nuns. A comparison of communities with only nuns and with both monks and nuns might reveal different institutional patterns and teaching and leadership styles, as well as the problems special to mixed-gender celibate communities.

5. See the article by Chien-yu Julia Huang and Robert P. Weller, "Merit and Mothering: Women and Social Welfare in Taiwanese Buddhism," *Journal of Asian Studies* 57:2 (1998): 379–96. Also, see Robert Weller's book, *Alternate Civilities: Democracy and Culture in China and Taiwan* (Boulder, Colo.: Westview Press, 1999).

6. I interviewed Master Wuyin, head of the Luminary Buddhist Seminary, and Venerable Mingjia, head of the Luminary Buddhist Temple, and their nun disciples; Venerable Hengqing, professor of philosophy at National Taiwan University; Venerable Jianshen, professor of education, Hsuan Chuang University; Venerable Shanhui of the Xianguang Temple; Venerables Guangguo and Xianyue of Lingjiu Mountain Monastery; Professor Jiang Canteng, National Tsinghua University; and Dr. Li Yuzhen, professor at National Qinghua University, Taiwan. Many thanks to Professor Dominique Tyl of the Socio-Cultural Research Center, Fujen University, who organized and carried out the phone survey in August of 1999. The number of Chinese sources is growing and includes official publications by the temples and monasteries themselves, as well as scholarly articles by monastics and laypersons. There are a vast number of English sources from many disciplines about women and the female in Buddhism, but they rarely, if ever, mention Taiwan's nuns and the Buddhist renaissance. International organizations such as Sakyadhita: International

Association of Buddhist Women and the Women Active in Buddhism website offer some general information about Taiwan's nuns.

7. In late Imperial China, "convents" were commonly stigmatized as repositories for orphans, abandoned girls and wives, runaway wives, widows, and other women without means of support. And according to Neo-Confucian moralists, to choose the monastic life was to commit the sin of unfiliality, which damages the honor and well-being of one's family (ancestors and future descendents included). The phrase for becoming a monastic is "to leave the family" (*chujia*), which is unfilial in itself. Then, to renounce marriage and children means one failed in one's duties to continue the descent line. In addition the rituals of tonsure and marking the scalp with burns, upon ordination, also is unfilial, as these rituals mutilate the original body given by one's parents.

8. Though each monastery must obey the Vinaya for general guidance, the details about daily operations, fiscal and personnel administration, and long-term missions are decided by each master and his or her disciples. Monastic education and training is also based on the Vinaya, but the actual courses of study, length of novitiate period, selection process, and so on, are decided by each monastery. Each monastery is an autonomous authority unto itself, according to the principles of "self-regulation, self-examination" (*zilu, ziqing*). Each monastery forms its own customary laws as well as constitution and bylaws (*mufa, zifa*, literally, mother and child laws), usually reached through group consensus. This aspect of monastic life deserves further inquiry, especially because the requirements of the modern world demand modification to, or liberal interpretation of, the Vinaya.

9. I interviewed Venerable Mingjia from June 27 to 29, 1999, at Xiangguang Temple.

10. Even if this is a generic answer that echoes their master's voice, we should not dismiss the kernel of authenticity that may lie within it.

11. Here arises another thorny problem: Due to different sociopolitical contexts after 1949, we should examine the definitions of "femininity" and "feminism" in the two contexts of Taiwan and mainland China.

12. Zhaohui Shi, "Buddhism and Women: Deconstructing Male Chauvinism in Buddhism," in *Luxue jinguan* (Vinaya Studies: Contemporary Interpretations) (Taipei: Fajie Press, 1999), pp. 335–88.

Chapter 15

Resistance without Borders: An Exploration of Buddhist Nuns across Cultures

CAREN I. OHLSON

When I began my research on Buddhist nuns, I was excited to explore the links between Asian Buddhism and Western feminism. As a Western Buddhist and a student of women's studies, this seemed a likely topic for me. I was expecting to write mostly about the ways that Buddhism has changed since its migration to the West, and what this has meant for women. Specifically, I was excited to explore the lives of nuns. I held many assumptions about the spiritual freedom that nuns must experience, based on my own sense of empowerment as a student of Buddhism. Imagine my surprise as I began to discover that the teachings I found so liberating when practiced within the context of my individualistic middle-class American life were also used in Asian countries to support a hierarchical, male-dominated religious institution that has kept nuns in poverty and denied them access to many religious teachings. Needless to say, I was confused and disheartened by this fact. As I continued my research, I discovered many of the revolutionary models of resistance nuns had made to their institutional subordination—some that knew no parallel in my studies of the American feminist movement. My focus shifted to an exploration of the theoretical models present in nuns' activism across different cultural, traditional, racial, and ethnic borders.

This study offers an overview of some of the models of resistance to institutional subordination represented by Buddhist nuns. In it, I meld my own personal interest in Buddhist teachings and my attempt to reveal some of the more complex layers of the Buddhist nun's experience. I have structured this exploration as a general overview of the textual and social representations of women in Buddhism. I have selected examples of how these representations have been played out in specific regions, and the ways that women have responded or resisted. First, I have narrowed the view to an examination of the foundational textual/social basis for the original formation of nuns' participation in Buddhist monastic tradition, and, second, to an exploration of how this foundation has expressed itself in the twenty-first century. Within the context of today, I describe the models of resistance to institutional subordination that nuns have exhibited. The first is represented by the self-defined marginal culture of nuns in Sri Lanka, and the second is revealed in a crosscultural, multiethnic, multitraditional dialogue aimed at achieving full institutional recognition for nuns.

The evolution that has taken place since the involvement of Western women in Buddhism has resulted in a tendency for many scholars to fall into a "West saves East" mentality. With my background in feminist/race/ethnic theory, I have found this mentality closely linked with the same race, class, and sexual exclusions that are often found in American feminism. I encourage the reader to think about these issues when reading about the nuns, because the purpose of this chapter is to illuminate the respectful mutual growth and integration that is taking place between Asian and Western women in the Buddhist tradition and it is my intent to present this model as one that can carry over to women of all traditions and social/cultural contexts. The dedication of Buddhist nuns of all cultures and traditions to open their minds and hearts to one another in their pursuit of the common goal of female spiritual advancement has created a revolutionary, integrated, collaborative model that can be used for activism on all fronts.

SOCIETAL INFLUENCE ON BUDDHIST SACRED TEXTS: SPONBERG'S "VOICES"

The story of Mahāprajāpatī, the Buddha's aunt and foster mother, provides a foundation for looking at the ways in which social norms have influenced the ways in which women have been portrayed in Buddhist sacred texts. Though a complex analysis of the many contradictions about "female nature" existent in the writings that form Buddhism's textual authority is beyond the scope of this chapter,[1] the archetypal story of Mahāprajāpatī aptly demonstrates the contradictions that currently exist within Buddhist doctrine about the roles and "nature" of women. The presence of the conflicting messages in Buddhist texts about the role of women displays the ways that male/female relationships in larger society have clouded the minds of monks who record Buddhist teachings.

To illustrate this phenomenon, Alan Sponberg has identified four distinct "voices" of Buddhism that can be heard in the traditional Buddhist texts.[2] Sponberg coins the terms "soteriological inclusiveness" and "soteriological androgyny" for the voices in Buddhist sacred texts that assert that sex/gender differences present no barriers to spiritual enlightenment. The difference between the two is that soteriological inclusiveness presents the message that sex/gender is insignificant, while soteriological androgyny suggests that there is a distinct difference between male and female spiritual aspirants, yet it is important for men and women to learn from each other, and to embody the other's strengths in order to be more fully on the Buddhist path. As we shall see, both of these voices are present in the story of Mahāprajāpatī. These voices are muted, however, by those of "institutional androcentrism," which posits men as the central authority figures in Buddhism, and "ascetic misogyny," which links femaleness with impurity and represents women as dangerous to the spiritual lives of men.

The version of Mahāprajāpatī's story that will be told in this section is from the *Cullavagga*[3] and reworded by Sponberg:

> *Scene 1. Mahāprajāpatī Beseeches Sākyamuni.* While staying among his kinsmen . . . the Buddha is approached by his aunt Pajāpati, who raised him as a child after his mother's death. She suggests that it would be good if women were allowed to become nuns, taking up the homeless life as full-time disciples rather than lay followers. The Buddha tells her to be wary of this idea, without specifying precisely what danger he has in mind. Pajāpati repeats her request three times, without avail, and then retires unhappy and distraught.
>
> *Scene 2. Mahāprajāpatī Meets with Ananda* in Vesali. Having shaved their heads and put on monastic robes, Pajāpati and a large group of Sakyan women follow the Buddha to Vesali, where

Pajāpati waits outside the Buddha's door with "her feet swollen . . . . sobbing and in tears." Disturbed at their appearance, the Buddha's personal attendant Ananda inquires about her distress and offers to take up their cause.

Scene 3. Ananda Intercedes on Mahāprajāpatī's Behalf. Telling Pajāpati to wait outside, Ananda leaves to seek out the Buddha. Making the same request, he gets the same answer. But then Ananda tries a different approach, asking, "Lord, are women, having gone forth from home into homelessness in the Dharma and Discipline proclaimed by the Truthfinder [i.e., capable of arhatship]?" The Buddha replies that indeed they are. Thereupon Ananda points out that the women should then be allowed to become nuns, both because the Buddha acknowledges that they are capable of arhatship and because he owes a great debt to Pajāpati, "foster-mother, nurse, giver of milk, who suckled him as a child."

Scene 4. The Buddha Assents, Conditionally. Conceding Ananda's point, the Buddha agrees to Pajāpati's ordination if she will accept eight rules (in addition to the normal monastic rules): 1) Nuns, no matter how senior, must always defer to monks, no matter how junior. 2) Nuns must not spend the rainy season retreat in a residence where there is no monk. 3) Nuns must observe the fortnightly monastic observances under the direction of monks. 4) After the rainy season retreat nuns must formally report to a convocation of monks as well as to the other nuns. 5) A nun who has broken a monastic rule must be disciplined by both the order of monks and by that of the nuns. 6) Both monks and nuns are necessary for the ordination of new nuns. 7) Monks must never be abused or reviled in any way by a nun. 8) Nuns may be formally admonished by monks, but not monks by nuns.

Scene 5. Ananda Communicates the Decision. Ananda then returns to Pajāpati and reports the Buddha's decision. Honored, Pajāpati accepts the eight conditions as readily as "a youth fond of ornaments would accept a garland of lotus or jasmine flowers," vowing she will never transgress them.

Scene 6. Ananda Communicates Mahāprajāpatī's Acceptance. On hearing Pajāpati's reply, the Buddha then declares the prophecy that this compromise will result in the Dharma enduring for only 500 years rather than 1000, adding several somewhat obscure analogies of robbers attacking households, mildew attacking rice, and rust attacking sugar cane. Finally, he says that establishing the eight rules is like prophylactically building a dam so that water will not overflow a reservoir.[4]

Sponberg claims that the above story is by no means a historical account of the establishment of the nuns' order. On the contrary, he asserts that that the story was *fabricated* by monks in response to the instability of the order after the death of the Buddha. Buddhism did not become a dominant religion in India until 250 CE,[5] over two hundred years after the Buddha's death. Since no teachings were recorded by the Buddha himself, the task was taken on by his male disciples who, needless to say, wanted the order to survive. Survival, for the monks, was dependent on full economic support from the laity. This crucial relationship forged an inseparable connection between monastics and lay Buddhists, which caused monks to alter the teachings of the Buddha in order to make them acceptable to the larger community.

> ... The two [portrayals of women] arise out of very different sets of concerns, and ... the latter attitude of androcentrism represents a response to a problem that became increasingly more an issue after the community had reached a certain degree of success in establishing a place for itself within the broader society. In contrast to the attitude of inclusiveness, which focused on the capability of women to pursue the path, the focus here is not on women themselves, but rather on a perceived threat to the integrity of the monastic institution as it existed within the broader social community.[6]

This claim is supported by the explicit contradictions about women's capabilities as reflected in the story. For instance, in scene 3, the Buddha asserts that women are equal. However, in scene 1 as well as scenes 4 and 6, their equality is denied. The portrayal of the Buddha as unwilling to explain his decision to deny female ordination suggests that there is social pressure behind this representation.

To ensure economic support from the laity, the monks who were interpreting the Buddha's teachings succumbed to the pressure of socially constructed, androcentric roles of the ideal "woman." Thus, the construction of women as passive, docile, and in need of male supervision was woven into the sacred texts. In the case of the nuns, their choice to follow a spiritual path could be perceived as an explicit rejection of socially prescribed roles, since part of the process of taking refuge in the Buddha's teachings is to give up worldly identities. Though it was socially acceptable for men to leave their wives and children behind in pursuit of spiritual enlightenment (the Buddha himself did this), the construction of "woman" as the center of the home made it more difficult for nuns to fully renounce family obligations. Because of their independence as spiritual practitioners and the absence of their traditional dependency and need for protection by men, nuns posed a threat to the dominant social order. Therefore, to justify the presence of women to lay donors who were needed for the monastic order's survival, the societal voice of androcentrism uncovered by Sponberg was woven into sacred text. By insisting that women could not teach, discipline, or admonish monks, the eight special rules that were created to govern nuns' behavior represented a mirror image of the husband/wife relationship in the lay community.[7]

In addition to the demotion that nuns suffered in order to maintain the economic status of the monastic community, they also were subjected to misogynist representation as sexual objects. The social stereotypes of "woman" as lustful and sexually deviant have been particularly demeaning as they have provided justification for female subordination. If a woman is perceived to have a dangerous sexuality, it follows that she is unable to advance spiritually, and it is best for her to be confined to the home where she can be supervised. Monks, despite their spiritual calling, were born into this misogynist society and were also subjected to these views of women:

> Although Sakyamuni Buddha preached a way of liberation patterned after his own awakening and rethinking of reality, the budding sect of Buddhism was not able to liberate itself completely from the confines of its own social and cultural context.[8]

The close relationship between the outside world and the inner workings of the monastic order also gave rise to the voice that Sponberg calls "ascetic misogyny," which reveals how this relationship came to be represented in Buddhist sacred text:

> Monks, a woman, even when going along, will stop to ensnare the heart of a man; whether standing, sitting or lying down, laughing, talking or singing, weeping, stricken or dying, a woman will stop to ensnare the heart of a man.[9]

> As the filth and decay of a dead dog or dead snake are burned away, So all men should burn filth and detest evil. The dead snake and dog are detestable, But women are even more detestable than they are. . . . Women are like fishermen; their flattery is a net. Men are like fish caught by the net.[10]

There is little doubt that the Buddha warned his followers against succumbing to desire in any form, whether for money, power, possessions, or sex. However, when Buddhism became more institutionalized, an original warning against excess or desire could have been easily reworded, as in the above passages, to reflect the socially constructed dichotomy of "woman" as the temptress and "man" as the tempted.

As Buddhist texts affected society, so did society affect Buddhist texts. As women were forced into dependence on their husbands in the wider society, this role was recreated and solidified for the nuns by the pressures of "institutional androcentrism" and "ascetic misogyny." Instead of enjoying the freedom of spiritual life, nuns remained tied to their "female nature," and thus were forced to the margins of the Buddhist monastic community while men have maintained central roles in the development of Buddhism. This dynamic has affected the spiritual development, education, and economic status of nuns up until the present day.

Despite the obstacles that have been erected by these negative textual and social representations of nuns, women still leave their homes in pursuit of the Buddhist path. This is especially true in the case of Sri Lanka, a home to many nuns whose lives have been lived in strong resistance to social convention. However, the autonomy of the nuns' marginal culture has done little to affect change at the institutional level—a fact that raises questions about the importance of official spiritual recognition. Do women need to be institutionally accepted in order to be "real" nuns? Are there advantages in remaining outside? What are the losses? These complex questions will be explored in the following sections.

THE EFFECTS OF MUTUALLY INTERACTIVE TEXTUAL/SOCIAL OPPRESSIONS ON SRI LANKAN NUNS

In Sri Lanka, the close relationship between the textual and social constructions of women has maintained their exclusion from the official Buddhist monastic order since the eleventh century. Androcentric and misogynistic textual representations have secured power for the monks, and the social status quo primarily confines women to the home. In light of these obstacles, there is much to be learned from the Sri Lankan women that Tessa Bartholomeusz calls "lay nuns."[11] These women don the traditional robes and hold the traditional ten precepts of Buddhist monastics, but have no official recognition and thus remain isolated. Though recent developments in Sri Lanka have given these nuns the right to an official ordination, Bartholomeusz's work reveals that Sri Lankan nuns have, despite their exclusion, created a marginal culture outside of the official monastic order. As we shall see, the recreation of socially constructed systems of domination in Buddhist monastic communities continues to play out in the everyday experience of these nuns and this has had serious economic and educational consequences for them.

According to Bartholomeusz, there has been no social (and thereby no institutional) interest in encouraging women to renounce the world because it would remove them from their ideal role in the home. In the context of Buddhist Sri Lanka, this means that the narrowly defined gender role of the laywoman has been elevated. Women are encouraged to be lay practitioners of Buddhism because they can still be defined as subordinates in their roles as wives, mothers, and sexual beings. However, for women to shave their heads, don robes, take vows of celibacy, and leave their families is a threat to socially constructed definitions of womanhood because it allows for a degree of female autonomy. This view is shown in Bartholomeusz's interviews with Sri Lankan lay Buddhists:

> In contemporary Buddhist Sri Lanka, the ideal woman is she who nurtures her family and the monastic order, not she who renounces the world. The majority of the lay Buddhists I interviewed remarked that even though they do, or would, offer danaya (alms) to female renunciants, they believe that world-renunciation is not a suitable concern for women.[12]

The above passage reflects my earlier exploration of the dual influence of androcentrism and misogyny on textual interpretation and societal practice. The status of the laywoman was elevated by the economic influence that the lay community had on the livelihood of the monastic order at the expense of the nuns. Therefore, one can see why there is little social interest in allowing women to participate in the Saṅgha and great interest in encouraging women to remain in lay life.

Despite these social obstacles, thousands of Sri Lankan women live the life of a nun. In fact, as is revealed in Bartholomeusz's interviews, these women enjoy feelings of autonomy and empowerment. What Bartholomeusz's work shows is that women enter nunhood largely to gain freedom from the confines of socially prescribed gender roles. Many women feel that becoming a nun increases their freedom:

> I did not want to marry; I never married. From early in my childhood, I never wanted to marry. If I had married, I would have had to have children, and I would have had no independence. Some men are not good; they drink...and neglect their wives and children. By becoming a [nun], I do not have to worry about these things; I can do what I please.[13]
>
> ...Who wants to marry? When girls marry, they have many children. It is too much work for us. As soon as they rise in the morning until they go to sleep at night, women are working for their children and husband. They have no freedom to meditate. We have a better life. Their lives are not good.[14]
>
> ...I wanted to die during most of my married life. I was miserable...I loved my children, but I wanted to die. Without telling anyone, I went to Anuradhapura to worship the eight holy places and decided to become a [nun].[15]

As these comments reveal, there is little opportunity for a woman to find time for herself in playing her "ideal" role. Though there are many textual examples of laywomen who were able to achieve enlightenment,[16] which were probably—at least in part—fabricated to somehow commodify enlightenment as something that could be achieved by women at home, the reality is that overwhelmingly large numbers of women become nuns to escape this life.[17]

While honoring the feelings expressed by the nuns quoted above and acknowledging their revolutionary actions in self-defining a nuns' order that allows them to practice and teach the Dharma, I also question the extent of the empowerment they describe in becoming nuns. It is apparent that there are many obstacles that cannot be overcome by simply rejecting the role of wife and mother, for we have seen that stereotypical gender roles are largely replicated in Buddhist teachings and institutions. My studies have revealed that, in practice, the lives of these nuns allow them only slightly more freedom than the life of a laywoman. Bartholomeusz calls them "lay nuns" and witnessed firsthand this recreation of socially constructed male/female roles in situations where both monks and nuns were present:

> ...If the laity has gathered together both monks and nuns for an alms-giving, the lay nuns help the laity (usually women) distribute the alms to monks. In other words, the women serve and the men eat....Only when the monks are fed, do the lay nuns themselves receive [alms]....Monks...play no role in offering [alms] to the lay nuns.[18]

Bartholomeusz cites the above example as a deliberate reinforcement of male domination on the part of the nuns,[19] who are also affected by what society dictates that a "woman's role" should be. In addition, the restructuring of the "mother" role is enacted by the lay nuns:

> In the majority of lay nunneries I visited, the renunciants spent hours baby sitting for those who support them, devoted much time and energy to sewing and stitching their own robes, and cooked their own meals.[20]

These examples are indicative of the ways in which the monk/nun relationship has come to reflect an only moderately distorted mirror image of the roles of husband/wife in larger society. Thus the question arises as to how much autonomy these female world renouncers have. Though they are not mothers and wives, they are still engaged in domestic work.

Not only are nuns expected to serve the needs of monks in the same way that wives are expected to serve husbands and families, but also the aforementioned hesitancy of the laity to give them alms has had serious economic consequences for the nuns. Here I will draw on Hanna Havnevik's work with Tibetan nuns to show the ways in which the autonomous culture of institutionally marginalized nuns is not an insulated experience of Sri Lankans. In each culture, the fundamentally similar androcentric, misogynist social construction ensures nuns will receive less economic support. This economic challenge, however, entails more than just not receiving adequate donations of food from the laity. Many nuns live in abject poverty, to the extent of sometimes being called "female beggars."[21] Both the lack of economic support and the poverty of the nuns all over Asia affect the amount of access nuns have to the education that could potentially elevate their status.

Education is probably the most important catalyst for change in the movement for nuns' equality. The mutual interaction of textual and social oppressions has resulted in less support for nuns from the lay community, and the construction of "woman" as less intelligent has encouraged and supported notions of "woman" as sexually deviant and inherently domestic. This not only justifies denying women access to the higher learning that would allow them to become interpreters of text, but also teaches women that they should not concern themselves with pursuing such knowledge. The exclusion of women from higher education is a hierarchical tool that ensures that nuns will not be able to gain access to the very texts that support their oppression.

Many monasteries function as institutions of higher learning because they are given the economic support to do so.[22] Socially constructed notions of women as less intelligent encourage little interest among the laity to support their intellectual pursuits. In addition, nuns are unable to access the teaching sessions in the monasteries because of the perceived threat of the "female nature" to the celibacy vows of the monks.[23] It is also rare for a high lama to come to a nunnery to teach for the same reasons:

> ...The reason why lamas so seldom go to the nunneries is because they are afraid of breaking their vows.... A western nun told me that once when H. H. Karmapa visited Tilokpur [a nunnery], he stayed for half an hour. Afterwards he spent several days at the Drugpa Kagyu monastery....[24]

In the above passage we see the mutually interactive forces of textual, economic and educational oppressions. Since women have been constructed as subordinates who fit only into the role of wife, mother, and sexual object, it naturally follows that they be discouraged from seeking out the education that would more directly inform them of their conditions because they are told they are "naturally" unfit to do so. However, the widespread acceptance of this "natural" inability further complicates the marginal status of nuns in areas such as Sri Lanka and Tibet.

Despite the strength of institutional barriers, the nuns interviewed by Havnevik and Bartholomeusz express no sense of loss about the lack of higher education.[25] It seems the marginal autonomy they enjoy outside the official Buddhist monastic community surpasses any concern they might have for the possibility of institutional change. This makes sense in that nuns were brought up as girls and young women in a culture that devalued women's minds. Because of their participation in society, most nuns are brought up to believe they have little use for higher learning, and that it is only good for participation in nonreligious lifestyles such as those of politicians or businesspeople:

> ...The lay nuns argue that renunciation is a life-long commitment, and not something one does lightly to obtain a degree.... According to one lay nun, the goal of Buddhism is to attain [enlightenment], and not to acquire "fat bellies, money, a secular education, and fancy cars, as many monks are prone to do."[26]

Also, the nuns interviewed by Bartholomeusz showed no interest in associating with monks at all, and declared they would not accept full ordination if it were offered because they would have to adhere to the eight rules and be subordinate to monks:

> ...The traditional relationship between the monks and the nuns would be reestablished, and the autonomy which we presently enjoy would therefore be relinquished. Though I wish that there were a nuns' lineage in Sri Lanka...I do not want to be subordinate to the order of monks. I do not believe that the Eight Weighty Rules are good or that the Buddha gave them.[27]

> ...If the nuns' lineage is reintroduced, then we would have to live by the Eight Rules which Lord Buddha gave to his foster mother when she became a member of the monastic order. I do not wish for this to happen; I do not want monks to be involved in my life.[28]

Due to a lack of awareness about the importance of education and general disinterest in associating with monks, many nuns remain confined to the basic practice of reciting prayers, performing prostrations, and sitting in meditation. These are the very practices that—although important—tend to insulate nuns within their own culture and tradition, blinding them to mutually interactive systems of oppression that keep them poor and unrecognized by the larger society. Thus, the question arises: Do nuns need institutional recognition to attain spiritual freedom? The next section presents one alternative to marginal autonomy and asks questions about what true spiritual freedom entails.

ASIAN AND WESTERN NUNS: COALITION-BUILDING ACROSS THE BORDERS OF DIFFERENCE

As we have already seen, one model of nuns' resistance to institutional subordination has been the creation of a self-defined marginal community. This model is admirable, but also problematic, because it insulates nuns within their own particular region and tradition, separating them from their sisters in other places. As a result, many nuns are not aware that full ordination and official recognition are given to nuns in China, Vietnam, and Korea, and that powerful monks such as the Dalai Lama of Tibet have recently allowed nuns to receive ordination from these lineages.[29] Nuns confined to their own traditions also remain naive about the coalitions being formed crossculturally and crosstraditionally in pursuit of female recognition within the monastic world. These days, instead of creating marginal cultures, many nuns are uniting across traditional and cultural boundaries, sharing and combining ideas from many different Buddhist traditions to create an international nuns' order. The purpose of this is to raise awareness about female subordination in Buddhism and fight for admittance into the official monastic order.

Before discussing the various ways that nuns are connecting cross-culturally in pursuit of institutional recognition, it is pertinent to consider the arguments that support this objective. As I have tried to convey, nuns in areas such as Sri Lanka and Tibet have built a successful, self-defined spiritual community, but remain overshadowed by socially constructed notions of the essential "woman." Their inability to fully disassociate themselves from their "female nature" in the eyes of larger society causes them to suffer economically, spiritually, and educationally. Those involved with the international nuns' order offer a counterargument to the claims of nuns who believe that official recognition would diminish their position. In the following paragraphs, I will provide a brief overview of the main arguments supporting the struggle for equal recognition of nuns within the Buddhist monastic tradition, based on the work of Karma Lekshe Tsomo and others.

Tsomo's work supports Sponberg's argument that the creation of the eight rules for women was a later interpretation by monks of the Buddha's hesitance to admit women into the Saṅgha, and was a response of other monks to the social and economic pressures of the time. Though it may have been that Buddhism would have died out unless it mirrored the male-dominant culture, in today's context Tsomo calls the story of Mahāprajāpatī's price of admission to the Saṅgha "unreasonable" and "demeaning."[30] She states that women are an essential part of the Buddhist community, and that denying them equal access to ordination only supports the status quo, not Buddhist tradition, and that such a denial also blatantly contradicts the egalitarian teachings of the Buddha.[31] Although times have changed since the first interpretations of Buddhist texts, Tsomo asserts that the Saṅgha is incomplete without fully ordained nuns.

According to Tsomo, one main reason women are excluded from the monastic order today is because monks do not wish to relinquish the power, support, and privilege their institutional recognition accords them. Influential monks argue that where the nuns' lineages have died out or were never established, there is no possibility to include nuns as members equal to the monks. To compensate for this exclusion of women from the official Buddhist monastic tradition, laywomen have been elevated to serve the purpose of maintaining male power within the spiritual community because the support of women is necessary for the order to survive, and laywomen do not pose a threat to the status quo:

> . . . to give the nuns equal status might erode the [monks'] basis of support. In many traditional Buddhist countries, it is mostly women who patronize the [monks]; if they began patronizing the [nuns], it would cause a conflict of interests.[32]

For reasons previously discussed, nuns are subject to poverty and lack support from the laity because it is not socially acceptable for women to renounce their role in the home. Tsomo argues for full ordination as the only way for nuns to begin to gain institutional recognition. This recognition will ideally cause a chain reaction that would allow nuns access to the education and authority that would position them as interpreters of sacred texts and as respected teachers within the tradition. From this, economic status would also improve.

The denial of education to nuns has limited their access to advanced spiritual teachings as well as to the reading and interpreting of sacred texts. Tsomo argues that it will not be until women reach a position of intellectual power within Buddhism that the androcentric and misogynist texts presented earlier will begin to be challenged:

> Unless structured systems of religious education are implemented soon, Buddhist women . . . will remain disadvantaged for several generations hence. Though [nuns] may well progress spiritually despite learning handicaps, they will not be able to take their rightful places in the religious hierarchy as teachers, administrators, role models, and perpetrators of the *Dharma*.[33]

In other words, it is only when women gain access to the texts previously discussed that the subordinating voices of "ascetic misogyny" and "institutional androcentrism" will be institutionally challenged and extracted.

Sakyadhita, or "Daughters of the Buddha" was created to help reach the above goals. The movement is a global network of nuns and laywomen that began in 1987. Since the establishment of this coalition, many conferences have been organized in Asian countries and in the West to address specific issues related to the status of nuns. The focus of the movement is: 1. to create a network of communications among the Buddhist women of the world; 2. to educate women as teachers of Buddhism; 3. to conduct research on women in Buddhism; and 4. to work for the establishment of the order of fully ordained nuns where it does not currently exist.[34] According to Tsomo, the migration of Buddhism to the West has opened up lines of communication not only between Asian and Western continents, but among Asian Buddhist countries as well. She states that, until recently, most Asian nuns remained insular, "...well aware of the historical background of their own traditions, but less aware of historical developments in other Buddhist countries. Until fairly recently, many did not realize that the Chinese, Korean, and Vietnamese traditions have preserved the [nuns'] lineage intact."[35] This increase in awareness has encouraged the participation of nuns in Sakyadhita who might otherwise never have been exposed to the possibility for change.

REVOLUTIONARY DIALOGUE

The nuns' movement is unique in that women are organizing not only across racial or ethnic boundaries, but also across language differences, opposing cultural viewpoints, and conflicting Buddhist traditions in an attempt to form a collective compromise. This collective compromise is a tricky idea because it offers a new model with which to view women's activism. Though the formation of marginal communities does little for institutional change, it would be naïve to assume that Buddhist nuns can unite solely on the basis of their status as women or as Buddhists given the different cultural and traditional contexts from which they come. To do this would be to relive the mistakes of white, liberal feminists who managed (inadvertently or not) to alienate women of color, lesbians, and working-class women by attempting to create an umbrella of "woman" under which all women could unite. What is unique about Sakyadhita is that the movement has been created around the "multiplicity of voices and experiences"[36] of nuns rather than a contrived "singular" experience of the group. Though these variations are many, I have chosen to present briefly the East/West distinction as it relates to this dialogue. This decision is based on the simple, obvious differences reflected in Asian and Western cultural values, rendering it one of the most illuminating examples of the ways in which nuns must address conflicting viewpoints in order to form a collective compromise.

The conflict between Asian and Western cultural values is just one example of the challenges faced by Sakyadhita. Western focus on individual goals and the cultivation of a "unique" identity grate against the Asian idea of identity in connection to family and community, not to a sense of individual uniqueness. Sara Shneiderman explains this difference expertly:

> ... Western culture tends to focus on the development of the individual self, praising separation and "special," "unique" qualities as legitimating personhood, while ... Buddhist thought posits the self as a fluid, only tentatively boundaried component of a larger, cosmically interconnected reality.[37]

This culturally based difference among women of Asian and Western descent provides a pertinent example through which to view just how revolutionary of a movement Sakyadhita is. To organize across these boundaries, Western nuns must not only begin to deconstruct their perceived individuality in the practice of Buddhism, but must be careful not to lose sight of their connection to their Asian sisters. At the same time, Asian nuns must begin to understand the nature of Western women's behavior, whose practice is often seen as more of a "spectacle" than a serious endeavor.

To explain further the miscommunication that often arises between Asian and Western nuns as a result of conflicting cultural concepts of the "self," let us return once again to Havnevik's study. The following excerpt from an interview with a Tibetan nun can be used to show both how nuns are interacting crossculturally and the difficulty of conflicting cultural viewpoints discussed above.

> ... I do not think that [Western nuns] influence us in any way. They do not stay in the nunneries. The way that a few western nuns have behaved in India is more like a spectacle to us. Tibetan nuns are more humble and simple, we do not have the same ambitions that the western nuns have, but maybe this will change.[38]

As we can see, the interviewee is acutely aware that the assertiveness and individualism that allows Western nuns to access such institutions as monasteries and universities where they are a "spectacle"[39] is contradictory to the way she has been taught to behave. However, she is also aware of the influence of Western nuns on her own life. By asserting that the attitude of Tibetan nuns may change as they begin to see other ways of behaving displayed by Westerners, we see one example of the thought process that is taking place within Sakyadhita. The point is not to devalue one's own views, but more specifically to alter one's view to *make room* to *acknowledge* the perceptions of others without discounting them. Instead of suggesting, as some nuns did,[40] that Western nuns are incapable of pursuing the Buddhist path because of their individualistic behavior, it is more conducive to acknowledge, as the above nun has, one's own differences and create space for change in one's own perception.

Though there is little research about this interlocking model of resistance as it pertains to nuns specifically, many scholars[41] have addressed the need to break free of systems of thought that emphasize binary distinctions such as either/or, bad/good, high/low and replace them with systems that encourage a both/and point of view. I find it interesting that Buddhist teachings themselves emphasize this all-encompassing mentality in their focus on the interconnectedness of all sentient beings, even despite the institutional binarisms that have been revealed. As a Westerner, I was inspired by the both/and system of thought, because it helped me begin creating what Shneiderman calls a "collective consciousness." It is because of the connection between the model of Sakyadhita that I have presented and the work of many scholars grappling with issues of women's coalition-building that this exploration is not only about Buddhist nuns. Its message extends into the lives of many women who are attempting to organize across the boundaries of race, class, and sexuality. The cultivation of collective consciousness can be translated as an open-mindedness and acceptance of views and experiences different from our own. Instead of searching for the "right" way to organize (as opposed to the "wrong" way), why not follow the nuns' example and look for where "we" can make room for all of the differences, ambiguities, and changes that dominate our lives, and work within them, rather than against them. I hope that these ideas sensitize readers to the plight of Buddhist nuns, but I also hope that they will be able to see themselves reflected in their resistance.

NOTES

1. For a more detailed analysis, see Diana Y. Paul, *Women in Buddhism: Images of the Feminine in Mahayana Buddhism* (Berkeley: University of California Press, 1985).

2. For a detailed analysis of these voices, see Alan Sponberg, "Attitudes Toward Women and the Feminine in Early Buddhism," in *Buddhism, Sexuality, and Gender,* José Ignacio Cabezón, ed. (Albany, N.Y.: State University of New York Press, 1992), pp. 3–36.

3. There are several different versions of this story that differ in only a few significant details. All follow the same basic structure and hold the same basic outcome, though the "eight rules" are sometimes ranked differently.

4. Sponberg, "Attitudes Toward Women," pp. 14–16.

5. There is some question about the exact dates in Buddhist history. This particular claim is quoted from Noble Ross Reat, *Buddhism: A History* (Fremont: Jain Publishing, 1994), p. 24.

6. Sponberg, "Attitudes Toward Women," pp. 15–16.

7. For further support of this claim, see Sandra A. Wawrytko, "Sexism in the Early Saṅgha: Its Social Basis and Philosophical Dis-solution" in *Buddhist Behavioral Codes and the Modern* World, Charles Wei-hsun Fu and Sandra A. Wawrytko, eds. (Westport, Conn: Greenview Press, 1994), pp. 278–79.

8. Ibid., p. 278.

9. Sponberg, "Attitudes Toward Women," p. 20.

10. Ibid., p. 21.

11. See Tessa Bartholomeusz, *Women Under the Bō Tree* (Cambridge: Cambridge University Press, 1994).

12. Ibid., p. 22.

13. Ibid., p. 133.

14. Ibid., p. 134.

15. Ibid.

16. For one such story, see Wawrytko, "Sexism in the Early Saṅgha," pp. 286–87.

17. See Hanna Havnevik, *Tibetan Buddhist Nuns* (Oslo: Norwegian University Press, 1990), pp. 94–98.

18. Ibid., p. 152.

19. Bartholomeusz, *Women Under the Bō Tree*, p. 152.

20. Ibid., p. 131.

21. Nancy Auer Falk, "The Case of the Vanishing Nuns: The Fruits of Ambivalence in Ancient Indian Buddhism," in *Unspoken Worlds: Women's*

Refigious Lives, Nancy Auer Falk and Rita M. Gross, eds. (San Francisco: Harper & Row, 1980), pp. 207–24.

22. Havnevik, *Tibetan Buddhist Nuns*, p. 51.

23. Ibid., p. 118.

24. Ibid., p. 119

25. Since Bartholomeusz and Havnevik, as well as myself, come from a Western context, feelings of contentment may be merely our own interpretations of nuns' responses to questions of education. Thus, it would be easy to miss any culturally specific nonverbal cues that may have been present in these interviews.

26. Bartholomeusz, *Women Under the Bō Tree*, p. 153.

27. Ibid., pp. 136–37.

28. Ibid., p. 137.

29. For a conversation with the Dalai Lama about nuns' status, see Karma Lekshe Tsomo, *Sakyadhita, Daughters of the Buddha* (Ithaca, N.Y.: Snow Lion, 1988) pp. 267–76.

30. Ibid., p. 218.

31. See chapter 6 of Bartholomeusz's *Women Under the Bō Tree* for a discussion of ways in which nuns have been either encouraged or discouraged from becoming Saṅgha members depending on the stability of the religion at a given period in time.

32. Tsomo, *Sakyadhita*, p. 217.

33. Ibid., p. 164.

34. Karma Lekshe Tsomo, ed., *Buddhist Women Across Cultures: Realizations* (Albany, N.Y.: State University of New York Press, 1999), p. 2.

35. Tsomo, *Sakyadhita*, p. 218–19.

36. Tsomo, *Buddhist Women Across Cultures*, p. 32.

37. Sara Shneiderman, "Appropriate Treasure? Reflections on Women, Buddhism, and Crosscultural Exchange," in Tsomo, *Buddhist Women Across Cultures*, p. 228.

38. Havnevik, *Tibetan Buddhist Nuns*, p. 192.

39. For more information about the experience of Western nuns in monasteries and universities, see Havnevik, *Tibetan Buddhist Nuns*, pp. 190–206, and Vicki Mackenzie, *Cave in the Snow: Tenzin Palmo's Quest for Enlightenment* (London: Bloomsbury Publishing, 1998).

40. Havnevik, *Tibetan Buddhist Nuns*, p. 192.

41. See the work of Patricia Hill Collins, Gloria Anzaldua, bell hooks, Minnie Bruce Pratt, Adrienne Rich, Eve Sedgwick, and others for varied standpoints.

Bibliography

Allione, Tsultrim. *Women of Wisdom*. London: Routledge and Kegan Paul, 1984.

Amarasingham, Loma Rhodes. "The Misery of the Embodied: Representations of Women in Sinhalese Myth." In *Women in Ritual and Symbolic Roles*. Edited by J. Hock-Smith and Anita Spring. New York: Plenum Press, 1978.

Anderson, Richard W. "Rissho Koseikai and the Bodhisattva Way: Religious Ideals, Conflict, Gender, and Status." *Japanese Journal of Religious Studies* 21 (June–September 1994): 311–37.

Aoyama, Shundo. *Zen Seeds: Reflections of a Female Priest*. Tokyo: Kosei Publishing Company, 1990.

Arai, Paula Kane Robinson. *Women Living Zen: Japanese Soto Buddhist Nuns*. Oxford: Oxford University Press, 1999.

Aziz, Barbara Nimri, "Ani Chodon: Portrait of a Buddhist Nun." In *Loka 2: A Journal from Naropa Institute*. Edited by Rick Fields. Garden City, N.Y.: Anchor Press, 1976, pp. 43–46.

Bancroft, Anne. "Women Disciples in Zen Buddhism." In *Women As Teachers and Disciples in Traditional and New Religions*, (*Studies in Women and Religion*, Vol. 32). Edited by Elizabeth Puttick and Peter B. Clarke. Lewiston, N.Y.: Edwin Mellen Press, 1993, pp. 91–96.

Barnes, Nancy Schuster. "Buddhist Women and the Nuns' Order in Asia." In *Engaged Buddhism: Buddhist Liberation Movements in Asia*. Edited by Christopher S. Queen and Sallie B. King. Albany, N.Y.: State University of New York Press, 1996, pp. 259–94.

Bartholomeusz, Tessa. *Women Under the Bō Tree*. Cambridge: Cambridge University Press, 1994.

———. "Mothers of Buddhas, Mothers of Nations: Kumaratunga and Her Meteoric Rise to Power in Sri Lanka." *Journal of Feminist Studies* 25:1 (Spring 1999): 211–25.

Batchelor, Martine. *Walking on Lotus Flowers: Buddhist Women Living, Loving and Meditating*. London: Thorsons, 1996.

Beyer, Stephan. *The Cult of Tara: Magic and Ritual in Tibet.* Berkeley: University of California Press, 1973.

Bianchi, Ester. *The Iron Statue Monastery, "Tienxiangsi": A Buddhist Nunnery of Tibetan Tradition in Contemporary China.* Firenze: Leo S. Olschki Editore, 2001.

Blackstone, Kathryn R. *Women in the Footsteps of the Buddha:* Struggle for *Liberation in the Therīgāthā.* Richmond, Surrey: Curzon Press, 1998.

Blakiston, Hilary. *But Little Dust: Life Amongst the "Ex-Untouchables."* Cambridge: Allborough Press, 1990.

Bloss, Lowell W. "The Female Renunciants of Sri Lanka: The *Dasasil mattawa.*" *Journal of the International Association of Buddhist Studies* 10:1 (1987): 7–32.

Boucher, Sandy. *Opening the Lotus: A Woman's Guide to Buddhism.* New York: Ballantine Books, 1997.

———. *Turning the Wheel. American Women Creating the New Buddhism.* Boston: Beacon Press, 1993.

Brazell, Karen, trans. *The Confessions of Lady Nijo.* Garden City, N.Y.: Anchor Books, 1973.

Brown, Sid. *The Journey of One Buddhist Nun: Even Against the Wind.* Albany, N.Y.: State University of New York Press, 2001.

Butler, Alex. *Feminism, Nationalism and Exiled Tibetan Women.* New Delhi: Kali for Women, 2003.

Byles, Marie B. *Journey into Burmese Silence.* George Allen and Unwin, London, 1962.

Cabezón, José Ignacio, ed. *Buddhism, Sexuality, and Gender.* Albany, N.Y.: State University of New York Press, 1992.

Campbell, June. *Traveller in Space: In Search of Female Identity in Tibetan Buddhism.* New York: George Braziller, 1996.

Chang, Pao. *Biographies of Buddhist Nuns.* Translated by Li Jung-hsi. Osaka: Tohokai, 1981.

Ching, Yu-Ing. *Master of Love and Mercy: Cheng Yen.* Nevada City, Calif: Blue Dolphin Publications, 1995.

Chodron, Thubten. *Blossoms of the Dharma: Living as a Buddhist Nun.* Berkeley: North Atlantic Books, 1999.

Chonam, Lama and Sangye Khandro, trans. *The Lives and Liberation of Princess Mandarava: The Indian Consort of Padmasambhava.* Boston: Wisdom Publications, 1998.

Chung, Inyoung. "A Buddhist View of Women: A Comparative Study of the Rules for *Bhikṣus* and *Bhikṣuṇī*s based on the Chinese *Prātimokṣa*." MA thesis, Graduate Theological Union, Berkeley, 1995.

Davids, Caroline A. F. Rhys, trans. *Poems of Early Buddhist Nuns: Therīgāthā.* London: Wisdom Publications, 1989.

de Silva, Padmasiri. "The Concept of Equality in the Theravāda Buddhist Tradition." In *Equality and the Religious Traditions of Asia.* Edited by R. Siriwardena. New York: Palgrave Macmillan, 1987, pp. 74–97.

Devine, Carol. *Determination: Tibetan Women and the Struggle for an Independent Tibet.* Toronto: Vauve Press, 1991.

Dharmasena. *Portraits of Buddhist Women: Stories from the* Saddharmaratnavaliya. Translated by Ranjini Obeyesekere. Albany, N.Y.: State University of New York Press, 2001.

Dowman, Keith. *Sky Dancer: The Secret Life and Songs of the Lady Yeshe Tsogyel.* London: Routledge and Kegan Paul, 1984.

Dresser, Marianne. *Buddhist Women on the Edge: Contemporary Perspectives from the Western Frontier.* Berkeley: North Atlantic Books, 1996.

Edou, Jerome. *Machig Labdron and the Foundations of Chod.* Ithaca, N.Y.: Snow Lion, 1995.

Eisler, Riane. *The Chalice and the Blade: Our History, Our Future.* San Francisco: Harper & Row, 1987.

Falk, Nancy Auer. "The Case of the Vanishing Nuns: The Fruits of Ambivalence in Ancient Indian Buddhism." In *Unspoken Worlds: Women's Religious Lives in Non-Western Cultures.* Edited by Nancy Auer Falk and Rita M. Gross. San Francisco: Harper & Row, 1980, pp. 207–24.

———. An Image of Women in Old Buddhist Literature: The Daughters of Māra." In *Women and Religion.* Edited by Judith

Plaskow and June Arnold. Missoula: Scholars Press, 1974, pp. 105–12.

Farrer-Halls, Gill. *The Feminine Face of Buddhism.* Wheaton, Ill.: Quest Books, 2002.

Faure, Bernard and Stephen F. Teiser, eds. *The Power of Denial: Buddhism, Purity, and Gender.* Princeton: Princeton University Press, 2003.

Findly, Ellison Banks, ed. *Women's Buddhism, Buddhism's Women: Tradition, Revision, Renewal.* Boston: Wisdom Publications, 2000.

Friedman, Lenore. *Meetings with Remarkable Women: Buddhist Teachers in America.* Boston: Shambhala, 1987.

Friedman, Lenore and Susan Moon. *Being Bodies: Buddhist Women on the Paradox of Embodiment.* Boston: Shambhala, 1997.

Goonatilake, Hema. "Buddhist Nuns: Protests, Struggle, and the Reinterpretation of Orthodoxy in Sri Lanka." In *Mixed Blessings: Gender and Religious Fundamentalism Cross Culturally.* Edited by Judy Brink and Joan Mencher. New York: Routledge, 1997, pp. 25–39.

Goonesekera, S. "Status of Women in the Family Law of Sri Lanka." In *Women at the Crossroads: A Sri Lankan Perspective.* Edited by Sirima Kiribamune and Vidyamali Samarasinghe. New Delhi: Vikas, 1990.

Grimshaw, Anna. *Servants of the Buddha: Winter in a Himalayan Convent.* Cleveland: Pilgrim Press, 1994.

Gross, Rita M. *Buddhism After Patriarchy: A Feminist History, Analysis, and Reconstruction of Buddhism.* Albany, N.Y.: State University ofNew York Press, 1993.

———. "Buddhism and Feminism: Toward Their Mutual Transformation." *The Eastern Buddhist* 19:2, (Autumn 1986): 62–74.

———. "Buddhism from the Perspective of Women's Bodies." *Buddhist-Christian Studies I* (1981) 72–82.

———. "Helping the Iron Bird Fly: Western Buddhist Women and Issues of Authority in the Late 1990s." In *The Faces of Buddhism in America.* Edited by Charles S. Prebish and Kenneth K. Tanaka. Berkeley: University of California Press, 1998.

Gross, Rita M. and Rosemary Radford Ruether. *Religious Feminism and the Future of the Planet: A Buddhist-Christian Conversation.* London and New York: Continuum, 2001.

Gunawardena, R. A. L. H. "Subtile Silks of Ferreous Firmness: Buddhist Nuns in Ancient and Early Medieval Sri Lanka and Their Role in the Propagation of Buddhism." *The Sri Lankan Journal of the Humanities* 14:1, 2 (1988): 1–59.

Hardacre, Helen. *Marketing the Menacing Fetus in Japan.* Berkeley: University of California Press, 1997.

Harrison, Elizabeth G. "Women's Responses to Child Loss in Japan: The Case of Mizuko Kuyo." *Journal of Feminist Studies in Religion* 11 (Fall 1995): 67–93.

Havnevik, Hanna. "On Pilgrimage for Forty Years in the Himalayas: The Female Lama Jetsun Lochen Rinpoche's (1865–1951) Quest for Sacred Sites." In *Pilgrimage in Tibet.* Edited by Alex McKay. Richmond, Surrey: Curzon Press, 1998, pp. 85–107.

———. *Tibetan Buddhist Nuns.* Oslo: Norwegian University Press, 1990.

Heikkila-Horn, Marja-Leena. *Buddhism with Open Eyes: Belief and Practice of Santi Asoke.* Bangkok: Fah Apai, 1997.

Heirman, Ann, *The Discipline in Four Parts: Rules for Nuns according to the Dharmaguptakavinaya.* Delhi: Motilal Banarsidass, 2002.

———. "Some Remarks on the Rise of the *bhikṣuṇī saṃgha* and on the Ordination Ceremony for *bhikṣuṇī*s, according to the Dharmaguptaka, Vinaya.," *Journal of the International Association of Buddhist Studies* 19:2 (1988) 33–85.

Hirakawa, Akira. "The History of Buddhist Nuns in Japan." *Buddhist-Christian Studies* 12 (1992): 147–58.

Hopkinson, Deborah. *Not Mixing up Buddhism: Essays on Women and Buddhist Practice.* Buffalo, N.Y.: White Pine Press, *1992.*

Horner, I. B. *Women Under Primitive Buddhism: Laywomen and Almswomen.* Delhi: Motilal Banarsidass, 1930.

Huang, Chien-yu Julia and Robert P. Wellnew. "Merit and Mothering: Women and Social Welfare in Taiwanese Buddhism," *Journal of Asian Studies* 57:2 (May 1998): 379–96.

Ingram, Paul O. "Reflections on Buddhist-Christian Dialogue and the Liberation of Women," *Buddhist-Christian Studies* 17 (1997): 49–60.

Jayawardena, Kumari. "Some Aspects of Religious and Cultural Identity and the Construction of Sinhala Buddhist Womanhood." In *Religion and Political Conflict in South Asia: India, Pakistan, and Sri Lanka.* Edited by Douglas Allen. Delhi: Oxford University Press, 1993.

Kabilsingh, Chatsumarn. "The Future of the *Bhikkuni Samgha* in Thailand." In *Speaking of Faith: Global Perspectives on Women, Religion, and Social Change.* Edited by Diana L. Eck and Devaki Jain. Philadelphia: New Society Publishers, 1987, pp. 148–58.

———. *Thai Women in Buddhism.* Berkeley: Parallax Press, 1991.

Kajiyama, Yuichi. "Women in Buddhism." *Eastern Buddhist* 15:2 (1982): 53–70.

Kalyanavaca, ed. *The Moon and Flowers: A Woman's Path to Enlightenment.* New York: Weatherhill, 1997.

Kawahashi, Noriko. "Jizoku (Priests' Wives) in Soto Zen Buddhism: An Ambiguous Category." *Japanese Journal of Religious Studies* 22 (Spring 1995): 161–83.

Kawanami, Hiroko. "The Religious Standing of Burmese Buddhist Nuns *(thileá-shin):* The Ten Precepts and Religious Respect Words." *Journal of the International Association of Buddhist Studies* 13:1 (1990): 17–39.

———. "Buddhist Nuns in Transition: The Case of Burmese *thilá-shin.*" In *Indian Insights: Buddhism, Brahmanism and Bhakti.* Edited by Peter Connolly and Sue Hamilton. London: Luzac Oriental, 2003.

Kaza, Stephanie. "Acting with Compassion: Buddhism, Feminism, and the Environmental Crisis." In *Ecofeminism and the Sacred.* Edited by Carol J. Adams. London and New York: Continuum, 1993, pp. 50–69.

Keller, Catherine. "More on Feminism, Self-Sacrifice, and Time: Or, Too Many Words for Emptiness." *Buddhist-Christian Studies* 13 (1993): 211–19.

Keyes, Charles F. "Mother or Mistress but Never a Monk: Buddhist Notions of Female Gender in Rural Thailand." *American Ethnologist* 11:2 (May 1984): 223–35.

Khaing, Mi Mi. *The World of Burmese Women.* London: Zed Books, 1984.

Khema, Ayya. I *Give You My Life: The Autobiography of a Western Buddhist Nun.* Boston: Shambhala, 1998.

Khong, Chan, Cao Ngoc Phuong, and Maxine Hong Kingston. *Learning True Love: How I Learned and Practiced Social Change in Vietnam.* Berkeley: Parallax Press, 1993.

Kikuchi, Shigeo. *Memoirs of a Buddhist Woman Missionary in Hawaii.* Honolulu: Buddhist Study Center Press, 1991.

King, Sallie B. "Egalitarian Philosophies in Sexist Institutions: The Life of Satomi-san, Shinto Miko and Zen Buddhist Nuns." *Journal of Feminist Studies in Religion* 4 (Spring 1988): 7–26.

Kitamura, Mariko. "The Best Way is to Keep Away from Them: Kamo No Chomei's Views of Women in the *Hosshinshu.*" *Journal of Asian Culture* (UCLA) 4 (Spring 1980): 1–20.

Klein, Anne Carolyn. "Finding a Self: Buddhist and Feminist Perspectives." In *Sharing New Vision: Gender and Values in American Culture.* Edited by Clarissa W. Atkinson, Constance H. Buchanan, and Margaret R. Miles. Ann Arbor: UMI Research Press, 1987, pp. 191–218.

———. *Meeting the Great Bliss Queen: Buddhists, Feminists, and the Art of the Self.* Boston: Beacon Press, 1994.

———. Presence with a Difference: Buddhists and Feminists on Subjectivity." *Hypatia* 9:4 (Fall 1994): 133-44.

———. Nondualism and the Great Bliss Queen: A Study in Tibetan Buddhist Ontology and Symbolism." *Journal of Feminist Studies in Religion* 1:1 (1985): 73–98.

———."Primordial Purity and Everyday Life: Exalted Female Symbols and the Women of Tibet." In *Immaculate and Powerful: The Female in Sacred Image and Social Reality.* Edited by Clarissa W. Atkinson, Margaret R. Miles, and Constance H. Buchanan. Boston: Beacon Press, 1985, pp. 111-38.

Kloppenborg, Ria. "Female Stereotypes in Early Buddhism: The Women of the *Therigatha.*" In *Female Stereotypes in Religious Traditions.* Edited by Ria Kloppenborg and W. J. Hanegraaff. Leiden: Brill, 1995, pp. 15–69.

Koh, Hesung Chun. "Religion and Socialization of Women in Korea." In *Religion and the Family in East Asia.* Edited by George De Vos and Takao Sofue. Berkeley: University of California Press, 1986, pp. 237–57.

Ku Cheng-Mei. "The Mahayanic View of Women: A Doctrinal Study." PhD dissertation, University of Wisconsin-Madison, 1983.

Kyi, Aung San Suu. *Freedom from Fear.* London: Viking, 1991.

———. *Letters from Burma.* London: Penguin Book, 1997.

———. *The Voice of Hope.* New York: Seven Stories Press, 1997.

LaFleur, William R. "Silences and Censures: Abortion, History, and Buddhism in Japan." *Japanese Journal of Religious Studies* 22 (Spring 1995): 185–96.

Lang, Karen Christina. "Lord Death's Snare: Gender-Related Imagery in the Theragatha and the Therigatha." *Journal of Feminist Studies in Religion* 2:2 (Fall 1986): 63–79.

———. "Shaven Heads and Loose Hair: Buddhist Attitudes Toward Hair and Sexuality." In *Off with Her Head! The Denial of Women's Identity in Myth, Religion, and Culture.* Edited by Howard Eilberg-Schwartz and Wendy Doniger. Berkeley: University of California Press, 1995, pp. 32–52.

Levering, Miriam. "The Dragon Girl and the Abbess of Mo-Shan: Gender and Status in Ch'an Buddhist Tradition." *Journal of the International Association of Buddhist Studies* 5:1 (1982): 19–35.

———. Stories of Enlightened Women in Ch'an and the Chinese Buddhist Female Bodhisattva/Goddess Tradition." In *Women and Goddess Traditions.* Edited by Karen L. King. Minneapolis, Minn.: Fortress Press, 1997, pp. 137–76.

Mackenzie, Vicki. *Cave in the Snow: Tenzin Palmo's Quest for Enlightenment.* London: Bloomsbury Publishing, 1998.

Minamato, Junko. "Buddhist Attitudes: A Woman's Perspective." In *Women, Religion, and Sexuality.* Edited by Jeanne Beche. Philadelphia: Trinity Press International, 1991, pp. 154–71.

Mohr, Thea. *Weibliche Identität und Leerheit: Eine ideengeschichtliche Rekonstruktion der buddhistischen Frauenbewegung Sakyadhīta International.* Frankfurt am Main: Peter Lang, 2002.

Murcott, Susan. *The First Buddhist Women: Translations and Commentaries on the Therigatha.* Berkeley: Parallax Press, 1991.

Nakamura, Kyoko. "Women and Religion in Japan." *Japanese Journal of Religious Studies* 10 (June-September 1983): 115–272.

Neumaier-Dargyay, Eva K. "Buddhist Thought from a Feminist Perspective." In *Gender, Genre, and Religion.* Edited by

Morny Joy, E. K. Neumaier-Dargyay, and Mary Gerhart. Waterloo, Ont.: Wilfrid Laurier University Press, 1995, pp. 145–70.

Obeyesekere, Ranjini. *Portraits of Buddhist Women: Stories from the* Saddharmaratnāvaliya. Albany, N.Y.: State University of New York Press, 2001.

Ogoshi Aiko. "Women and Sexism in Japanese Buddhism: A Reexamination of Shinran's View of Women." *Japan Christian Review* 59 (1993): 19–25.

Ong, Aihwa and Michael G. Peletz, eds. *Bewitching Women, Pious Men: Gender and Body Politics in Southeast Asia*. Berkeley: University of California Press, 1995.

Ortner, Sherry B. "The Founding of the First Sherpa Nunnery and the Problem of 'Women' as an Analytic Category." In *Feminist Re-Visions: What Has Been and What Might Be*. Edited by Vivian Paraka and Louise Tilly. Ann Arbor: University of Michigan Press, 1983.

Overmyer, Daniel L. "Women in Chinese Religions: Submission, Struggle, Transcendence." In *From Benares to Beijing: Essays on Buddhism and Chinese Religion*. Edited by Koichi Shinohara and Gregory Schopen. Niagara Falls, N.Y.: Mosaic Press, 1992, pp. 91–120.

Paul, Diana. "Buddhist Attitudes Toward Women's Bodies." *Buddhist-Christian Studies* 1 (1981): 63–71.

———. *The Buddhist Feminine Ideal: Queen Srimala and the Tathagatagarbha*. Missoula: Scholars Press, 1980.

———. "Empress Wu and the Historians: A Tyrant and Saint of Classical China." In *Unspoken Worlds: Women's Religious Lives in Non-Western Cultures*. Edited by Nancy Auer Falk and Rita M. Gross. San Francisco: Harper & Row, 1979, pp. 191–206.

———. *Women in Buddhism: Images of the Feminine in Mahāyāna Tradition*. Berkeley: University of California Press, 1985.

Peach, Lucinda Joy. "Buddhism and Human Rights in the Thai Sex Trade." In *Religious Fundamentalisms and the Human Rights of Women*. Edited by Courtney W. Howland. New York: St. Martin's Press, 1999, pp. 215–26.

———. *Women and World Religions*. Upper Saddle River, N.J.: 2002.

Phuong, Cao Ngog. "Days and Months." In *The Path of Compassion: Writings on Socially Engaged Buddhism.* Edited by Fred Eppsteiner. Berkeley: Parallax, 1988, pp. 155–69.

Queen, Christopher S., ed. *Engaged Buddhism in the West.* Boston: Wisdom Publications, 2000.

Queen, Christopher S. and Sallie B. King, eds. *Engaged Buddhism: Buddhist Liberation Movements in Asia.* Albany, N.Y.: State University of New York Press, 1996.

Roth, Gustav. *Bhikṣuṇī-Vinaya: Manual of Discipline for Buddhist Nuns.* Patna: K. P. Jayaswal Research Institute, *1970.*

Ruch, Barbara, ed. *Engendering Faith: Women and Buddhism in Premodern Japan.* Ann Arbor: University of Michigan Center, 2002.

Sakya, Jamyang and Julie Emery. *Princess in the Land of Snows: The Life of Jamyang Sakya in Tibet.* Boston: Shambhala, 1988.

Salgado, Nirmala S. "Equality and Inequality in the Religious and Cultural Traditions of Hinduism and Buddhism." In *Equality and the Religious Traditions of Asia.* Edited by R. Siriwardena. London: Pinter, 1987, pp. 51–73.

Schuster, Nancy. "Striking a Balance: Women and Images of Women in Early Chinese Buddhism." In *Women, Religion, and Social Change.* Edited by Yvonne Yazbeck Haddad and Ellison Banks Findly. Albany, N.Y.: State University of New York Press, 1985, pp. 87–112.

Sidor, Ellen S. *A Gathering of Spirit: Women Teaching in American Buddhism.* Cumberland, R.I.: Primary Point Press, 1987.

Simmer-Brown, Judith. *Dakini's Warm Breath: The Feminine Principle in Tibetan Buddhism.* Boston and London: Shambhala, 2001.

Smith, Kendra. "Sex, Dependency, and Religion: Reflections from a Buddhist Perspective." In *Women in the World's Religions, Past and Present.* Edited by Ursula King. New York: Paragon House, 1987, pp. 219–31.

Tollifson, Joan. *Bare Bones Meditation: Waking Up from the Story of My Life.* New York: Bell Tower, 1996.

Tsai, Kathryn Ann, trans. *Lives of the Nuns: Biographies of Chinese Buddhist Nuns from the Fourth to Sixth Centuries: A*

Translation of the Pi-Ch'iu-Ni Chuan. Honolulu: University of Hawaii Press, 1994.

Tsomo, Karma Lekshe, ed. *Buddhism Through American Women's Eyes.* Ithaca, N.Y.: Snow Lion, 1995.

———. "Buddhist Nuns: Changes and Challenges." In *Westward Dharma: Buddhism Beyond Asia.* Edited by Martin Baumann and Charles Prebish. Berkeley: University of California Press, 2002, pp. 255–74.

———. "Buddhist Nuns: New Roles and Possibilities." In *Exile as Challenge: The Tibetan Diaspora.* Edited by Dagmar Bernstorff and Hubertus von Welck. Delhi: Orient Longman, 2003.

———. *Buddhist Women Across Cultures: Realizations.* Albany, N.Y.: State University of New York Press, 1999.

———. *Innovative Women in Buddhism: Swimming Against the Stream.* Richmond, Surrey: Curzon Press, 2000.

———. *Sisters in Solitude: Two Traditions of Buddhist Monastic Ethics for Women, A Comparative Analysis of the Dharmagupta and Mūlasarvāstivāda* Bhikṣuṇī Prātimokṣa Sūtras. Albany, N.Y.: State University of New York Press, 1996.

———. *Sakyadhita: Daughters of the Buddha.* Ithaca, N.Y.: Snow Lion, 1988.

Turner, Karen Gottschang. *Even the Women Must Fight: Memories of War from North Vietnam.* John Wiley and Sons, 1999.

Uchino, Kumiko. "The Status Elevation Process of Soto Sect Nuns in Modem Japan." In *Speaking of Faith: Global Perspectives on Women, Religion and Social Change.* Edited by Diana Eck and Devaki Jain. Philadelphia: New Society Publishers, 1987, pp. 177–94.

Ueki, Masatoshi. *Gender Equality in Buddhism.* New York: Peter Lang, 2001.

Walters, Jonathan S. "A Voice from the Silence: The Buddha's Mother's Story." *History of Religions* 33 (May 1994): 358–79.

Watkins, Joanne C. *Spirited Women: Gender, Religion, and Cultural Identity in the Nepal Himalaya.* New York: Columbia University Press, 1996.

Wawrytko, Sandra A. "Sexism in the Early Saṅgha: Its Social Basis and Philosophical Dis-solution." In *Buddhist Behavioral Codes and the Modem World*. Edited by Charles Wei-hsun Fu and Sandra A. Wawrytko. Westport, Conn.: Greenwood Press, 1994, pp. 277–96.

Wessinger, Catherine. "Woman Guru, Woman Roshi: The Legitimation of Female Religious Leadership in Hindu and Buddhist Groups in America." In *Women's Leadership in Marginal Religions: Explorations Outside the Mainstream*. Edited by Catherine Wessinger. Urbana and Chicago: University of Illinois Press, 1993, pp. 125–46.

Willis, Janice D. *Feminine Ground. Essays on Women and Tibet*. Ithaca, N.Y.: Snow Lion, 1989.

———. "Nuns and Benefactresses: The Role of Women in the Development of Buddhism." In *Women, Religion, and Social Change*. Edited by Yvonne Yazbeck Haddad and Ellison Banks Findly. Albany, N.Y.: State University of New York Press, 1985, pp. 59–85.

———. "Tibetan Ani-s: The Nun's Life in Tibet." In *Feminine Ground: Essays on Women and Tibet*, edited by Janice D. Willis. Ithaca, N.Y.: Snow Lion, 1989, pp. 96–117.

Wilson, Liz. *Charming Cadavers: Horrific Figurations of the Feminine in Indian Buddhist Hagiographic Literature*. Chicago: University of Chicago Press, 1996.

———. "Seeing Through the Gendered 'I': The Self-Scrutiny and Self-Disclosure of Nuns in Post-Asokan Buddhist Hagiographic Literature." *Journal of Feminist Studies in Religion* 11 (Spring 1995): 41-80.

Women and Buddhism: A Special Issue of the Spring Wind-Buddhist Cultural Forum 6, Nos. 1, 2, and 3, 1986.

Wurst, Rotraut. *Identität im exil. Tibetisch-Buddhistische Nonnen und das Netzwerk Sakyadhita*. Berlin: Dietrich Reimer Verlag, 2001.

Wu Yin, Bhikshuni. *Choosing Simplicity: Commentay on the* Bhikshuni Pratimoksha. Ithaca, N.Y.: Snow Lion, 2001.

Yifa, Venerable. *Sisters of the Buddha: Women's Roles in Buddhism Through the Centuries*. New York: Lantern Books, 2003.

Young, Serinity. *Buddhism and Gender: The Biographical Traditions*. New York: Routledge, 2002.

Contributors

Lin Chew is a graduate of the University of Singapore and has been active in advocacy work with nongovernmental organizations since the 1970s. A native of Singapore, she has lived and worked in Malaysia, the Netherlands, and Hong Kong. From 1999 to 2002, she worked with the Asian Human Rights Commission as the project officer for Human Rights Education at AHRC. At present she is the research project officer with the Gender Research Center of the Chinese University of Hong Kong. Her primary commitment is to the defense and promotion of human rights for women migrant workers.

Meenakshi Chhabra is an SGI Buddhist and an instructor at Lesley University in Cambridge, Massachusetts. She holds a BA in Political Science from the University of Delhi and a master's degree in Intercultural Relations from Lesley University. She is a scholar-practitioner in the field of conflict transformation and conducts conflict transformation workshops with women and youth groups from India, Pakistan, Israel, and the United States. She has been a Fulbright scholar and published her work in peace journals. She is a doctoral candidate in education at Lesley University.

Margaret Coberly is a registered nurse with a doctorate in psychology. She is on the faculty at the University of Hawaii—Windward. Her recent book, *Sacred Passage: How to Provide Fearless Compassionate Care for the Dying*, is based on her experience as a hospice nurse and her doctoral research in Tibetan Buddhism and cognitive psychology. She serves on the Board of Directors of the International Foundation of Transpersonal Studies and Jamyang Foundation, a nonprofit organization that supports education for Buddhist women.

Elise Anne DeVido is an associate professor in the Department of History at National Taiwan Normal University, Taipei, and is a researcher at the Taipei Ricci Institute. She is the editor of *Reinventing Confucianism: The New Confucian Movement*, by Umberto Bresciani, and coeditor (with Benoît Vermander) of *Creeds, Rites, and Videotapes: Narrating Religious Experience in East Asia.* She has authored various articles on Taiwanese Buddhism and the Shandong communist movement, and is completing a book on Taiwanese Buddhist nuns.

Ranjani de Silva is a founding member of Sakyadhita: International Association of Buddhist Women and served as its president from 1995 to 2002. Since 1987, she has been an active force in promoting the welfare of Buddhist women and coordinating higher ordinations to restore the lineage of full ordination for nuns in Sri Lanka. She served as president of Sakyadhita: International Association of Buddhist Women from 1995 to 2001. In 2000, she established the Sakyadhita Training and Meditation Center outside of Colombo for the training and education of nuns.

David N. Gellner is a lecturer in the anthropology of South Asia at the University of Oxford. Among his books are *Monk, Householder, and Tantric Priest: Newar Buddhism and Its Hierarchy of Ritual*; *Contested Hierarchies: A Collaborative Ethnography of Caste among the Newars of the Kathmandu Valley* (ed. with D. Quigley); *Nepal, Nationalism and Ethnicity in a Hindu Kingdom* (ed. with J. Pfaff-Czarnecka and John Whelpton); *The Anthropology of Buddhism and Hinduism: Weberian Themes*; *Resistance and the State: Nepalese Experiences* (ed.); and *Rebuilding Buddhism: Theravāda Revivalism in Nepal* (coauthored with Sarah LeVine and in preparation).

Paula Green is the founder and director of Karuna Center for Peacebuilding and a professor of Conflict Transformation at the School for International Training (SIT) in Vermont. At SIT, she created and directs the Conflict Transformation Across Cultures (CONTACT) program, to develop professional skills for international peacebuilders. Dr. Green facilitates intercommunal dialogue in war-threatened or war-recovering countries in the Middle East, Asia, Africa, and Eastern Europe. She is the coauthor of *Psychology and Social Responsibility:*

Facing Global Challenges, as well as chapters and professional articles published in the United States and abroad.

Anne Carolyn Klein is a professor of Religious Studies at Rice University in Houston, Texas. She is the author of four books, including *Meeting the Great Bliss Queen: Buddhists, Feminists, and the Art of the Self*. She is also founding director of Dawn Mountain, a Tibetan practice and research center in Houston. Her writing focuses on ways of knowing and the significance of the body in Tibetan philosophy and practice. Outside the Academy she teaches meditation, including "Buddhism in the Body" and contemplative programs with Phyllis Pay, and translates for visiting Tibetan lamas.

Khandu Lama is a native of Helambu, one of the most remote areas of Nepal. She taught English at the local high school from 1991 to 1999. She is the founder and chairperson of the Hyolmo Women's Development Association (HWDA), the only womens' organization in Helambu. She has been actively involved with the organization since its founding in 1993. She became the chairperson of the association in 1998.

Sarah LeVine is a research associate in Human Development and Psychology at Harvard Graduate School of Education. She is the author of *Mothers and Wives: Gusii Women of East Africa* and *Dolor Y Alegria: Women and Social Change in Urban Mexico*, and is coauthor (with David Gellner) of *Rebuilding Buddhism: Theravāda Revivalism in Nepal.*

Kathryn L. Norsworthy is a licensed psychologist in private practice and associate professor of Counseling at Rollins College, Winter Park, Florida. She works in collaboration with local partners in the United States and in Southeast Asia to analyze and prevent structural violence against women in their communities and to develop culturally relevant, community-based helping programs for women survivors of trauma. Her areas of specialization include women and trauma, integration of Engaged Buddhist and feminist theory and practice, and liberatory models of pedagogy and counseling.

Caren I. Ohlson holds a degree in Womens' Studies from Mills College with emphasis on social justice activism. She is a recipient of the

Leavens Undergraduate Research Award for excellence in Womens' Studies and Religion, and the 2000 winner of the Mills Essay Award for Women's Studies. She resides in Berkeley, California, where she is currently engaged with other Buddhists committed to exploring diversity issues and utilizing spiritual practice to dismantle oppression in our own minds, relationships, cultures, and the world.

Karma Lekshe Tsomo is an assistant professor of Theology and Religious Studies at the University of San Diego. She is the president of Sakyadhita: International Association of Buddhist Women and director of Jamyang Foundation, a nonprofit organization that supports education for women, especially in developing countries. She completed her doctorate in philosophy at the University of Hawai'i and has edited a number of books on women and Buddhism.

Diana E. Wright is an associate professor of Japanese History at Western Washington University. She completed her doctorate at the University of Toronto in 1996, with a focus on women, crime, and other features of life in the Edo period. She is the author of several articles on Mantokuji (the "divorce temple"), the Aizu Women's Platoon, and other historical events involving women in this period of Japanese history.

Index